"How deep can priestly spirituality go? Msgr. Michael Becker's work demonstrates it has no bottom. It is easy to see the priesthood as a series of daily ritual functions. Becker identifies the sacred uniqueness within these functions by drawing us into the mystical side of priests, a side that is often overlooked in our busy, distracted culture. As meditation draws us into the depths, so too does Becker uncover the spiritual depths of being a priest. The renowned theologian Karl Rahner once said that Christianity must be mystical or it won't exist. Becker identifies the mystical in the priesthood upon which its very existence exists."

> —Rev. Eugene F. Hemrick
> Director of the National Institute for the Renewal of the Priesthood

"When parish priests are trying to find time for meditation, reflection and discernment, this resource is an excellent opportunity to be engaged with scripture, theologians and prayer."

> —Very Reverend James A. Wehner
> Rector of Notre Dame Seminary, New Orleans

A Life of Daring Simplicity

*Daily Meditations on
the Priesthood*

Edited by Michael A. Becker

LITURGICAL PRESS

Collegeville, Minnesota

www.litpress.org

1	2	3	4	5	6	7	8	9

Library of Congress Cataloging-in-Publication Data

A life of daring simplicity : daily meditations on the priesthood / edited by Monsignor Michael A. Becker.

     pages   cm

   ISBN 978-0-8146-3824-8 — ISBN 978-0-8146-3849-1 (ebook)

   1. Priests—Prayers and devotions.   2. Priesthood—Meditations.

 3. Devotional calendar.   I. Becker, Michael A., Monsignor, editor.

BX1912.7.L54   2014

242'.692—dc23   2014015153

To my parents,
Clarence and Eileen

Contents

Preface

The "daily reading" genre has become a staple for countless men and women whose lives are already full but nevertheless desire a "still point" for personal reflection. There are books, websites, apps, newsletters that offer a wide array of daily, thematic readings taken from saints and popes, poets and seekers—all with the intention of offering the reader some inspiring food for reflection. Such collections grace the breakfast table or the night stand, offering a daily page of wisdom.

I am one of the countless. I readily confess to a full life. And to maintain that "still point" I have often kept at my bedside such collections of daily readings. In my four decades as a priest, however, I have been unable to discover any collection that offered everyday verse for those living the vocation to priestly life and ministry. If I felt this need to live more consciously this call of Christ to serve God as a priest, perhaps others may have felt a similar need. Hence, *A Life of Daring Simplicity*.

This book of daily readings has been prepared for priests, for those aspiring to the priesthood, and for every Christian who seeks to understand the priestly life. While there are a great many volumes that offer a single, cohesive spirituality of the priesthood, this one seeks to provide a wide variety of daily insights, each limited to a single page. It is designed to provide for each day of the year a prayerful daily meditation on some facet of priestly life. Each day begins with a verse or two from Sacred Scripture, followed by a few paragraphs from the writer for the day. At the bottom of each page I have included a brief prayer or question meant to prompt further reflection on the text.

The reader will notice that the writings of Saint John Paul II are the single greatest source of meditations. Few have written more extensively and regularly on this topic than he, whose annual Holy Thursday letters have been for so many of us an inexhaustible fountain of wisdom. From the first year of his papacy to his last, these personal reflections flowed from his own lived experience of over half a century of priestly life. Saint John XXIII's personal diary, *Journal of a Soul*, has also offered very personal and pastoral insights. Dozens of other writers, those living priesthood and those observing it, our contemporaries and our Church Fathers, popes, and parish priests also provide glimpses of this unique and blessed way of discipleship.

The greater part of this collection was done—using Cardinal Carlo Maria Martini's phrase—"in the thick of ministry." I am most grateful to my family and brother priests who continued to encourage this work over the past many years. I especially appreciate the counsel of my friend Fr. William Cawley, who has been invaluable in editing, my students at St. Vincent Seminary who offered ready comments and suggestions, and the staff at Liturgical Press, whose attention to innumerable details has made this work a reality.

It is Saint John XXIII who uses the expression "daring simplicity" in his *Journal of a Soul*. Pope Francis gives vibrant witness to these words and calls us in our time to embody such priestly virtue. Day by day, may it become our reality!

August 4, 2014
Memorial of Saint John Vianney, Priest

> And Mary said: / "My soul proclaims the greatness of the Lord; / my spirit rejoices in God my savior." (Luke 1:46)

The Second Vatican Council presents the life of the Church as a pilgrimage of faith. Each one of us, dear brothers, by reason of our priestly vocation and ordination, has a special part in this pilgrimage. As ministers of the Good Shepherd we are called to go forward guiding others, helping them along their way. As stewards of the mysteries of God we must therefore possess a maturity of faith corresponding to our vocation and our tasks. Indeed, "it is required of stewards that they be found trustworthy," since the Lord commits his inheritance to them.

It is appropriate, then, that on this pilgrimage of faith each one of us should fix his soul's gaze on the Virgin Mary, the Mother of Jesus Christ, the Son of God. For as the Council teaches, following the Fathers of the Church she "precedes" us in this pilgrimage . . . and she offers us a sublime example. . . .

In Mary, who is the Immaculate Virgin, we also discover the mystery of that supernatural fruitfulness through the power of the Holy Spirit, which makes her the "figure" of the Church. For the Church "becomes herself a mother . . . because by her preaching and by Baptism she brings forth to a new and immortal life children who are conceived of the Holy Spirit and born of God," as witnessed to by the Apostle Paul: "My children, I must go through the pain of giving birth to you all over again." This the Church does, suffering as a mother who "has sorrow, because her hour has come; but when she is delivered of her child, she no longer remembers the anguish, for joy that a child is born into the world."

—Saint John Paul II, Letter to Priests for
Holy Thursday, 1987

Lord Jesus, may I continually look to your Mother Mary as a model of prayerful and priestly service to your people.

"For the bread of God is that which comes down from heaven and gives life to the world." (John 6:33)

As Our predecessor of immortal memory, Pius XII, has said—"The wonderful example of St. John Mary Vianney retains all of its force for our times." For the lengthy prayer of a priest before the adorable Sacrament of the Altar has a dignity and an effectiveness that cannot be found elsewhere nor be replaced. And so when the priest adores Christ Our Lord and gives thanks to Him, or offers satisfaction for his own sins and those of others, or finally when he prays constantly that God keep special watch over the causes committed to his care, he is inflamed with a more ardent love for the Divine Redeemer to whom he has sworn allegiance and for those to whom he is devoting his pastoral care. And a devotion to the Eucharist that is ardent, constant and that carries over into works also has the effect of nourishing and fostering the inner perfection of his soul and assuring him, as he carries out his apostolic duties, of an abundance of the supernatural powers that the strongest workers for Christ must have.

We do not want to skip over the benefits that accrue to the faithful themselves in this way, as they see the piety of their priests and are drawn by their example. For, as our predecessor of happy memory, Pius XII, pointed out in a talk to the clergy of this dear city: "If you want the faithful who are entrusted to your care to pray willingly and well, you must give them an example and let them see you praying in church. A priest kneeling devoutly and reverently before the tabernacle, and pouring forth prayers to God with all his heart, is a wonderful example to the Christian people and serves as an inspiration." The saintly Curé of Ars used all of these helps in carrying out his apostolic office, and without a doubt they are suitable to all times and places.

—Saint John XXIII,
Sacerdotii Nostri Primordia, 48–49

Lord Jesus, as you are truly present in the Blessed Sacrament, so may I be truly and fully present to you!

The Priest Belongs to All January 3

"As you sent me into the world, so I sent them into the world. And I consecrate myself for them . . . " (John 17:18-19)

To be a pastor the priest must be both a minister and an apostle. But to whom? The faithful themselves need this double ministry: the Gospel and the sacramental life. So priests, already overburdened because of their small numbers wonder whether they ought not to make a choice and confine themselves either only to believers or only to those outside the Church. The definition and experience of Catholic Action answers their doubts; not by a magic formula, in this realm of mystery and free gift, but by throwing a light on the way to a solution.

The priest, as a minister of God, and the father of a community which, through him, must render to the Lord the worship which is His due, has charge of the souls of the people entrusted to him, whether they are "inside" or "outside" the Church.

He belongs to all, equally and without distinction. So he would have a poor grasp of what the Church expects of him, if he thought that the sad circumstances of contemporary atheism entitled him to neglect the faithful. Progress will not be made with unbelievers by jeopardizing the faith, charity, and moral life of believers, or by allowing the source of their apostolic generosity and spiritual energy to dry up. The care of the baptized must not be considered as a ministry of secondary importance, still less as a necessary evil. On the contrary, it is the open road, the predestined passage of grace, to the masses who are separated from Christ.

. . . In everything and everywhere it should contribute to the creation and education of the faithful so that they will become the Christian Leaven . . . The faithful will bring about a profound transformation of their whole environment.

—Emmanuel-Célestin Cardinal Suhard,
The Church Today, 280–81

How do I understand my ministry to those "outside" the church? How inclusive or exclusive have I become?

> "I consecrate myself for them, so that they also may be consecrated in truth." (John 17:19)

This is what stands out clearly in the priestly prayer of Jesus in the Upper Room: "I have manifested your name to the men whom you gave me out of the world; yours they were, and you gave them to me, and they have kept your word."

Following Jesus' example, the priest, "the steward of the mysteries of God," is truly himself when he is "for others." Prayer gives him a special sensitivity to these "others," making him attentive to their needs, to their lives and destiny. Prayer also enables the priest to recognize those whom "the Father has given to him." These are, in the first place, those whom the Good Shepherd has as it were placed on the path of his priestly ministry, of his pastoral care. They are children, adults and the aged. They are the youth, married couples, families, but also those who are alone. They are the sick, suffering, the dying; they are those who are spiritually close and willing to collaborate in the apostolate, but also those who are distant, those who are absent or indifferent, though many of them may be searching and reflecting. Those who for different reasons are negatively disposed, those who find themselves in difficulties of various sorts, those who are struggling against vices and sins, those who are fighting for faith and hope. Those who seek the priest's help, and those who reject it.

How can one be "for" all of these people and "for" each one of them according to the model of Christ? How can we be "for" those whom "the Father has given to us," committing them to us in trust? Ours will always be a test of love—a test that we must accept, first of all, in the realm of prayer.

—Saint John Paul II, Letter to Priests for
Holy Thursday, 1987

What evidence is there in my daily life that I have consecrated the whole of my life and my prayer "for others"?

The Fruits of a Priest's Prayer

"Whoever remains in me and I in him will bear much fruit . . . "
(John 15:5)

All movements of the spirit, and all forms of prayer, are measured by their fruits. "You will know them by their fruits," says Matthew's Gospel. Prayer is far too deep, mysterious, and personal to attest to its authenticity on its own. . . .

The first encounters of the risen Jesus with his followers were experiences in which he forgave their infidelities. John's Gospel relates the words of Jesus to his disciples, cowering behind closed doors, "Peace be with you. As the Father has sent me, even so I send you. And when he had said this, he breathed on them and said to them, 'Receive the Holy Spirit. If you forgive the sins of any, they are forgiven; if you retain the sins of any, they are retained'" (John 20:19, 21-22). Peace and forgiveness are the first gifts of the risen Lord. The forgiveness of others is inseparable from the forgiveness of self, the last and perhaps most difficult link in the chain. These fruits show themselves as a life of charity in word and deed, the complement of a genuine life of prayer. It is hard to imagine a true spirit of prayer resting in an ungenerous heart. . . .

Perhaps the most enduring way in which the power of prayer manifests itself is as a source of strength that goes beyond normal powers and capacities. This is what William James observed, and this capacity remains an accurate gauge of the power of prayer, indeed, of religious faith. Religious experience, above all prayer, gives people an inner resource they can tap at critical moments. Equally important is a sense of perspective. Prayer sheds light and perspective on all aspects of human life.

—Howard P. Bleichner, *View from the Altar*, 81–82

In what way is the spirit of my prayer reflected in my daily ministry?

> May the eyes of [your] hearts be enlightened, that you may know what
> is the hope that belongs to his call, what are the riches of glory in his
> inheritance among the holy ones . . . (Eph 1:18)

Dear friends, how could the saving waters of Redemption flow to all generations if it were not for you? The clarity and certainty of your identity give rise to an awareness of your absolute indispensability in the Church and in the world.

Through you the Good Shepherd continues to teach, to sanctify, to guide and to love all peoples of every culture, every continent and every age. For this reason you alone enjoy the title of pastor and, since there is no salvation except in Christ and since he must be proclaimed to the ends of the earth, it is impossible to cross the threshold of the third millennium without making the pastoral care of vocations a priority. If the world cannot do without Christ, it also cannot do without his priests.

Dear priests, from the land of the Incarnation of the Word, from the land he traveled, immersed in the air he breathed, illumined by the sun which lit his footsteps, proclaim to everyone who Jesus of Nazareth is; tell them that in him we find total human fulfillment, in him alone true progress, in him alone the fullness of justice and peace, in him alone joy without darkness, in him alone the true and complete humanism whose crown is eternal salvation.

By your very presence you tell people who a priest is and what is his identity; you show your indispensability and the need to devote yourselves totally to your pastoral ministry within the presbyterate gathered closely round its Bishop. Try to make every person understand that if the place of the Eucharist is absolutely essential in the community, precisely in relation to it the priest is equally essential. Wherever priests are scarce, nothing can substitute for them, but rather the whole community should beg for them with greater insistence, by personal and community prayer, by repentance and with the specific holiness of priests.

—Saint John Paul II, Message to the Participants in the
Fourth International Meeting of Priests, June 19, 1999

What is there about my life of service as a priest that attracts others to follow Christ in the priesthood? Do I, by word and action, say with Saint Paul, "Imitate me as I imitate Christ"?

> So whoever is in Christ is a new creation: the old things have passed away; behold, new things have come. And all this is from God, who has reconciled us to himself through Christ and given us the ministry of reconciliation . . . (2 Cor 5:17-18)

The Redemption remains connected in the closest possible way with forgiveness, God has redeemed us in Jesus Christ; God has caused us to become, in Christ, a "new creation," for in Him He has granted us the gift of forgiveness.

God has reconciled the world to Himself in Christ. And precisely because He has reconciled it in Jesus Christ, as the firstborn of all creation, the union of man with God has been irreversibly consolidated. This union—which the "first Adam" had, in himself, once consented to be taken away from the whole human family—cannot be taken from humanity by anyone, since it has been rooted and consolidated in Christ, the "second Adam." And therefore humanity becomes continually, in Jesus Christ, a "new creation." It becomes this, because in Him and through Him the grace of the remission of sins remains inexhaustible before every human being: "With him is plenteous redemption."

Dear brothers, during the Jubilee Year we must become particularly aware of the fact that we are at the service of this reconciliation with God, which was accomplished once and for all in Jesus Christ. We are the servants and ministers of this sacrament, in which the Redemption is made manifest and is accomplished as forgiveness, as the remission of sins.

How eloquent is the fact that Christ, after His resurrection, once more entered that Upper Room in which on Holy Thursday He had left to the Apostles, together with the Eucharist, the sacrament of the ministerial Priesthood, and that He then said to them: "Receive the Holy Spirit; whose sins you shall forgive, they are forgiven them; and whose sins you shall retain, they are retained."

—Saint John Paul II, Letter to Priests for
Holy Thursday, 1983

Within and beyond the sacrament of penance, I consider how the whole of my priestly life is at the service of reconciliation.

> Then the LORD extended his hand and touched my mouth, saying to me,
> See, I place my words in your mouth! (Jer 1:9)

We live in a world in which many people deeply appreciate the Church and the priesthood. But there are others who have difficulty understanding why a group of talented, intelligent, energetic people like yourselves would want to spend their lives as priests. It's not a highly remunerative occupation. It's not the kind of position which provides much opportunity to become a mover or shaker in our society. You sacrifice a wife and family of your own in order to serve the kingdom of God. It is not a ready avenue to fame or fortune. You know all of that. So why are you taking this step today?

Why? Because you have become increasingly aware of the deep hungers of the human spirit. You are aware of people who try to have it all, only to discover that possessions do not satisfy the profound yearnings of the human spirit. You realize that the priest is the unique person who is privileged to be invited by so many to enter into the key events of life as the Church's representative—indeed, as God's representative. You realize that you will be privileged to baptize babies and catechumens, celebrate weddings and First Communions, anoint the sick and comfort the dying, and lead the confused or brokenhearted to the experience of God's compassion, mercy, and forgiveness. You will gather the community to break the bread of the Eucharist and to ponder the mysterious meaning of God's holy word. You will be the shepherds of the flock, the heralds of the Good News, the mediators between God and his beloved people.

—Joseph Cardinal Bernardin, Homily for
Priesthood Ordination, May 21, 1994

Am I more aware of acting in the person of Christ each time I administer the sacraments?

The Year of the Priest Proclaimed January 9

I am the good shepherd, and I know mine and mine know me, just as the Father knows me and I know the Father; and I will lay down my life for the sheep. (John 10:14-15)

I have decided to inaugurate a "Year for Priests" in celebration of the 150th anniversary of the *"dies natalis"* of John Mary Vianney, the patron saint of parish priests worldwide. This Year [is] meant to deepen the commitment of all priests to interior renewal for the sake of a more forceful and incisive witness to the Gospel in today's world. . . . "The priesthood is the love of the heart of Jesus," the saintly Curé of Ars would often say. This touching expression makes us reflect, first of all, with heartfelt gratitude on the immense gift which priests represent, not only for the Church, but also for humanity itself. I think of all those priests who quietly present Christ's words and actions each day to the faithful and to the whole world, striving to be one with the Lord in their thoughts and their will, their sentiments and their style of life. How can I not pay tribute to their apostolic labours, their tireless and hidden service, their universal charity? And how can I not praise the courageous fidelity of so many priests who, even amid difficulties and incomprehension, remain faithful to their vocation as "friends of Christ," whom He has called by name, chosen and sent?

I still treasure the memory of the first parish priest at whose side I exercised my ministry as a young priest: he left me an example of unreserved devotion to his pastoral duties, even to meeting death in the act of bringing viaticum to a gravely ill person. I also recall the countless confreres whom I have met and continue to meet, not least in my pastoral visits to different countries: men generously dedicated to the daily exercise of their priestly ministry.

—Pope Benedict XVI, Letter Proclaiming
a Year for Priests, June 16, 2009

I ponder the ways in which my priestly life is "the love of the heart of Jesus."

19

[W]e always pray for you, that our God may make you worthy of his calling and powerfully bring to fulfillment every good purpose and every effort of faith, that the name of our Lord Jesus may be glorified in you, and you in him . . . (2 Thess 1:11-12)

The primary reason for evangelizing is the love of Jesus which we have received, the experience of salvation which urges us to ever greater love of him. What kind of love would not feel the need to speak of the beloved, to point him out, to make him known? If we do not feel an intense desire to share this love, we need to pray insistently that he will once more touch our hearts. We need to implore his grace daily, asking him to open our cold hearts and shake up our lukewarm and superficial existence. Standing before him with open hearts, letting him look at us, we see that gaze of love which Nathaniel glimpsed on the day when Jesus said to him: "I saw you under the fig tree" (Jn 1:48). How good it is to stand before a crucifix, or on our knees before the Blessed Sacrament, and simply to be in his presence! How much good it does us when he once more touches our lives and impels us to share his new life! What then happens is that "we speak of what we have seen and heard" (1 Jn 1:3). The best incentive for sharing the Gospel comes from contemplating it with love, lingering over its pages and reading it with the heart. If we approach it in this way, its beauty will amaze and constantly excite us. But if this is to come about, we need to recover a contemplative spirit which can help us to realize ever anew that we have been entrusted with a treasure which makes us more human and helps us to lead a new life. There is nothing more precious which we can give to others.

—Pope Francis, *Evangelii Gaudium*, 264

I was ordained to preach! I pray that my preaching may be renewed by my contemplation of the Gospel with love. I will linger over its pages, and read it with my heart.

> But when [God], who from my mother's womb had set me apart and called me through his grace, was pleased to reveal his Son to me, so that I might proclaim him to the Gentiles, I did not immediately consult flesh and blood, nor did I go up to Jerusalem to those who were apostles before me; rather, I went into Arabia and then returned to Damascus. (Gal 1:15-17)

The missionary dimension of the priesthood is born from the priest's sacramental configuration to Christ. As a consequence it brings with it a heartfelt and total adherence to what the ecclesial tradition has identified as *apostolica vivendi forma*. This consists in participation in a "new life," spiritually speaking, in that "new way of life" which the Lord Jesus inaugurated and which the Apostles made their own. Through the imposition of the Bishop's hands and the consecratory prayer of the Church, the candidates become new men, they become "presbyters." In this light it is clear that the *tria munera* are first a gift and only consequently an office, first a participation in a life, and hence a *potestas*. Of course, the great ecclesial tradition has rightly separated sacramental efficacy from the concrete existential situation of the individual priest and so the legitimate expectations of the faithful are appropriately safeguarded. However, this correct doctrinal explanation takes nothing from the necessary, indeed indispensable, aspiration to moral perfection that must dwell in every authentically priestly heart. . . .

The priest's mission . . . is carried out "in the Church." This ecclesial, communal, hierarchical and doctrinal dimension is absolutely indispensable to every authentic mission and, alone guarantees its spiritual effectiveness. The four aspects mentioned must always be recognized as intimately connected: the mission is "ecclesial" because no one proclaims himself in the first person, but within and through his own humanity every priest must be well aware that he is bringing to the world Another, God himself. God is the only treasure which ultimately people desire to find in a priest.

—Pope Benedict XVI, Address to the Members of
the Congregation for the Clergy, March 16, 2009

Daily I need to be more aware that "God is the only treasure" that people desire to find in me.

I have competed well; I have finished the race; I have kept the faith.
(2 Tim 4:7)

In four years of war, passed in the midst of a world in agony, how good the Lord has been to me! He has enabled me to go through so much, and granted me so many occasions of doing good to my fellow men! My Jesus, I thank you and I bless you. I call to mind all those young souls I have come to know during these years, many of whom I accompanied to the threshold of the other life; the memory of them moves me deeply, and the thought that they will pray for me is comforting and encouraging.

While we are all re-awakening as if to the light of a new day, those supreme principles of faith and Christian and priestly life which by the grace of God were the nourishment of my youth are once more clear to me and now seem even brighter and firmer than before: the glory of God, the sanctification of my soul, paradise, the Church, the souls of men. The contacts with the world during these four years have transformed these principles into action, ennobled them and imbued them with a more burning apostolic zeal. I am now of mature years: either I achieve something positive, or I bear a terrible responsibility for having wasted the Lord's mercies.

As the foundation of my apostolate I want an inner life spent in the search for God in myself and for close union with him, and in the habitual and tranquil meditation on the truths which the Church teaches me, a meditation which, according to the teaching of the Church, shall be expressed in religious practices which will become more and more dear to me.

—Saint John XXIII, *Journal of a Soul*, 255–56

In what way are the challenges of my own priestly ministry inviting me to a deeper inner life?

> For God did not give us a spirit of cowardice but rather of power and love and self-control. (2 Tim 1:7)

The priestly life is built upon the foundation of the sacrament of Orders, which imprints on our soul the mark of an indelible character. This mark, impressed in the depths of our being, has its "personalistic" dynamism. *The priestly personality must be for others a clear and plain sign and indication.* This is the first condition for our pastoral service. The people from among whom we have been chosen and for whom we have been appointed want above all to see in us such a sign and indication, and to this they have a right. It may sometimes seem to us that they do not want this, or that they wish us to be in every way "like them"; at times it even seems that they demand this of us. And here one very much needs a profound "sense of faith" and "the gift of discernment." In fact, it is very easy to let oneself be guided by appearances and fall victim to a fundamental illusion in what is essential. Those who call for the secularization of priestly life and applaud its various manifestations will undoubtedly abandon us when we succumb to temptation. We shall then cease to be necessary and popular. Our time is characterized by different forms of "manipulation" and "exploitation" of man, but we cannot give in to any of these. *In practical terms, the only priest who will always prove necessary to people is the priest who is conscious of the full meaning of his Priesthood: the priest who believes profoundly, who professes his faith with courage, who prays fervently, who teaches with deep conviction, who serves, who puts into practice in his own life the program of the Beatitudes, who knows how to love disinterestedly, who is close to everyone, and especially to those who are most in need.*

—Saint John Paul II, Letter to Priests for
Holy Thursday, 1979

I read again the final lines of this meditation, and consider the full meaning of priesthood for me.

> See, I place my words in your mouth! / Today I appoint you / over nations and over kingdoms, / To uproot and to tear down, / to destroy and to demolish, / to build and to plant. (Jer 1:9-10)

What the priest does surrounded by happy friends on the day of his first solemn Mass, he will do every day of his life. Every day in youth and old age, on the gray mornings that begin the daily grind and at the terrible moments that find their way into every life. And each time this poor little celebration will hold the content of all the riddles of existence, and the solution of all the riddles: the body which was handed over and the blood which was spilt for the forgiveness of sin. Everything will be contained together in this short half hour every day; for here we have present as Victim and as Conqueror the one who is in Himself the real union of the riddle with its solution, the union of earth with heaven, the union of man with God, in the celebration of that one instant in which on the cross the greatest distance between the two became the inseparable nearness.

The priest is man, messenger of God's truth, dispenser of the divine mysteries, one who makes Christ's single sacrifice present again. What great good fortune! Of course every man has his calling from God, his fortune decided for him from eternity, his commission too in the body of Christ which is the Church. A purely profane existence cannot be found; nobody has one. But the reality of God, which for most men appears most exclusively in the depths of their inmost conscience and in the silent secrecy of their private life, that reality, under the call of God to the priest, forces its way up out of the depths and floods every reach of his life. All of it must be consumed by God or pressed into His own glorious but demanding service.

—Karl Rahner, *Meditations on the Sacraments*, 67–68

Lord Jesus, may your call penetrate the whole of my life, and make it a total gift of faith-filled service to your people.

> But you, man of God, avoid all this. Instead, pursue righteousness, devotion, faith, love, patience, and gentleness. (1 Tim 6:11)

The priest must, first of all, strive in his following of Christ to be a "man of God" as described in the "ordination sermon" of 1 Timothy: that is, he must ensure that his life belongs to God and that God's kingdom has the first place in it.

This existential demand on the disciple with a particular mission becomes particularly clear in the numerous vocation texts in the Gospels (especially Mt 10:5ff.; 8:18ff.; 16:24ff.). These demonstrate what Jesus expects from those whom he chooses to send to preach the kingdom. The essential point is that the disciple who is commissioned should, like Jesus, show visibly in this world by his personal life and mode of living the beginning of God's kingdom and its "complete otherness." For this reason, the disciple must be different, must maintain an "alternative lifestyle"; he must leave everything behind and set out on his way without power and money; he must be poor and available and must set up a sign of peace and reconciliation. It is precisely in this way that he will become a sign of God's supremacy which in its otherness exposes the standards of this world. In what other way can the supremacy of God be credibly proclaimed, if the messenger does not seek to make it actual in his own life? If he is no more than a religious bureaucrat, his words and his actions are not credible, cannot touch the heart.

Since the disciple is sent "to where the Lord himself wishes to come" (cf. Lk 10:11), the priest cannot carry out his mission if he is not permanently filled and touched by Jesus Christ. He must be one who before everything else listens to God: how else would he bring the will of God to men?

—Gisbert Greshake, *The Meaning of Christian Priesthood*, 114

In what ways is my "lifestyle" an alternative to that of the culture?

> I do not ask that you take them out of the world but that you keep them from the evil one. (John 17:15)

Nourished by the Second Vatican Council which has felicitously placed the priest's consecration within the framework of his pastoral mission, let us join Saint John Mary Vianney and seek the dynamism of our pastoral zeal in the Heart of Jesus, in his love for souls. If we do not draw from the same source, our ministry risks bearing little fruit!

In the case of the Curé of Ars, the results were indeed wonderful, somewhat as with Jesus in the Gospel. . . . First his parish—which numbered only 230 people when he arrived—which will be profoundly changed. One recalls that in that village there was a great deal of indifference and very little religious practice. . . . The bishop had warned John Mary Vianney: "There is not much love of God in that parish, you will put some there." But quite soon, far beyond his own village, the Curé becomes the pastor of a multitude coming . . . from different parts of France and from other countries. It is said that 80,000 came in the year 1858! . . . What attracted them to him was . . . the realization of meeting a saint, amazing for his penance, so close to God in prayer, remarkable for his peace and humility . . . , and above all so intuitive in responding to the inner disposition of souls and in freeing them from their burdens, especially in the confessional. Yes, God chose as a model for pastors one who could have appeared poor, weak, defenseless and contemptible in the eyes of men. While recognizing the special nature of the grace given to the Curé of Ars, is there not here a sign of hope for pastors today who are suffering from a kind of spiritual desert?

> —Saint John Paul II, Letter to Priests for
> Holy Thursday, 1986

Good Shepherd of Souls, give me the grace that you gave to St. John Vianney, that like him I may bring forgiveness and healing for souls.

A Life in Harmony with Christ

> To the weak I became weak, to win over the weak. I have become all things to all, to save at least some. All this I do for the sake of the gospel, so that I too may have a share in it. (1 Cor 9:22-23)

Teach me your way of relating to disciples, to sinners, to children, to Pharisees, Pilates, and Herods; also to John the Baptist before his birth and afterward in the Jordan. Teach me how you deal with your disciples, especially the most intimate: with Peter, with John, with the traitor Judas. How delicately you treat them on Lake Tiberius, even preparing breakfast for them! How you washed their feet!

May I learn from you and from your ways, as St. Ignatius did: how to eat and drink; how to attend banquets; how to act when hungry or thirsty, when tired from the ministry, when in need of rest or sleep.

Teach me how to be compassionate to the suffering, to the poor, the blind, the lame, and the lepers; show me how you revealed your deepest emotions, as when you shed tears, or when you felt sorrow and anguish to the point of sweating blood and needed an angel to console you. Above all, I want to learn how you supported the extreme pain of the cross, including the abandonment of your Father.

Your humanity flows out from the Gospel, which shows you as noble, amiable, exemplary and sublime, with a perfect harmony between your life and your doctrine. Even your enemies said: "Master, we know that you are truthful, that you teach the way of God in truth and care not for anyone's opinion, for you regard not a person's status" (Matt. 22:16). The Gospel shows your virile manner, hard on yourself in privations and wearying work, but for others full of kindness, with a consuming longing to serve.

—Pedro Arrupe, "Our Way of Proceeding,"
The Spiritual Legacy of Pedro Arrupe, S.J., 80–81

Lord Jesus, you desire to live your life again in me. May I surrender my humanity to you for the greater glory of God.

The Priest: Entirely from Christ, Entirely for Us

> Those who fear the Lord prepare their hearts / and humble themselves before him. (Sir 2:17)

The priest, then, is to become fully that which he is . . . . The active element of righteousness must become realized as he cooperates with God's grace in living out that which he has become. As we all know, this is manifested publicly and ritually in the holy Mass, to which sacrament the priest is preeminently ordered *(PO, 12)*. . . . As the Holy Father has pointed out, "the celebrant, by reason of this special sacrament, identifies himself with the eternal high priest, who is both author and principal agent of his own sacrifice in which truly no one can take his place" *(Dominicae Cenae, 8)*. But the sacrifice of Christ was the total surrender of his life to the Father in the Spirit for his friends as well as the total surrender of his life to his friends for his Father's sake. This is the holiness that comes to mark the life of the priest. The Council tells us that the source of all pastoral charity is the Eucharistic sacrifice, for here the priest is most sublimely configured to his Lord. In the words of the Council, "This sacrifice is . . . the center and root of the whole life of the priest, so that the priestly soul strives to make his own what is enacted on the altar of sacrifice" *(PO, 14)*.

Through his ordination the priest has entered more fully into the paschal mystery. As Jesus was entirely from God and entirely for us, so the priest is entirely from Christ and entirely for us. He is consumed in his surrender to God and to us faithful. His entire life is an oblation. As with Christ, one cannot separate his person and his work.

> —John M. Haas, "The Sacral Character of the Priest as the Foundation for his Moral Life and Teaching," 144–45

As I begin each day I renew the oblation of my life for the glory of God and the service of his people.

The Priest as Brother

> Accompanying him were the Twelve and some women who had been cured of evil spirits and infirmities, Mary, called Magdalene, from whom seven demons had gone out, Joanna, the wife of Herod's steward Chuza, Susanna, and many others who provided for them out of their resources. (Luke 8:1-3)

The dimensions of mother and sister *are the two fundamental dimensions* of the relationship between women and priests. If this relationship develops in a serene and mature way, women will find no particular difficulties in their contact with priests. For example they will not find difficulties in confessing their faults in the Sacrament of Penance. Even less will they encounter any in undertaking various kinds of *apostolic activities* with priests. Every priest thus has the great *responsibility of developing an authentic way of relating* to women *as a brother,* a way of relating which does not admit of ambiguity. In this perspective, Saint Paul exhorts his disciple Timothy to treat "older women like mothers, younger women like sisters, in all purity" (1 Tim 5:2).

In view of this, women can only be sisters for the priest, and their dignity as sisters needs to be consciously fostered by him. The Apostle Paul, who lived a celibate life, writes in the First Letter to the Corinthians: "I wish that all were as I myself am. *But each one has his own special gift from God,* one of one kind and one of another" (7:7). For him there is no doubt: marriage and celibacy are both gifts of God, to be protected and fostered with great care. . . . Each has its own specific *charism;* each of them is a *vocation* which individuals, with the help of God's grace, must learn to discern in their own lives.

—Saint John Paul II, Letter to Priests for
Holy Thursday, 1995

Lord Jesus, in your relationships to Martha and Mary you model for priests the path of authentic relationships with women. Bless me with the grace to imitate you.

For I am not ashamed of the gospel. It is the power of God for the salvation of everyone who believes: for Jew first, and then Greek. (Rom 1:16)

Your first responsibility is the Word of God. Proclaim the Gospel and comment on it. When you read the Gospel, Christ is truly present. Through you he speaks. The Gospel contains his thoughts, his actions, his love. The words of the Gospel are received into the minds and hearts of those who hear them or read them. In his words, known and loved, the Word himself makes his abode in people's minds and hearts, but in a manner beyond our understanding. It is the work of the Spirit. . . . It is important that we do our task well and, in commenting on the Word do so with the respect that the Church has shown from one generation to the next.

The sacraments are your next responsibility, especially the celebration of the Eucharist. You give the Body and Blood of the Lord to the community of believers. Meditate on that special presence of Christ in the bread and wine marvelously changed into his Body and Blood. Faith, not reason, enables us to explore this great change. Your gestures and bearing when handling the Blessed Sacrament will express your faith; your faith in that Sacrament will inspire and shape your attitude, your actions, your spirituality.

Your responsibility, indeed privilege, of charity is ever-present. Our status in life has an important bearing on the way we relate in love to God and to each other. Our love of others, generous and giving, will always mean making space in our hearts for all . . .

—Basil Cardinal Hume, *Light in the Lord*, 30–31

In what ways does my sharing of Word and Sacrament shape me as a man of genuine pastoral charity?

The Call to Be More Widely Human

I am grateful to him who has strengthened me, Christ Jesus our Lord, because he considered me trustworthy in appointing me to the ministry. (1 Tim 1:12)

As far as my strength will allow me, because I am a priest, I would henceforth be the first to become aware of what the world loves, pursues, suffers. I would be the first to seek, to sympathize, to toil; the first in self fulfillment, the first in self denial—I would be more widely human in my sympathies and more nobly terrestrial in my ambitions than any of the world's servants. . . .

That is why I have taken on my vows and my priesthood (and it is this that gives me my strength and my happiness), in a determination to accept and divinize the powers of the earth. . . . I speak to you, my fellow-priests, who share the battle: if there be any among you who are at a loss in so unforeseen a situation—with your Mass unsaid and your ministry unaccomplished—remember that over and above the administration of the sacraments, as a higher duty than the care of individual souls, you have a universal function to fulfill: the offering to God of the entire world. . . .

You are the leaven spread by providence throughout the battlefield, so that, by your mere presence, the huge mass of our toil and agony may be transformed. Never have you been more priests than you are now, involved as you are and submerged in the tears and blood of a generation—never have you been more active—never more fully in the line of your vocation. I thank you, my God, in that you have made me a priest. . . .

—Pierre Teilhard de Chardin, "The Priest"

I pause to reflect upon the abundance of blessings that have been given to me in my priestly life.

As you sent me into the world, so I sent them into the world. (John 17:18)

It is within the Church's mystery, as a mystery of Trinitarian communion in missionary tension, that every Christian identity is revealed, and likewise the specific identity of the priest and his ministry. Indeed, the priest, by virtue of the consecration which he receives in the sacrament of orders, is sent forth by the Father through the mediatorship of Jesus Christ, to whom he is configured in a special way as head and shepherd of his people, in order to live and work by the power of the Holy Spirit in service of the Church and for the salvation of the world.

In this way the fundamentally "relational" dimension of priestly identity can be understood. Through the priesthood which arises from the depths of the ineffable mystery of God, that is, from the love of the Father, the grace of Jesus Christ and the Holy Spirit's gift of unity, the priest sacramentally enters into communion with the bishop and with other priests in order to serve the People of God who are the Church and to draw all mankind to Christ in accordance with the Lord's prayer: "Holy Father, keep them in your name, which you have given me, that they may be one, even as we are one . . . even as you, Father, are in me, and I in you, that they also may be in us, so that the world may believe that you have sent me" (Jn. 17:11, 21).

—Saint John Paul II, *Pastores Dabo Vobis*, 12

Lord Jesus, I know my truest self only in relationship with you.

For this reason, I remind you to stir into flame the gift of God that you have through the imposition of my hands. (2 Tim 1:6)

The renewal of ordination is *God's work* in us. This day of renewal is not merely a day of our good will, our resolutions, *ours* "in spite of everything." God's grace takes place in us just as on the first day, as long as we have faith and love. On the day when God called us and when he tore us out of the world to be his property and when he sent us out, as those set apart for him (cf. Heb 7:26), right into the midst of the world, our whole life was already present to the regard of his all-knowing love and of his loving knowledge. He already then knew all about us, about what we have experienced and suffered only gradually since the day of our priestly ordination: the puzzle of our own being which is only completely unveiled to us once we have arrived at the end; our tasks, our work, the condition of our age, our needs, our temptations, and even our darkest hours when we sinned. He has not made us priests, like someone who knows the beginning without having any idea of the end. He knew everything, and yet he placed everything precisely the way it is under the law of the priesthood. He has freely given us his Holy Spirit to help with everything, so that each one of us should become the very one whom God conceived and loved.

This Spirit which was "poured out" in us on the day of our ordination is now also in us in the hour of the renewal of ordination.

—Karl Rahner, "The Renewal of Priestly Ordination,"
Theological Investigations III, 174

Lord Jesus, renew the gift of priesthood within me, a life that is fully embraced by your infinite love and compassion.

Hear, O Israel! The LORD is our God, the LORD alone! Therefore you shall love the LORD, your God, with your whole heart, and with your whole being, and with your whole strength. Take to heart these words which I command you today. (Deut 6:4-6)

The Christian priesthood, being of a new order, can be understood only in the light of the newness of Christ, the Supreme Pontiff and eternal Priest, who instituted the priesthood of the ministry as a real participation in His own unique priesthood. The minister of Christ and dispenser of the mysteries of God, therefore, looks up to Him directly as his model and supreme ideal. The Lord Jesus, the only Son of God, was sent by the Father into the world and He became man, in order that humanity which was subject to sin and death might be reborn, and through this new birth might enter the kingdom of heaven. Being entirely consecrated to the will of the Father, Jesus brought forth this new creation by means of His Paschal mystery; thus, He introduced into time and into the world a new form of life which is sublime and divine and which radically transforms the human condition.

Matrimony, according to the will of God, continues the work of the first creation; and considered within the total plan of salvation, it even acquired a new meaning and a new value. Jesus, in fact, has restored its original dignity, has honored it and has raised it to the dignity of a sacrament and of a mysterious symbol of His own union with the Church. Thus, Christian couples walk together toward their heavenly fatherland in the exercise of mutual love, in the fulfillment of their particular obligations, and in striving for the sanctity proper to them. But Christ, "Mediator of a superior covenant," has also opened a new way, in which the human creature adheres wholly and directly to the Lord, and is concerned only with Him and with His affairs. . . .

—Blessed Pope Paul VI,
Sacerdotalis Caelibatus, 19–21

I quietly consider how I might deepen my dedication to Christ, first as a Christian and then as a priest. What does "total" dedication look like in my life?

The Unique Vocation of Christ the Priest   January 25

[W]hen I saw it [the vision of "the likeness of the glory of the LORD"], I fell on my face and heard a voice speak. The voice said to me: Son of man, stand up! I wish to speak to you. As he spoke to me, the spirit entered into me and set me on my feet . . . (Ezek 1:28–2:2)

The priesthood is a call, a particular vocation: "one does not take this honour upon himself, but he is called by God" (Heb 5:4). The Letter to the Hebrews . . . leads us to an understanding of the mystery of Christ the Priest: "Christ did not exalt himself to be made a high priest, but was appointed by him who said to him: . . . You are a priest for ever, after the order of Melchizedek" (5:5-6).

Christ the Son, of one being with the Father, has been made priest of the New Covenant according to the order of Melchizedek: therefore he too was called to the priesthood. It is the Father who "calls" his own Son, whom he has begotten by an act of eternal love, to "come into the world" (cf. Heb 10:5) and to become man. He wills that his only-begotten Son, by taking flesh, should become "a priest for ever": the one priest of the new eternal Covenant. The Son's vocation to the priesthood expresses the depth of the Trinitarian mystery. For only the Son, the Word of the Father, in whom and through whom all things were created, can unceasingly offer creation in sacrifice to the Father, confirming that everything created has come forth from the Father and must become an offering of praise to the Creator. Thus the mystery of the priesthood has its beginning in the Trinity and is, at the same time, a consequence of the Incarnation. By becoming man, the only-begotten and eternal Son of the Father is born of woman, enters into the created order and thus becomes a priest, the one eternal priest.

—Saint John Paul II, Letter to Priests for
Holy Thursday, 1996

Lord Jesus, eternal High Priest, fashion my heart after your own, that I might daily live my priestly vocation with humility and great love.

January 26   Celibacy and the Hope of Eternal Life

> Therefore you shall love the LORD, your God, with your whole heart, and with your whole being, and with your whole strength. Take to heart these words which I command you today. (Deut 6:5-6)

Keep praying your way into what Jesus says about discipleship; place yourself with your whole concrete life before the cross of Christ. Really and honestly face up to the cross and death of your Lord. Accept the solitude which celibacy brings with it. Have the incredible courage to keep asking for grace to understand this way of life that is yours, even if your heart seems unwilling to utter the prayer. Do not think only of yourself and your happiness, think first of those others that you are to serve as a priest. Keep telling yourself that it is a slow business, calling for much patience, to acquire a certain understanding of what one has begun in God's name, in the strength of the Crucified, in reliance on the Gospel. Then you will find yourself being drawn ever deeper into the mystery of that life which springs from the death of Christ.

Your life is steeped in that mystery. Even if we bleed in silence from other wounds that we would be justified in speaking of, perhaps celibacy is a wound which heartens one to attest the hope of eternal life. Remember, this is a chapter of theology that cannot be dealt with by the lecturer's logic or widespread discussion or desultory talk at a meeting of parish priests. It is part of a theology on its knees, at prayer.

—Karl Rahner, *Servants of the Lord*, 167

How have I kept focus upon the spiritual dimensions of my call to priestly celibacy?

> But they urged him, "Stay with us, for it is nearly evening and the day is almost over." So he went in to stay with them. (Luke 24:29)

The Curé of Ars was particularly mindful of the permanence of Christ's real presence in the Eucharist. It was generally before the tabernacle that he spent long hours in adoration, before daybreak or in the evening; it was towards the tabernacle that he often turned during his homilies, saying with emotion: "He is there!" It was also for this reason that he, so poor in his presbytery, did not hesitate to spend large sums on embellishing his church. The appreciable result was that his parishioners quickly took up the habit of coming to pray before the Blessed Sacrament, discovering, through the attitude of their pastor, the grandeur of the mystery of faith.

With such a testimony before our eyes, we think about what the Second Vatican Council says to us today on the subject of priests: "They exercise this sacred function of Christ most of all in the Eucharistic Liturgy." And more recently, the Extraordinary Synod in December 1985 recalled: "The liturgy must favour and make shine brightly the sense of the sacred. It must be imbued with reverence, adoration and glorification of God. . . . The Eucharist is the source and summit of all the Christian life."

Dear brother priests, the example of the Curé of Ars invites us to a serious examination of conscience: what place do we give to the Mass in our daily lives? Is it, as on the day of our Ordination—it was our first act as priests!—the principle of our apostolic work and personal sanctification? What care do we take in preparing for it? And in celebrating it? In praying before the Blessed Sacrament? In encouraging our faithful people to do the same? In making our churches the House of God to which the divine presence attracts the people of our time who too often have the impression of a world empty of God?

> —Saint John Paul II, Letter to Priests for
> Holy Thursday, 1986

Lord Jesus, eternal High Priest, strengthen my love and reverence for the daily celebration of the Eucharist.

January 28   A Life of Constant and Generous Charity

"Amen, I say to you, whatever you did for one of these least brothers of mine, you did for me." (Matt 25:40)

The presbyter is also called to be involved personally in the works of charity, sometimes even in extraordinary forms, as has happened in the past and does so today as well. Here I especially want to underscore that simple, habitual, almost unassuming but constant and generous charity which is manifested not so much in huge projects, but in the daily practice of goodness, which helps, supports and comforts according to each one's capacity.

Clearly the principal concern, and one could say the preference, must be for "the poor and weaker ones, to whom the preaching of the gospel is given as a sign of messianic mission"; for the "sick and dying," to whom the priest should be especially devoted, "visiting them and comforting them in the Lord"; for "young people, who must be looked after with special diligence, as well as for "married couples and parents."

In particular, the priest must devote his time, energy and talents to young people, who are the hope of the community, in order to foster their Christian education and their growth in living according to the gospel.

Even when the presbyter must devote his time and concern to the local community entrusted to him, his heart must remain open to the "fields ripe for the harvest" beyond all borders, as the universal dimension of the spirit and as the personal participation in the Church's missionary tasks.

—Saint John Paul II, "The Priest Is a Shepherd to the Community," General Audience, May 19, 1993

In what ways have I made the young, the poor, and the afflicted a priority in my ministry?

God of My Vocation

"You are the light of the world" (Matt 5:14)

You have made me your priest, and have chosen me to be an earthly sign of Your grace to others. You have put your grace into my hands, Your truth into my mouth. And although it doesn't surprise me that men should recognize You when they come to meet You in Your only begotten Son, or in the chaste waters of baptism, or in the silent form of the host, or in the words of Scripture so simple and yet so profound, still I find it all but incredible that you desire to come into your kingdom in the hearts of others through *me*. How can men possibly recognize you in *me*?

Your grace remains pure, even when it is dispensed through my hands. Your gospel is still the good tidings of great joy, even when it's not particularly noticeable that my soul is exulting in God my Savior. And Your light continues to shine forth, changing the dark death-shadows of our earth into the brilliant noonday of Your grace, even when this light has to find its way to your people through the cracked and dusty pains of my tiny lantern.

Your charge to me, Your commission itself has become my very life. It ruthlessly claims all my energies for itself; it lives from my own life. As your messenger, I can live my own personal life only by passing on Your word. I am Your messenger, and nothing more. Your lamp, Lord, burns with the oil of my life.

—Karl Rahner, *Encounters with Silence*, 70–71

I am humbled to consider my life as Christ's light in the world.

For I received from the Lord what I also handed on to you . . .
(1 Cor 11:23)

The priest, ordained precisely to be a Eucharistic person, is, of necessity, at the heart of the Church and most himself when he stands at the altar of Christ. His identity, as a priest, flows from the words of consecration, "This is my body . . . This is my blood." Uniquely among the People of God, St. Paul's words are proper to the priest, "For me to live is Christ." At the Last Supper, our Lord revealed his intended way to continually become present in our midst. It is through the transformation of bread and wine into his body and blood at the hands of the priest. "Do this in remembrance of me."

We can only conclude that a priestly spirituality is always, fundamentally, a Eucharistic spirituality. The often expressed desire for a more developed spirituality of the priesthood, particularly for diocesan priests, must always find its foundation and fulfillment in the Eucharist. It is in the Mass that the priest will find his true identity and the means to become more perfectly conformed to Christ the High Priest who is also the immaculate Lamb of Sacrifice and the Shepherd of Souls. As a consequence, the priest becomes a living sacramental sign of the presence of Jesus Christ in our midst, in our world. This is a heavy office to bear because the priest is held to a higher standard than the ordinary Christian. The Catholic faithful have expectations regarding the depth of the priest's interior life and the example of his exterior behavior. Accepting his human frailty and imperfections, they nonetheless look for spiritual inspiration and moral guidance from their priests. A priest must live close to the Eucharist if he is to fulfill the expectations of the Church and the people in his pastoral ministry.

—Gabriel B. O'Donnell, "The Eucharist—
Heart of the Priest's Life," 130

I am resolved to better prepare myself for the celebration of the Eucharist, and to take ample time thereafter in thanksgiving.

> But you are "a chosen race, a royal priesthood, a holy nation, a people of his own, so that you may announce the praises" of him who called you out of darkness into his wonderful light. (1 Pet 2:9)

During the sacred Triduum, the one Priesthood of the new and everlasting covenant is made visible to the eyes of our faith, the Priesthood which is in Christ himself. To him indeed can be applied the words about the high priest who, "chosen from among men is appointed to act on their behalf." As man, Christ is priest; he is "high priest of the good things that have come." At the same time, however, this man-priest is the Son, of one being with the Father. For this reason his Priesthood—the Priesthood of his redemptive sacrifice—is one and unrepeatable. It is the transcendent fulfillment of all that Priesthood is.

This very same Priesthood of Christ is shared by everyone in the Church through the sacrament of Baptism. Although the words "a priest chosen from among men" are applied to each of us who shares in the ministerial Priesthood, they refer first of all to membership in the messianic people, in the royal Priesthood. They point to our roots in the common Priesthood of the faithful, which lies at the base of our individual call to the priestly ministry.

The "lay faithful" are those from among whom each one of us "has been chosen," from among whom our Priesthood has been born. First of all, there are our parents, then our brothers and sisters as well as the many people of the different backgrounds from which each of us comes, human and Christian backgrounds, which are sometimes also de-Christianized. The priestly vocation, in fact, does not always emerge in an atmosphere favorable to it; sometimes the grace of vocation passes through an unfavorable environment and even through occasional resistance by parents or family.

—Saint John Paul II, Letter to Priests for
Holy Thursday, 1989

I pause to prayerfully reflect upon the beginnings of my vocation within my family and my community, upon all the positive and/or negative influences.

> Therefore, we are not discouraged; rather, although our outer self is wasting away, our inner self is being renewed day by day. (2 Cor 4:16)

Dearly beloved brothers! Day after day, year after year, we discover the content and substance, which are truly inexpressible, of our Priesthood in the depths of the mystery of the Redemption. And I hope that the present Year of the extraordinary Jubilee will serve this purpose in a special way! *Let us open our eyes ever wider*—the eyes of our soul—in order to understand better what it means to celebrate the Eucharist, the Sacrifice of Christ Himself, entrusted to our priestly lips and hands in the community of the Church.

Let us open our eyes ever wider—the eyes of our soul—in order to understand better what it means to forgive sins and reconcile human consciences with the infinitely holy God, with the God of Truth and Love.

Let us open our eyes ever wider—the eyes of our soul—in order to understand better what it means to act "in persona Christi," in the name of Christ; to act with His power with the power which, in a word, is rooted in the salvific ground of the Redemption.

Let us open our eyes ever wider—the eyes of our soul—in order to understand better what the mystery of the Church is. We are men of the Church! . . .

My brothers! To each of us "grace was given . . . according to the measure of Christ's gift . . . for building up the body of Christ." May we be faithful to this grace! May we be heroically faithful to this grace!

—Saint John Paul II, Letter to Priests for
Holy Thursday, 1984

I consider the various ways that my fidelity to Christ is expressed in my priestly life.

And I have given them the glory you gave me, so that they may be one, as we are one, I in them and you in me, that they may be brought to perfection as one, that the world may know that you sent me, and that you loved them even as you loved me. (John 17:22-23)

At the April 17, 2008, Mass with the Pope at Nationals Stadium in Washington, D.C., as I was praying in thanksgiving during the silence after the distribution of Holy Communion, I looked into the stadium from the sanctuary and had a profound experience of the unity in Christ that is the essence of the Church's life. The Pope is the visible center of universal communion, but Jesus, risen from the dead in the body that we had just received sacramentally, works invisibly to unite, ever more closely, all those who come to know him in his body, the Church. We know this, but sometimes we feel it; and such an experience was given me during this moment of Pope Benedict's visit to our country. After all the preparations, the security concerns, the programming to the minute, the care that all would go as planned, the Lord acts as he will to remind us who we are and to draw us into the center of our lives: life with him . . .

The Eucharist is the sacrament of unity, and unity is a mark of the Church. Unity is first of all a gift from Christ, prayed for at the Last Supper, bestowed at Pentecost with the gift of the Holy Spirit, guaranteed through visible communion with the successor of Peter. Often, perhaps, we don't think about the fullest extent of this unity as willed by Christ himself. It is the will of Christ that all those he died to save should be gathered visibly into his body, the Church, and there receive sacramentally his Eucharistic body in Holy Communion.

It is the Church's mission in this world to extend this unity. How can we receive the body of the Lord in the Eucharist and not be driven to invite all to come to know him intimately in sharing his gifts?

—Francis Cardinal George,
"Universal Communion," 45–46

How do the blessings of the Eucharist impel me to work more fervently to promote unity within the local and universal church?

February 3 A Priest's Friendship with Christ

"You are my friends if you do what I command you. I no longer call you slaves, because a slave does not know what his master is doing. I have called you friends, because I have told you everything I have heard from my Father." (John 15:14-15)

"Friends": this is what Jesus calls the Apostles. This is what he also wishes to call us who, thanks to the Sacrament of Holy Orders, share in his priesthood. Let us listen to these words with great emotion and humility. They contain the truth. First of all, the truth about friendship, but also a truth about ourselves who share in the priesthood of Christ as ministers of the Eucharist. Could Jesus have expressed to us his friendship any more eloquently than by enabling us, as priests of the New Covenant, to act in his name, *in persona Christi Capitis?* Precisely this takes place in all our priestly service, when we administer the sacraments and especially when we celebrate the Eucharist. We repeat the words that he spoke over the bread and wine and, through our ministry, the same consecration that he brought about takes place. Can there be a fuller expression of friendship than this? It goes to the very heart of our priestly ministry.

Christ says: "You did not choose me, but I chose you and appointed you that you should go and bear fruit and that your fruit should abide" (Jn 15:16). At the end of this Letter, I offer these words to you as a wish. On the day of the institution of the sacrament of the priesthood let us make this our wish for one another, dear Brothers: that we may go and bear fruit, like the Apostles, and that our fruit may abide.

—Saint John Paul II, Letter to Priests for
Holy Thursday, 1997

In my daily ministry as Christ's priest, I seek to be ever more conscious of my friendship with him.

The Domain of God's Voice   February 4

> Oh, that today you would hear his voice: / Do not harden your hearts
> . . . (Ps 95:7-8)

Although the Gospels first relate how the apostles straightaway forsook everything to follow the Lord and only later speak of the difficulties of their chosen road, we cannot conclude from this that the first step was easy for them. The following of Christ always represents a painful break in life. The renunciation is real but the import of the call outweighs everything else . . .

The consenter knows that much struggle awaits him. He will not always have joy; hours of doubt will overfall him; his mistakes and weaknesses will not abandon him. He will be in the danger of increasing the multitude of the lukewarm. He does not have the feeling that the monastery, seminary or community receiving him is gaining much. He is a questionable gift with which they will be able to do less than with most of the others who could have applied. He, nevertheless, has no choice, since God has precisely pointed to him . . .

If God gives him the strength to consent, He can also give him the strength to persevere in letting himself be changed. His awareness that this strength is being bestowed by God allows him to draw the line of demarcation and to sacrifice whatever is demanded. He derives the strength to avoid always computing in a petty way the value of each individual thing he must give up. Rather, he learns to appreciate rightly the value of things from the one great gift he makes. For him, they are gifts which he is allowed to give away. In this way, he will be able to renounce things in order to remain in the domain of God's voice. His place is not alongside the voice, nor in the space of an echo, but right in the middle of the voice, where the Word is a living thing and has the name of God.

—Adrienne von Speyr, *They Followed His Call*, 31–33

Amidst the cacophony of modern society and contemporary ministry, bless me, Lord, with that inner silence that allows your voice to be heard.

February 5   The Priest, Answering Love with Love

From his fullness we have all received, grace in place of grace . . .
(John 1:16)

A vocation to the priesthood or to practice of the evangelical counsels is in fact a sign of great love by him who has chosen you out from a large number and called you to share his friendship in a special way: " 'I shall not call you servants any more,' said Our Lord, 'because a servant does not know his master's business; I call you friends, because I have made known to you everything I have learned from my Father'" (Jn 15:5). May your hearts be ever filled with gratitude and joy for this precious gift of your vocation!

What a joy it is for the Pope to see you all gathered here in this sacred place of prayer . . . Coming as you do from varying backgrounds, united in fraternal love in one faith and dedicated to the service of one and the same Master, you have answered love with love. One is not always able to give due recognition to the depth of your sacrifice and to the sometimes heroic perseverance which you must have to live out your lives in the service of others, and most often of the poorest. Nor is it easy to appreciate fully the deep meaning of your lives, for they are not motivated by human interest, but illuminated by faith. "It is not everyone who can accept what I have said, but only those to whom it is granted" (Mt 19:11), as Our Lord likewise tells us.

The task which is yours is often exacting. Even though the world to which you devote yourselves manifests a surprising richness of natural virtues and a remarkable religious spirit, it demands your time, your skill and your heart, without allowing you rest. "The harvest is rich but the laborers are few" (Mt 9:37).

—Blessed Pope Paul VI, Homily in the Manila
Metropolitan Cathedral-Basilica, November 27, 1970

Lord, it is a grace and privilege to be asked to give of myself so completely—my time, my skill, my heart. All are yours!

Priesthood Interpreted in Christ Alone February 6

> Here is my servant whom I uphold, / my chosen one with whom I am
> pleased. / Upon him I have put my spirit; / he shall bring forth justice
> to the nations. (Isa 42:1)

Another grace of the synod [On the Formation of Priests] was a new
maturity in the way of looking at priestly service in the Church; a maturity
which keeps pace with the times in which our mission is being carried out.
This maturity finds expression in a more profound interpretation of the
very essence of the sacramental Priesthood and thus also of the personal
life of each and every priest, that is to say, of each priest's participation in
the saving mystery of Christ: *sacerdos alter Christus*. This is an expression which indicates how necessary it is that Christ be the starting point
for interpreting the reality of the Priesthood. Only in this way can we do
full justice to the truth about the priest, who, having been "chosen from
among men, is appointed to act on behalf of men in relation to God." The
human dimension of priestly service, in order to be fully authentic, must
be rooted in God. Indeed, in every way that this service is "on behalf of
men," it is also "in relation to God": It serves the manifold richness of this
relationship. Without an effort to respond fully to that "anointing with the
Spirit of the Lord" which establishes him in the ministerial Priesthood,
the priest cannot fulfill the expectations that people—the Church and the
world—rightly place in him.

. . . The need for priests—in some ways a growing phenomenon—
should help to overcome the crisis of priestly identity. The experience of
recent decades shows ever more clearly how much the priest is needed both
in the Church and in the world, not in some "laicized" form, but in the form
which is drawn from the Gospel and from the rich tradition of the Church.

—Saint John Paul II, Letter to Priests for
Holy Thursday, 1991

Lord Jesus, the whole of my life, all of it, is made sacred in your call to
priestly service. Bless me with the generosity to open my life completely
to your transforming grace.

I am the good shepherd, and I know mine and mine know me, just as the Father knows me and I know the Father; and I will lay down my life for the sheep. (John 10:14-15)

In times of rapid change and confusion, some people become frozen in fear, desperately searching for certitude, rigidly clinging to what is familiar and comfortable, closing themselves off from any possibility of an encounter with what might challenge or shake their carefully constructed worlds. You may know some people who live like that—insulated and isolated from the realities of life. It cannot be like that with you.

As priests, you will be called to exercise the prophetic ministry described by Isaiah in the first reading. Anyone who hopes to exercise this ministry effectively must be willing to get close to people, the kind of people Isaiah describes: the lowly, the brokenhearted, the captive, the imprisoned, those who mourn.

. . . To be an effective priest also means that you must be willing to get your hands dirty. No matter how confusing, messy, or bewildering life may seem, it is there that you will encounter the Lord. You will not find him in fancy vestments or fixed formulas; you will not find him in complex structures or in bricks and mortar, as important as these may be at times for the well-being and good order of the faith community.

But you will encounter him in the lives of the people you serve. So listen closely to them as they articulate their needs and wants, their hungers and aspirations. If you listen attentively, you cannot help but hear the voice of him who calls you out of your fear and doubt and anoints you to proclaim, boldly and lovingly, the glad tidings he has revealed to us. Yes, know them, really *know* them, so that you can recognize in them Christ's voice, and help them to celebrate those moments when their lives are transformed by his life-giving word.

—Joseph Cardinal Bernardin, Homily for
Priesthood Ordination, May 18, 1991

Sometimes it is so much easier to keep a distance, to treat my people as statistics rather than to deal with them as real people with real problems. I wonder how I might make myself more available to my flock.

He advanced a little and fell to the ground and prayed that if it were possible the hour might pass by him . . . (Mark 14:35)

Between the words of institution: "This is my Body which is given for you"; "This cup which is poured out for you is the new covenant in my Blood," and the effective fulfillment of what these words express, the prayer of Gethsemane is interposed. Is it not true that, in the course of the Paschal events, it is this prayer which leads to the reality which is also visible and which the sacrament both signifies and renews?

The Priesthood, which has become our inheritance by virtue of a sacrament so closely linked to the Eucharist, is always a call to share in the same divine-human, salvific and redemptive reality which precisely by means of our ministry must bear ever new fruit in the history of salvation: "that you should go and bear fruit and that your fruit should abide." The saintly Curé of Ars, the second centenary of whose birth we celebrated last year, appears to us precisely as a man of this call, reviving the awareness of it in us too. In his heroic life, prayer was the means which enabled him to remain constantly in Christ, to "watch" with Christ as his "hour" approached. This "hour" does not cease to decide the salvation of the many people entrusted to the priestly service and pastoral care of every priest. In the life of Saint John Mary Vianney, this "hour" was realized particularly by his service in the confessional.

The prayer in Gethsemane is like a cornerstone, placed by Christ at the foundation of the service of the cause "entrusted to him by the Father" at the foundation of the work of the world's redemption through the sacrifice offered on the Cross.

—Saint John Paul II, Letter to Priests for
Holy Thursday, 1987

Lord Jesus, may my prayer always reflect your own heart's desire to be totally one with the Father.

How can I repay the LORD / for all the great good done for me? / I will raise the cup of salvation / and call on the name of the LORD. (Ps 116:12-13)

We must orient our whole day towards the Mass. It is the central point and the sun of the day. It is, as it were, the focus from which there comes to us light, fervor and supernatural joy. We must hope that, little by little, our priesthood will take possession of our soul and our life so that it may be said of us: "he is always a priest." That is the effect of a Eucharistic life, embalmed in the perfume of the sacrifice which makes us an *alter Christus*.

How good it is to see a priest after long years of fidelity, living with the true spirit of the divine oblation! There are many priests entirely dedicated to Christ and to souls who realize this ideal fully; they are the glory of the Church and the joy of the divine Master.

If we also wish to rise to the heights of our priestly vocation, if we want it to impress its character on our whole existence so as to inflame us with love and zeal, we must prepare our souls to receive the graces of our Mass.

. . . Is it right that the priest should perpetuate the sacrifice of the Cross without conforming himself, whole-heartedly, to the immolation which he carries out on the altar? . . . In His oblation, Christ bore in Himself the whole human race. Following His example, let us open our hearts wide to the necessities and sufferings of all men; let us think of sinners, of the poor, of the sick, of the dying, as though we were charged with presenting all their supplications to the Lord. In this way we shall each be the spokesman of the whole Church.

—Blessed Columba Marmion,
Christ: The Ideal of the Priest, 206

I am too often in a hurry to get out of the sacristy after Mass and to get on with my day, leaving no time for a prayerful thanksgiving.

I look to you in the sanctuary / to see your power and glory. / For your love is better than life . . . My soul shall be sated as with choice food, / with joyous lips my mouth shall praise you! (Ps 63:3-4, 6)

We sincerely hope, Venerable Brethren, that these lessons from the life of St. John Mary Vianney may make all of the sacred ministers committed to your care feel sure that they must exert every effort to be outstanding in their devotion to prayer; this can really be done, even if they are very busy with apostolic labors.

But if they are to do this, their lives must conform to the norms of faith that so imbued John Mary Vianney and enabled him to perform such wonderful works. "Oh the wonderful faith of this priest"—one of his colleagues in the sacred ministry remarked—"It is great enough to enrich all the souls of the diocese!"

This constant union with God is best achieved and preserved through the various practices of priestly piety; many of the more important of them, such as daily meditation, visits to the Blessed Sacrament, recitation of the Rosary, careful examination of conscience, the Church, in her wise and provident regulations, has made obligatory for priests. As for the hours of the Office, priests have undertaken a serious obligation to the Church to recite them.

The neglect of some of these rules may often be the reason why certain churchmen are caught up in the whirl of external affairs, gradually lose their feeling for sacred things and finally fall into serious difficulties when they are shorn of all spiritual protection and enticed by the attractions of this earthly life. John Mary Vianney on the contrary "never neglected his own salvation, no matter how busy he may have been with that of others."

—Saint John XXIII,
Sacerdotii Nostri Primordia, 40–43

Bless me, Lord Jesus, with a deeper commitment to be a man of prayer, in the spirit and with the fervor of the Curé of Ars.

February 11   The Laity's Right to Our Service

[W]hoever wishes to be great among you shall be your servant; whoever wishes to be first among you shall be your slave. (Matt 20:26-27)

Each of us who shares by sacramental ordination in Christ's Priesthood must constantly reread this "inscription" of Christ's redeeming service. For each one of us is appointed "to act on behalf of men in relation to God." The council rightly affirms that "the laity have the right to receive in abundance from their pastors the spiritual goods of the Church, especially the assistance of the word of God and the sacraments."

This service is at the very heart of our mission. Certainly our brothers and sisters the lay faithful look to us as "servants of Christ and stewards of the mysteries of God." Here is found the full authenticity of our vocation, of our place in the Church. During the [1988] Synod of Bishops, in its discussion on the very question of the laity's apostolate, it was frequently mentioned that the laity have very much at heart the authenticity of vocations and priestly life. Indeed this is the first condition for the vitality of the lay state and for the apostolate proper to the laity. It is not at all a matter of "laicizing" the clergy any more than it is a matter of "clericalizing" the laity. The Church develops organically according to the principle of the multiplicity and diversity of "gifts," that is to say, charisms. Each one "has his own special gift" "for the common good." "As each one has received a gift, employ it for one another, as good stewards of God's varied grace." These statements by the apostles are fully relevant in our own time. Likewise the exhortation "to lead a life worthy of the calling" to which each one has been called is directed to everyone both the ordained and the laity.

—Saint John Paul II, Letter to Priests for
Holy Thursday, 1989

Lord Jesus, forgive me for the times that I have lorded "my" priesthood over the laity, for the times that I have sought to be served rather than to serve.

> In the days when he was in the flesh, he offered prayers and supplications with loud cries and tears to the one who was able to save him from death . . . (Heb 5:7)

If there were no Mass, all the offering in the world would be in vain, all offering of creation pointless. The entire effort of mankind to bring back the universe to God stands revealed as powerless and incomplete. For the Sacrifice of the Mass, since it continues the Sacrifice of the Cross, constitutes the essential act and culminating point of Christ's redemptive mediation.

In this way, through his power over Christ's Sacramental Body, the priest becomes, by extension, the privileged craftsman of the world's consecration. In the restricted space where, holding the Host in his hands, he lets the Sovereign Priest pronounce the words of consecration with his lips, the poorest and the humblest priest embraces the universe and continues its redemption.

The modern priest must make this stupendous certainty his own. . . . In this action he will, without any doubt, gather up all his pastoral intentions; all those he names in the two "Mementos," the parish where he is rector or curate, the work entrusted to him, the leaders he has to nourish with the living God. But he will not limit himself to his own sphere; he will extend his intention to the scale of the whole world.

Yet to be really co-extensive with the world's true dimensions, the priest's intention will have to become universal. It will not be satisfied with what he can see, or with what he knows. It will gather up more than the visible congregation. Beyond the limits of church or chapel, it will go seeking through time and space for every being, spiritual or inanimate, to bring them back from the four winds to the foot of the eternal Calvary. The Church herself sings in her liturgy: *"Terra, pontus, astra, mundus—Quo lavantur flumine*: Earth, sea, the stars, the universe, all are washed by this Blood."

> —Emmanuel-Célestin Cardinal Suhard,
> *The Church Today*, 310

Expand my heart, O Lord, that I may embrace with your love all the world, and upon your altar place its joys and sorrows, its strength and weakness, its failures and its triumphs.

It is due to [God] that you are in Christ Jesus, who became for us wisdom from God, as well as righteousness, sanctification, and redemption, so that, as it is written, "Whoever boasts, should boast in the Lord." (1 Cor 1:30-31)

How very deeply each one of us is constituted in his own priestly being through the mystery of the Redemption! It is precisely this that the liturgy of Holy Thursday brings home to us. It is precisely this that we must meditate upon during the Jubilee Year. It is upon this that our personal interior renewal must be concentrated, for the Jubilee Year is understood by the Church as a time of spiritual renewal for everyone. If we must be witnesses of this renewal for others, for our brothers and sisters in the Christian vocation, then we must be witnesses to it, and spokesmen for it, to ourselves: the Holy Year of the Redemption is a year of renewal in the priestly vocation.

By bringing about such an interior renewal in our holy vocation, we shall be able better and more effectively to preach "a year of favor from the Lord." In fact, the mystery of the Redemption is not just a theological abstraction, but an unceasing reality, through which God embraces man in Christ with His eternal love—and man recognizes this love, allows himself to be guided and permeated by it, to be interiorly transformed by it, and through it he becomes "a new creation." Man, thus created anew by love, the love that is revealed to him in Jesus Christ, raises the eyes of his soul to God and together with the psalmist declares: "With him is plenteous Redemption!"

In the Jubilee Year this declaration must rise with special power from the heart of the whole Church, and this must come about, dear brothers, through your witness and your priestly ministry.

—Saint John Paul II, Letter to Priests for
Holy Thursday, 1983

Lord Jesus, I pray that I might experience the infinite depth of your redeeming love, and generously proclaim this love in my priestly ministry.

Vessels of Clay February 14

> But we hold this treasure in earthen vessels, that the surpassing power may be of God and not from us. (2 Cor 4:7)

Clearly the appearances of the risen Jesus bestow a special gift. Jesus does not first appear to neutral bystanders but to the very disciples who denied and abandoned him. His first act is to forgive their betrayal, and this forgiveness becomes for them a moment of personal transformation. The Spirit who raised Jesus from the dead now changes his followers from weak, fearful men into forceful preachers, able now to carry the message of Jesus into the world. Their witness is always twofold. They testify that God's Spirit raised Jesus from the dead, and that the same Spirit changed and transformed their lives, bringing them from sin and death to new life in Christ.

The message of Jesus has always been carried on the shoulders of weak followers, and this has been both its genius and its Achilles' heel. What Chesterton wrote of Peter is true of the whole church. "All the empires and the kingdoms have failed, because of this inherent and continual weakness, that they were founded by strong men and upon strong men. But this one thing, the historic Christian church, was founded on a weak man, and for that reason it is indestructible. For no chain is stronger than its weakest link." Human weakness starkly underscores that God's Spirit carries the church. Though God uses the natural gifts and talents of his followers, human weakness offers a privileged moment for God's grace to shine through. . . .

The church has few illusions about the weaknesses of officeholders, of popes, bishops, and priests. Indeed, the promise of obedience by a priest to his bishop is made from one weak human vessel to another.

—Howard P. Bleichner, *View from the Altar*, 123–24

Painfully aware of the human weakness of the church's ministers, am I generous in giving myself and others the benefit of the doubt?

For the LORD, your God, has chosen him out of all your tribes to be in
attendance to minister in the name of the LORD, him and his descendants for all time. (Deut 18:5)

Holy Thursday is an occasion for us to ask ourselves over and over
again: to what did we say our "yes"? What does this "being a priest of
Jesus Christ" mean? The Second Canon of our Missal, which was probably
compiled in Rome already at the end of the second century, describes the
essence of the priestly ministry with the words with which, in the Book
of Deuteronomy (18: 5, 7), the essence of the Old Testament priesthood is
described: *astare coram te et tibi ministrare* ["to stand and minister in the
name of the Lord"].

There are therefore two duties that define the essence of the priestly
ministry: in the first place, "to stand in his [the Lord's] presence." In the
Book of Deuteronomy this is read in the context of the preceding disposition, according to which priests do not receive any portion of land in the
Holy Land—they live of God and for God. They did not attend to the usual
work necessary to sustain daily life. Their profession was to "stand in the
Lord's presence"—to look to him, to be there for him. Hence, ultimately,
the word indicated a life in God's presence, and with this also a ministry
of representing others. As the others cultivated the land, from which the
priest also lived, so he kept the world open to God, he had to live with his
gaze on him.

Now if this word is found in the Canon of the Mass immediately after
the consecration of the gifts, after the entrance of the Lord in the assembly
of prayer, then for us this points to being before the Lord present, that is,
it indicates the Eucharist as the centre of priestly life.

—Pope Benedict XVI, Homily for the Chrism Mass,
March 20, 2008

As I stand at the altar, Lord Jesus, keep me aware that you have called me
to represent your holy people.

Anointed with the Oil of Gladness February 16

You love justice and hate wrongdoing; / therefore God, your God, has anointed you / with the oil of gladness. (Ps 45:8)

In the eternal "today" of Holy Thursday, when Christ showed his love for us to the end (cf. Jn 13:1), we recall the happy day of the institution of the priesthood, as well as the day of our own priestly ordination. The Lord anointed us in Christ with the oil of gladness, and this anointing invites us to accept and appreciate this great gift: the gladness, the joy of being a priest. Priestly joy is a priceless treasure, not only for the priest himself but for the entire faithful people of God: that faithful people from which he is called to be anointed and which he, in turn, is sent to anoint.

Anointed with the oil of gladness so as to anoint others with the oil of gladness. Priestly joy has its source in the Father's love, and the Lord wishes the joy of this Love to be "ours" and to be "complete" (Jn 15:11). I like to reflect on joy by contemplating Our Lady, for Mary, the "Mother of the living Gospel, is a wellspring of joy for God's little ones" (Evangelii Gaudium, 288). I do not think it is an exaggeration to say that priest is very little indeed: the incomparable grandeur of the gift granted us for the ministry sets us among the least of men. The priest is the poorest of men unless Jesus enriches him by his poverty, the most useless of servants unless Jesus calls him his friend, the most ignorant of men unless Jesus patiently teaches him as he did Peter, the frailest of Christians unless the Good Shepherd strengthens him in the midst of the flock. No one is more "little" than a priest left to his own devices; and so our prayer of protection against every snare of the Evil One is the prayer of our Mother: I am a priest because he has regarded my littleness (cf. Lk 1:48). And in that littleness we find our joy.

—Pope Francis, Homily for the Chrism Mass,
April 17, 2014

It is not uncommon that we priests struggle at times with depression. Anoint me, Lord Jesus, in those times of darkness, with the healing oil of joy!

> I heard a loud voice from the throne saying, "Behold, God's dwelling is
> with the human race." (Rev 21:3)

When I was consecrated [a bishop] twenty years ago, I'm afraid I
thought I was God's gift to the Church. It was probably even worse thirty-
four years ago when I was ordained a priest. Like most young people, I
thought I had all the answers. All I needed was the opportunity to show
people how things should be done. My dear mother, who is here in the
cathedral with me this evening, sensed the problem. She wisely told me
just before the consecration ceremony began: "Joe, make sure you walk
straight, but don't look too pleased."

I understand much better now what she meant, because in the intervening years I have matured. I now realize—in a way I didn't before—that the
human condition is very complex and at times paradoxical. While there is
surely a wonderful clarity about our Catholic faith, just how that faith is to
be lived out each day in our highly secularized, consumer-oriented society
is not always so clear. So I have learned to be a little more realistic, a little
more humble in terms of my ability to set things right, to provide answers
to the challenges and problems of daily life.

In the final analysis, it is not so much our human efforts that are responsible for the good things in life as it is God's grace. So we should not
pretend that everything depends on us. Rather, we should see ourselves as
instruments in the Lord's hands. I know that my best planned efforts often
produce little or nothing while, at other times, in spite of my blundering,
things turn out well. I'm sure that you have experienced this also.

We simply have to place our faith and trust in the Lord. And why
shouldn't we?

> —Joseph Cardinal Bernardin, Homily for the Mass
> Commemorating the 20th Anniversary of
> Episcopal Ordination, April 26, 1986

Lord Jesus, help me always to recognize that in my ministry I am totally
dependent upon your amazing graces.

> [B]e watchful with all perseverance and supplication for all the holy
> ones and also for me, that speech may be given me to open my mouth,
> to make known with boldness the mystery of the gospel for which I am
> an ambassador in chains . . . (Eph 6:18-20)

I care nothing for the judgments of the world, even of the ecclesiastical world. My intention, before God, is upright and pure. I want a seal, a visible seal, set on the intention conceived in the first years of my clerical life. That is the intention of being entirely and solely under obedience, in the hands of my Bishop, even in matters of no importance. I intend that the promise which I make shall be a declaration before the whole Church that it is my will to be crushed, despised, neglected for the love of Jesus and for the good of souls, and to live always in poverty and detachment from all the interests and riches of this world.

During this retreat the Lord has been pleased to show me yet again all the importance for me, and for the success of my priestly ministry, of the spirit of sacrifice, which I desire, shall from now on ever more inspire my conduct "as a servant and prisoner of Jesus Christ." And also I want all the undertakings in which I shall take part during this present year to be done in this spirit, in so far as I have a share in them; all are to be done for the Lord and in the Lord: plenty of enthusiasm but no anxiety about their greater or lesser success. I will do them as if everything depended on me but as if I myself counted for nothing, without the slightest attachment to them, ready to destroy or abandon them at a sign from those to whom I owe obedience.

O blessed Jesus, what I am proposing to do is hard and I feel weak, because I am full of self-love, but the will is there and comes from my heart. Help me! Help me!

—Saint John XXIII, *Journal of a Soul*, 245–46

I consider the importance of my annual retreat and how my resolutions have brought me nearer to Christ.

> For my eyes are upon you, O LORD, my Lord; / in you I take refuge
> . . . (Ps 141:8)

"The eyes of all in the synagogue were fixed on him" (Lk 4:20). What the evangelist Luke says about the people in the synagogue at Nazareth that Sabbath, listening to Jesus' commentary on the words of the prophet Isaiah which he had just read, can be applied to all Christians. They are always called to recognize in Jesus of Nazareth the definitive fulfillment of the message of the prophets: "And he began to say to them, 'Today this Scripture has been fulfilled in your hearing'" (Lk 4:21). The "Scripture" he had read was this: "The Spirit of the Lord is upon me, because he has anointed me to preach good news to the poor. He has sent me to proclaim release to the captives and recovery of sight to the blind, to set at liberty those who are oppressed, to proclaim the acceptable year of the Lord" (Lk 4:18-19; cf. Is 61:1-2). Jesus thus presents himself as filled with the Spirit, "consecrated with an anointing," "sent to preach good news to the poor." He is the Messiah, the Messiah who is priest, prophet and king.

These are the features of Christ upon which the eyes of faith and love of Christians should be fixed. Using this "contemplation" as a starting point and making continual reference to it, the synod fathers reflected on the problem of priestly formation in present-day circumstances. This problem cannot be solved without previous reflection upon the ministerial priesthood . . . as a participation—in the Church—in the very priesthood of Jesus Christ.

—Saint John Paul II, *Pastores Dabo Vobis*, 11

Lord Jesus, you and you alone are the model for priestly life. My eyes are fixed on you.

Chastity: An Invitation to Full Humanity   February 20

[I]f I have all faith so as to move mountains but do not have love, I am nothing. (1 Cor 13:2b)

We have an urgent need to think together about the meaning of the vow of chastity. It touches issues central to our humanity: our sexuality, our bodiliness, our need to express and receive affection, and yet frequently we fear to talk. So often it is an area in which we struggle alone, afraid of judgment or incomprehension.

It is of course true that this vow is, like the others, a means. It gives us the freedom to preach, the mobility to respond to needs. But with this vow it is perhaps especially important that it is not merely endured as a grim necessity. Unless we can learn, perhaps through much time and suffering, to embrace it positively, then it can poison our lives. And we can do so because it is, like all the vows, ordered towards *caritas*, towards that love which is the very life of God. It is a particular way of loving. If it is not that, then it will lead us to frustration and sterility.

The first sin against chastity is a failure to love. It was said of Dominic that "since he loved all, he was loved by all." What is at issue, yet again, is the authority of our preaching. How can we speak of the God of love if that is not a mystery that we live? If we do so, then it will ask of us death and resurrection. Ultimately this vow demands of us that we follow where God has gone before. Our God has become human, and invites us to do so as well.

—Timothy Radcliffe, OP, *Sing a New Song*, 48–50

Do I live in fear or denial of my sexuality, or am I coming to embrace it as a pathway to the very life of God?

> When they brought their boats to the shore, they left everything and
> followed him. (Luke 5:11)

And when the bishop takes my hands in his hands, I shall promise the
Church obedience and loyalty: exacting and unwavering obedience, selfless
obedience, obedience whereby a man forgets his life in work that matters
more than he does, obedience whereby a man loses himself only to find
himself again in this steadfastness and constant generosity. Behold, I lay
my hands in Your hands, my God. So take my hands and lead me: through
joy and grief, through honor and disgrace, in labor and anguish, in my
ordinary life and at great moments, in the holy stillness of Your house but
also on the long, dusty roads of the world. Lead me today and always, lead
me into the kingdom of Your eternal life.

When You have called and elevated me in this way, anointed me with
power and sent me forth, I shall arise and walk again as Your priest for all
eternity. Ordination to the priesthood is really Your last great word spoken
in my life, Your last, crucial, final, irrevocable call that shapes my life now
for always. Whatever happens in my life now can only be my answer to,
my living of, this final call, only a carrying out of this one final command
that will rule my life always. Grant, therefore, that I may be found faithful.
You have called me and You will see to it (1 Thes 5:24). For You do not
repent of Your gifts. On the day of my ordination let the morning prayer of
my priestly life be these words from the spirit of Ignatius, the holy warrior:
*Eternal Word, only begotten Son of God, Teach me true generosity. Teach
me to serve You as You deserve. To give without counting the cost, to fight
heedless of wounds, to labor without seeking rest, to sacrifice myself without
thought of any reward, save the knowledge that I have done Your will. Amen.*

—Karl Rahner, *Prayers for a Lifetime*, 122–23

Lord Jesus, bless me with a growing awareness that every day of my life
is shaped by your irrevocable call.

A Priest: Anointed and Anointing   February 22

[It is like] fine oil on the head, / running down upon the beard, / Upon the beard of Aaron, / upon the collar of his robe. (Ps 133:2)

A good priest can be recognized by the way his people are anointed. This is a clear test. When our people are anointed with the oil of gladness, it is obvious: for example, when they leave Mass looking as if they have heard good news. Our people like to hear the Gospel preached with "unction," they like it when the Gospel we preach touches their daily lives, when it runs down like the oil of Aaron to the edges of reality, when it brings light to moments of extreme darkness, to the "outskirts" where people of faith are most exposed to the onslaught of those who want to tear down their faith. People thank us because they feel that we have prayed over the realities of their everyday lives, their troubles, their joys, their burdens and their hopes. And when they feel that the fragrance of the Anointed One, of Christ, has come to them through us, they feel encouraged to entrust to us everything they want to bring before the Lord: "Pray for me, Father, because I have this problem," "Bless me," "Pray for me"—these words are the sign that the anointing has flowed down to the edges of the robe, for it has turned into prayer. The prayers of the people of God. When we have this relationship with God and with his people, and grace passes through us, then we are priests, mediators between God and men. What I want to emphasize is that we need constantly to stir up God's grace and perceive in every request, even those requests that are inconvenient and at times purely material or downright banal—but only apparently so—the desire of our people to be anointed with fragrant oil, since they know that we have it.

—Pope Francis, Homily for the Chrism Mass,
March 28, 2013

In what ways is my priestly ministry a fragrant anointing of the people I serve?

"For as you judge, so will you be judged, and the measure with which you measure will be measured out to you." (Matt 7:2)

Presbyters must be sympathetic, merciful to all, guiding back the wanderers, visiting all the sick, neglecting neither widow nor orphan nor pauper, but "always providing what is good before God and men." They must refrain from all anger, from respect of persons, from unfair judgment, and keep far from all love of money; be not quick to believe anything against any man, not hasty in judgment, knowing that we are all under the debt of sin. If then, we beseech the Lord to forgive us, we should also forgive. For we stand before the eyes of the Lord God, and we "must all stand before the judgment seat of Christ," and "each must give an account of himself." Accordingly, let us so serve Him with fear and all reverence, as He has commanded and as did the Apostles who evangelized us, and the prophets who foretold of the coming of the Lord; being zealous for what is good, refraining from offenses and false brethren, and from those who carry the name of the Lord in hypocrisy, to mislead the foolish.

Stand fast, therefore, in this conduct and follow the example of the Lord, "firm and unchangeable in faith, lovers of the brotherhood, loving each other, united in truth," helping each other with the mildness of the Lord, despising no one. When you can do good, do not put it off, "for almsgiving frees from death."

—Saint Polycarp of Smyrna,
The Letter to the Philippians

How have I made pastoral charity the measure of my priestly life?

An Obedient "Man for Others"

> Although I am free in regard to all, I have made myself a slave to all so as to win over as many as possible. (1 Cor 9:19)

Obedience as a sacrifice of freedom, as a giving up when called upon, as a radical availability: these are the decisive structural elements of biblical obedience. . . . Freedom is at its greatest when it is exercised and voluntarily surrendered at God's call, a call which ever meets us afresh in the here and now.

Obedience of this kind is required of all Christians. . . . Nevertheless, Jesus expects a more radical, a more clearly significant form of this obedience from those to whom he gives a special commission of service for the kingdom. Thus, at the sending out of the disciples (Lk 9:57ff; 10:11ff), to the requirement of poverty is added the injunction to have that radical availability which keeps only one thing in mind—the service of the kingdom. The same attitude is clear in the life of St Paul: listening to each particular situation he becomes "all things to all men" (1 Cor 9:22) in order to win them for the kingdom of God.

Only the priest who is able to hear and be sensitive to the manifold call of reality has also the openness to let himself be touched by the needs, the anxieties and concerns of his brothers. . . . Only he who can surrender himself . . . is able to let himself be worn out by the justified and sometimes not so justified wishes and expectations of those around him. One who is available through obedience is able to put aside his own wishes, prejudices and favorite interests, for the sake of others. He can work together with them, he is able to accept criticism and is ready for what comes. Thus obedience is a prerequisite for being a "man for others" in a special way. But it is just this which is an essential part of priestly ministry in imitation of the obedient Lord.

—Gisbert Greshake, *The Meaning of Christian Priesthood*, 133–34

Can I sense a "willing surrender" of my life as I confront the myriad of demands which are placed upon me daily? How do I cope with the inevitable resentments that surface?

To him who loves us and has freed us from our sins by his blood, who has made us into a kingdom, priests for his God and Father, to him be glory and power forever [and ever]. Amen. (Rev 1:5-6)

The Council teaches that all the baptized share in the priesthood of Christ. But at the same time it clearly distinguishes between the priesthood of the People of God, common to all the faithful, and the hierarchical or ministerial priesthood. In this regard, it is worth-while quoting in full an instructive passage of the Constitution: "Christ the Lord, High Priest taken from among men (cf. Heb 5:1-5), 'made a kingdom and priests to God his Father' (Rev 1:6; cf. 5:9-10) out of this new people. The baptized, by regeneration and the anointing of the Holy Spirit, are consecrated into a spiritual house and a holy priesthood. Thus through all those works befitting Christian men and women they can offer spiritual sacrifices and proclaim the power of him who has called them out of darkness into his marvelous light (cf. 1 Pet 2:4-10). Therefore all the disciples of Christ, should present themselves as a living sacrifice, holy and pleasing to God (cf. Rom 12:1). Everywhere on earth they must bear witness to Christ and give an answer to those who seek an account of that hope of eternal life which is in them (cf. 1 Pet 3:15).

The common priesthood of the faithful and the ministerial or hierarchical priesthood are nonetheless interrelated. Each of them in its own special way is a participation in the one priesthood of Christ. . . . The ministerial priesthood is at the service of the common priesthood of the faithful. For when the priest celebrates the Eucharist and administers the sacraments, he leads the faithful to an awareness of their own particular sharing in the priesthood of Christ.

—Saint John Paul II, Letter to Priests for
Holy Thursday, 1996

Lord Jesus, may I always see my priestly ministry to be at the service of the common priesthood of the faithful.

A Prayer to Christ Our Model

But we have the mind of Christ. (1 Cor 2:16)

Lord . . . I have discovered that the ideal of our way of acting is your way of acting. For this reason I fix my eyes on you; the eyes of faith see your face as you appear in the Gospel. I am one of those about whom St. Peter says: "You did not see him, yet you love him, and still without seeing him, you are already filled with a joy so glorious that it cannot be described, because you believe" (1 Pet. 1:8).

Lord, you yourself have told us: "I have given you an example to follow" (John 13:15). I want to follow you in that way so that I can say to others: "Be imitators of me as I am of Christ" (1 Cor. 11:1). Although I am not able to mean it as literally as St. John, I would like to be able to proclaim, at least through the faith and wisdom that you give me, what I have heard, what I have seen with my eyes, what I have contemplated and touched with my hands concerning the Word of Life; the Life manifested itself, and I have seen it and give witness (1 John 1:1). Although not with bodily eyes, certainly through the eyes of faith.

Above all, give me that *sensus Christi* about which St. Paul speaks (1 Cor 2:16): that I may feel with your feelings, with the sentiments of your heart, which basically are love for your Father and love for humankind. No one has shown more charity than you, giving your life for your friends with that kenosis of which St. Paul speaks (Phil 2:7). And I would like to imitate you not only in your feelings but also in everyday life, acting, as far as possible, as you did.

—Pedro Arrupe, "Our Way of Proceeding,"
The Spiritual Legacy of Pedro Arrupe, S.J., 79–80

My daily desire is to think with the mind of Christ and to love with his most Sacred Heart.

> LORD, you have probed me, you know me: / you know when I sit and stand; / you understand my thoughts from afar. (Ps 139:1-2)

God has created me to do Him some definite service; He has committed some work to me which He has not committed to another. I have my mission—I never may know it in this life, but I shall be told it in the next. . . . I have a part in a great work; I am a link in a chain, a bond of connexion between persons. He has not created me for naught. I shall do good, I shall do His work; I shall be an angel of peace, a preacher of truth in my own place, while not intending it, if I do but keep His commandments and serve Him in my calling.

Therefore I will trust Him. Whatever, wherever I am, I can never be thrown away. If I am in sickness, my sickness may serve Him; in perplexity, my perplexity may serve Him; if I am in sorrow, my sorrow may serve Him. My sickness, or perplexity, or sorrow may be necessary causes of some great end, which is quite beyond us. He does nothing in vain; He may prolong my life, He may shorten it; He knows what He is about. He may take away my friends, He may throw me among strangers, He may make me feel desolate, make my spirits sink, hide the future from me—still He knows what He is about.

—Blessed John Henry Newman,
Meditations and Devotions, 400–401

In every circumstance of my priestly life, Lord Jesus, I trust your loving companionship.

A Cosmic Yet Pastoral Eucharist

> I am the living bread that came down from heaven; whoever eats this bread will live forever. (John 6:51)

In the celebration of the Eucharist the greatest participation takes place in the perfect worship which Christ the High Priest gives to the Father by representing and expressing the whole created order. The presbyter, who sees and recognizes that his life is thus deeply linked to the Eucharist, feels the horizons of his spirit broaden on a global scale, embracing even heaven and earth, and is also aware of the increased need and responsibility to impart this treasure—"the whole spiritual good of the Church"—to the community.

Therefore, the priest will make every effort to encourage participation in the Eucharist by catechesis, pastoral exhortation and the excellent quality of the celebration in its liturgical and ceremonial aspect. He will thus succeed, as the Council stresses, in teaching the faithful to offer the divine victim to God the Father in the sacrifice of the Mass and, in union with this victim, to make an offering of their own life in service to their brothers and sisters.

The faithful will also learn to seek pardon for their sins, to meditate on the word of God, to pray with sincere hearts for all the needs of the Church and the world and to put all their trust in Christ the Savior.

Every priest, at any level, in any area of work, is the servant and minister of the paschal mystery accomplished on the cross and lived anew on the altar for the redemption of the world.

—Saint John Paul II, "Priests Are Ordained to
Celebrate Mass," General Audience, May 12, 1993

I consider how I might more effectively encourage full participation in the celebration of the Eucharist.

> For this is the message you have heard from the beginning: we should
> love one another . . . (1 John 3:11)

A little while ago I read what St. Augustine said in Book X of his
Confessions: "I was tempted and I now understand that it was a temptation to enclose myself in contemplative life, to seek solitude with you, O
Lord; but you prevented me, you plucked me from it and made me listen
to St Paul's words: 'Christ died for us all. Consequently, we must die with
Christ and live for all.' I understood that I cannot shut myself up in contemplation; you died for us all. Therefore, with you, I must live for all and
thus practice works of charity. True contemplation is expressed in works of
charity. Therefore, the sign for which we have truly prayed, that we have
experienced in the encounter with Christ, is that we exist 'for others.'"

This is what a parish priest must be like. And St Augustine was a great
parish priest. He said: "In my life I also always longed to spend my life
listening to the Word in meditation, but now—day after day, hour after
hour—I must stand at the door where the bell is always ringing, I must
comfort the afflicted, help the poor, reprimand those who are quarrelsome,
create peace and so forth."

St. Augustine lists all the tasks of a parish priest, for at that time the
Bishop was also what the Kadi in Islamic countries is today. With regard
to problems of civil law, let us say, he was the judge of peace: he had to
encourage peace between the litigants. He therefore lived a life that for him,
a contemplative, was very difficult. But he understood this truth: thus, I am
with Christ; in existing "for others," I am in the Crucified and Risen Lord. I
think this is a great consolation for parish priests and Bishops. Even if little
time is left for contemplation, in being "for others," we are with the Lord.

> —Pope Benedict XVI, Address to the Lenten Meeting
> of the Clergy of Rome, February 22, 2007

When the demands of the ministry are great, I must be reminded that this
is my enduring vocation, to be a man "for others."

"Being with" Christ for Others

> It is [Christ] whom we proclaim, admonishing everyone and teaching everyone with all wisdom, that we may present everyone perfect in Christ. For this I labor and struggle, in accord with the exercise of his power working within me. (Col 1:28-29)

I believe that it is important to rekindle constantly an awareness of our divine vocation, which we often take for granted in the midst of our many daily responsibilities: as Jesus says, "You did not choose me, but I chose you" (*Jn* 15:16). This means returning to the source of our calling. For this reason, a Bishop, a priest, a consecrated person, a seminarian cannot be "forgetful": it would mean losing the vital link to that first moment of our journey. Ask for the grace, ask the Virgin for the grace, she who had a good memory; ask for the grace to preserve the memory of this first call. We were called by God and we were called to be with Jesus (cf. *Mk* 3:14), united with him. In reality, this living, this abiding in Christ marks all that we are and all that we do. It is precisely this "life in Christ" that ensures our apostolate is effective, that our service is fruitful: "I appointed you that you should go and bear fruit and that your fruit be authentic" (cf. *Jn* 15:16). It is not creativity, however pastoral it may be, or meetings or planning that ensure our fruitfulness, even if these are greatly helpful. But what assures our fruitfulness is our being faithful to Jesus, who says insistently: "Abide in me and I in you" (*Jn* 15:4). And we know well what that means: to contemplate him, to worship him, to embrace him, in our daily encounter with him in the Eucharist, in our life of prayer, in our moments of adoration; it means to recognize him present and to embrace him in those most in need. "Being with" Christ does not mean isolating ourselves from others. Rather, it is a "being with" in order to go forth and encounter others.

> —Pope Francis, Homily at Mass with Bishops, Priests,
> Religious, and Seminarians, July 27, 2013

In the daily routine of my priestly life, I am ever realizing that the priesthood is in every circumstance, "life in Christ." I do not shirk from its labor and struggle.

One thing I ask of the LORD; / this I seek: / To dwell in the LORD's house / all the days of my life, / To gaze on the LORD's beauty, / to visit his temple. (Ps 27:4)

How timely and how profitable this example of constant prayer on the part of a man completely dedicated to caring for the needs of souls is for priests in Our own day, who are likely to attribute too much to the effectiveness of external activity and stand ready and eager to immerse themselves in the hustle and bustle of the ministry, to their own spiritual detriment!

"The thing that keeps us priests from gaining sanctity"—the Curé of Ars used to say— "is thoughtlessness. It annoys us to turn our minds away from external affairs; we don't know what we really ought to do. What we need is deep reflection, together with prayer and an intimate union with God." The testimony of his life makes it clear that he always remained devoted to his prayers and that not even the duty of hearing confessions or any other pastoral office could cause him to neglect them. "Even in the midst of tremendous labors, he never let up on his conversation with God."

But listen to his own words; for he seemed to have an inexhaustible supply of them whenever he talked about the happiness or the advantages that he found in prayer: "We are beggars who must ask God for everything"; "How many people we can call back to God by our prayers!" And he used to say over and over again: "Ardent prayer addressed to God: this is man's greatest happiness on earth!"

. . . And the crowds of pilgrims who surrounded him in the temple could feel something coming forth from the depths of the inner life of this humble priest when words like these burst forth from his inflamed breast, as they often did: "To be loved by God, to be joined to God, to walk before God, to live for God: O blessed life, O blessed death!"

—Saint John XXIII, *Sacerdotii Nostri Primordia*, 36–39

Like St. John Vianney, may I never let up in my prayerful conversation with God.

> We have not received the spirit of the world but the Spirit that is from God, so that we may understand the things freely given us by God. And we speak about them not with words taught by human wisdom, but with words taught by the Spirit . . . (1 Cor 2:12-13)

Do not be afraid, I say, because great courage is required if we are to open the doors to Christ, if we are to let Christ enter into our hearts so fully that we can say with Saint Paul, "The life I live now is not my own; Christ is living in me" (Gal. 2: 20). Conquering fear is the first and indispensable step for the priest if he is to open the doors, first of his own heart, then of the hearts of the people he serves, to Christ the Redeemer. You need courage to follow Christ, especially when you recognize that so much of our dominant culture is a culture of flight from God, a culture which displays a not-so-hidden contempt for human life, beginning with the lives of the unborn, and extending to contempt for the frail and the elderly.

Therefore, dear Seminarians, you must not be afraid to confront the "wisdom of this world" with the certainty of the teachings of Christ in which you are grounded, but above all with the love of Christ, with the compassion and the mercy of Christ, who—like the Father—desires everyone to be saved and to come to the knowledge of the truth (Cf. 1 Tim. 2: 4). The disciple cannot be greater than the master (Cf. Mt. 10: 24). You will not become priests to be served, or to lord it over others (Cf. ibid. 20: 28), but to serve others, especially the poorest of the poor, the materially poor and the spiritually poor.

Open the doors of your hearts in order that Christ may enter and bring you his joy. The Church needs joyful priests, capable of bringing true joy to God's people, which is the Good News in all its truth and transforming power.

—Saint John Paul II, Homily at the Liturgy of Vespers,
October 6, 1995

To what extent is my ministry marked by generous portions of both courageous joy and joyful courage?

> Amen, amen, I say to you, unless a grain of wheat falls to the ground
> and dies, it remains just a grain of wheat; but if it dies, it produces much
> fruit. (John 12:24)

We shall take from the Mass and from the Ordination ceremony certain
gestures of the priest that will provide symbols . . . of his role in the world
in which we live.

The first symbol is the prostration ceremony. "Let all prostrate themselves," cries the Bishop's assistant to the ordinands assembled before him.
The priests-to-be with one movement stretch out on the sanctuary flooring,
with the immobility and silence of death, a death which the Church herself,
has just made a duty for them. A death which, according to the individual,
either gives joy or astonishment. The priest is dead! Let us live without him!
We have no need of the Priesthood! The world can stand on its own two feet!

This annihilating gesture is one a priest has to renew every day of
his life. Such "death to the world" is no transitory action for him. It is an
enduring state, a prolonged holocaust. He hears at every hour the jeers
which mock his sacrifice as a suicidal folly. While he offers himself as a
victim, civilizations pass by, men go on their way, unheeding or haughty
spectators of his voluntary annihilation. It is an enduring lesson: the priest
is and always will be in some way dead among the living.

Yet soon, when the supplications of the Litanies have brought down on
them the prayer of all the Saints, the ordinands, like Peter, James, and John,
after the vision on Tabor, which made them "fall flat on their faces on the
ground" (Matt., 17:6), stand up and "looking about them, see no one but
only Jesus" (Luke, 9:8). After the Bishop's consecration has made them
priests they go off into the world "transfigured" in the likeness of Christ,
transparent with his beauty, bearing his divine powers.

—Emmanuel-Célestin Cardinal Suhard,
The Church Today, 339–40

I am prompted to remember the day of my ordination, and my prostration
before the ordaining bishop. I remember as well those times in my ministry
when I have been face down before the living God and before those whom
I've been sent to serve.

> The spirit of the LORD shall rest upon him: / a spirit of wisdom and of understanding, / A spirit of counsel and of strength, / a spirit of knowledge and of fear of the LORD . . . (Isa 11:2)

The Spirit guides the baptized to the point where they are wholly configured to Christ and are in complete harmony with the horizon of the Kingdom of God . . . but, in order that they may exercise their demanding ministry with profit, the Spirit reserves a special attention for those who have received Holy Orders.

With the gift of *wisdom*, therefore, the Spirit leads the priest to evaluate all things in the light of the Gospel, helping him to read in his own experience and the experience of the Church the mysterious and loving plan of the Father. With the gift of *understanding*, the Spirit fosters in the priest a deeper insight into revealed truth, pressing him to proclaim with conviction and power the Good News of salvation. With the gift of *counsel*, the Spirit illuminates the ministry of Christ so that the priest may direct his activities according to the perspectives of Providence, never allowing himself to be swayed by the judgments of the world. With the gift of *strength*, the priest is sustained in the hardships of his ministry and provided with the boldness (*parresia*) required for the proclamation of the Gospel (cf. Acts 4:29, 31). With the gift of *knowledge*, the priest is able to understand and accept the sometimes mysterious interweaving of secondary causes with the First Cause in the turn of events in the universe. With the gift of *piety*, the Spirit revives in the priest the relationship of intimate communion with God and of trusting surrender to his Providence. Finally, with the gift of *fear of the Lord*, last in the hierarchy of gifts, the Spirit gives the priest a stronger sense of his own human weakness and of the indispensable role of divine grace, since "neither the one who plants nor the one who waters is anything, but only God who gives the growth" (1 Cor 3:7).

—Saint John Paul II, Letter to Priests for
Holy Thursday, 1998

Come, Holy Spirit, transform my priestly heart with those gifts which will more fully conform me to Christ the Good Shepherd.

As you sent me into the world, so I sent them into the world. (John 17:18)

That the church is one is a characteristic of its public life; such unity is grounded in its second mark, holiness, a quality of depth. The church as Catholic is the mark of its universality, which, in turn, is rooted in the faith of the apostles, a characteristic of historical origins.

The church does not possess these marks on its own. They are gifts of Christ. . . . These gifts come to full realization only in the kingdom. In history, the interplay between surface and depth, light and darkness, revelation and hiddenness characterize the church's life. . . . they serve as beacons, indicating that the church is on course toward its final destination.

If these marks are essential characteristics of the church and its mission, they must relate to the priesthood as well. In fact, these marks must also be defining characteristics of the priest. If the tasks of preaching, sanctifying, and shepherding are entrusted to those who publicly represent Christ in a special way, by the same token those same persons must be symbols and agents of the church's unity, holiness, catholicity, and apostolic origins. If preaching, sanctifying, and shepherding are the tasks, the marks provide a sense of mission. Their historical manifestations are signs to believer and unbeliever alike that the church is on course because its defining characteristics are visible. This is why they can function as motives of credibility. Likewise, these marks can be lost. But their continuing historical absence constitutes a witness against the church, indeed a scandal.

The marks of the church must be distinguishing characteristics of priests as walking symbols of Christ's presence: . . . Priests as symbols and agents of the church's unity, its holiness, its catholic and apostolic character bear special responsibility for keeping these marks visible. Both their successes and failures are as visible as the marks themselves.

—Howard P. Bleichner, *View from the Altar*, 156–57

I am invited to ponder seriously the way in which my priestly life is one, holy, catholic, and apostolic.

> Then [Jesus] said to them, "My soul is sorrowful even to death. Remain here and keep watch with me." (Matt 26:38)

If in our Holy Thursday meditation . . . we link the Upper Room with Gethsemane, it is in order to understand how deeply Our Priesthood must be linked with prayer, rooted in prayer. Surely this statement is obvious, but it does need to be continually pondered in our minds and hearts, so that the truth of it can be realized ever more deeply in our lives.

For it is a question of our life, our priestly existence itself, in all its richness, encompassed first of all in the call to Priesthood and then shown in that service of salvation which flows from it. We know that the sacramental and ministerial Priesthood is a special sharing in the Priesthood of Christ. It does not exist without him or apart from him. It neither develops nor bears fruit unless it is rooted in him. "Apart from me you can do nothing," Jesus said during the Last Supper at the conclusion of the parable about the vine and the branches.

When later, during his solitary prayer in the garden of Gethsemane, Jesus goes to Peter, James and John and finds them overcome with sleep, he awakens them saying: "Watch and pray that you may not enter into temptation." For the Apostles therefore prayer was to be the concrete and effective means of sharing in "Jesus' hour," of taking root in him and in his Paschal mystery. Thus it will always be for us priests. Without prayer, the danger of that "temptation" threatens us, the temptation to which the Apostles sadly succumbed when they found themselves face to face with "the scandal of the Cross."

—Saint John Paul II, Letter to Priests for
Holy Thursday, 1987

I hear the pain in Jesus' voice and heed the invitation: remain here and stay awake with me.

> They stood before the throne and before the Lamb, wearing white robes
> and holding palm branches in their hands. (Rev 7:9)

Putting on priestly vestments was once accompanied by prayers that helped us understand better each single element of the priestly ministry.

Let us start with the amice. In the past—and in monastic orders still today—it was first placed on the head as a sort of hood, thus becoming a symbol of the discipline of the senses and of thought necessary for a proper celebration of Holy Mass. My thoughts must not wander here and there due to the anxieties and expectations of my daily life; my senses must not be attracted by what there, inside the church, might accidentally captivate the eyes and ears. My heart must open itself docilely to the Word of God and be recollected in the prayer of the Church, so that my thoughts may receive their orientation from the words of the proclamation and of prayer. And the gaze of my heart must be turned toward the Lord who is in our midst: this is what the *ars celebrandi* means: the proper way of celebrating.

If I am with the Lord, then, with my listening, speaking and acting, I will also draw people into communion with him. The texts of the prayer expressed by the alb and the stole both move in the same direction. They call to mind the festive robes which the father gave to the prodigal son who had come home dirty, in rags.

When we approach the liturgy to act in the person of Christ, we all realize how distant we are from him; how much dirt there is in our lives. He alone can give us festive robes, can make us worthy to preside at his table, to be at his service.

—Pope Benedict XVI, Homily for the Chrism Mass,
April 5, 2007

These words of the Holy Father are a reminder to me that I could be more attentive to my preparation for Mass.

Being a Sacrificial Victim

> Every high priest is taken from among men and made their representative before God, to offer gifts and sacrifices for sins. (Heb 5:1)

And while the war rages, the peoples can only turn to the *Miserere* and beg for the Lord's mercy, that it may outweigh his justice and with a great outpouring of grace bring the powerful men of this world to their senses and persuade them to make peace.

What is happening in the world on a grand scale is reproduced on a small scale in every man's soul, is reproduced in mine. Only the grace of God has prevented me from being eaten up with malice. There are certain sins which may be called typical: this sin of David, the sins of St. Peter and St. Augustine. But what might I not have done myself, if the Lord's hand had not held me back? For small failings the most perfect saints underwent long and harsh penances. So many, even in our own times, have lived only to make atonement; and there are souls whose lives, even today, are one long expiation of their own sins, of the sins of the world. And I, in all ages of my life more or less a sinner, should I not spend my time mourning . . .

Far from seeking consolation by comparing myself with others, I should make the *Miserere* for my own sins my most familiar prayer. The thought that I am a priest and bishop and therefore especially dedicated to the conversion of sinners and the remission of sins should add all the more anguish to my feelings of grief, sadness and tears, as St. Ignatius says: What is the meaning of all these flagellations, or having oneself set on the bare ground, or on ashes, to die, if not the priestly soul's continual plea for mercy, and his constant longing to be a sacrificial victim for his own sins and the sins of the world?

—Saint John XXIII, *Journal of a Soul*, 296

How do I understand my own call to be united to Christ as a sacrificial victim?

> [L]iving the truth in love, we should grow in every way into him who is the head, Christ . . . (Eph 4:15)

I will never forget the night I first met all the priests here in the cathedral. My knees were literally knocking as I carried a heavy paschal candle down the middle aisle of the darkened church. But when the lights went on, what a tremendous reception they gave me. "As our lives and ministries are mingled together through the breaking of the Bread and the blessing of the Cup," I told them, "I hope that long before my name falls from the Eucharistic Prayer in the silence of death you will know me well. . . . You will know me as a friend, fellow priest, and bishop. You will know also that I love you. For I am Joseph, your brother."

. . . Today our task remains the same: to proclaim the gospel to every creature. To carry out such a task, as the Second Vatican Council told us, the Church must constantly scrutinize "the signs of the times," interpret them in the light of the gospel, and show how the gospel speaks to the hopes and aspirations, the anxieties and concerns of each generation. The genius of the council was that it addressed some of the most important issues of our time, setting the course for the Catholic community as we approach the third millennium of Christianity. Significantly, my episcopate began just four months after the close of the council, and I have spent the past quarter century implementing its teaching and insights.

I am convinced that we do not fully understand all the implications of the council's teaching, . . . it takes more than a single generation to assimilate fully the teaching of an ecumenical council, especially one whose purpose was primarily pastoral and whose scope embraced so many important topics and concerns.

> —Joseph Cardinal Bernardin, Homily for the Mass
> Commemorating the 25th Anniversary of
> Episcopal Ordination, April 28, 1991

Where do I find myself in relation to the council? Do I read and study the documents? What is it that nourishes my vision of priesthood and Church?

Recognizing the Dignity of the Lay Faithful

> God did not send his Son into the world to condemn the world, but that the world might be saved through him. (John 3:17)

Today, therefore, on a day so holy and filled with deep spiritual meaning for us, we should meditate once more, and in detail, on the particular character of our vocation and of our priestly service. Concerning priests, the council teaches that "their ministry itself by a special title forbids them to be conformed to this world. Yet at the same time this ministry requires that they live in this world among men." In the priestly vocation of a pastor there must always be a special place for these people, the lay faithful and their "lay state," which is also a great asset of the Church. Such an interior place is a sign of the priest's vocation as a pastor.

The Council has shown with great clarity that the lay state, which is rooted in the sacraments of Baptism and Confirmation—the lay state as a common dimension of sharing in the priesthood of Christ—constitutes the essential vocation of all the lay faithful. Priests "cannot be ministers of Christ unless they are witnesses and dispensers of a life other than this earthly one," yet at the same time "they cannot be of service to men if they remain strangers to the life and conditions of men." This indicates precisely that interior place given to the lay state, which is deeply inscribed in the priestly vocation of every pastor: It is the place for everything in which this "secularity" expresses itself. In all this the priest must try to recognize the "true Christian dignity" of each of his lay brothers and sisters; indeed, he must make every effort to convince them of it, to educate them in it through his own priestly service.

—Saint John Paul II, Letter to Priests for
Holy Thursday, 1989

What evidence is there that I make a concerted effort to understand the "life and conditions" of the people I serve?

> Blessed is the man who does not walk / in the counsel of the wicked
> . . . the law of the LORD is his joy; / and on his law he meditates day
> and night. / He is like a tree / planted near streams of water, / that yields
> its fruit in season; / Its leaves never wither; / whatever he does prospers.
> (Ps 1:1-3)

What is the function of a priest in the world? To teach other men? To advise them? To console them? To pray for them? These things enter into his life, but they can be done by anyone. Every man in the world is called to teach and to advise and to console some other man, and we are all bound to pray for one another that we may be saved. These actions require no special priesthood other than our baptismal participation in the priesthood of Christ, and they can be exercised even without this. Nor is the priest's distinctive vocation simply that he must be a man of God. The monk is a man of God, and he does not have to be a priest.

The priest is called to be another Christ in a far more particular and intimate sense than the ordinary Christian or the monk. He must keep alive in the world the sacramental presence and action of the Risen Savior. He is a visible human instrument of the Christ Who reigns in Heaven, Who teaches and sanctifies and governs the Church through His anointed priests. The words of the priest are not to be merely his own words or his own doctrine. They should always be the doctrine of the One Who sent him. The action of the priest upon souls should come from something more than his own poor human power to advise and to console. Human though his acts may be, poor and deficient in themselves, they must be supported by the sacramental action of Jesus Christ and vivified by the hidden working of the Divine Spirit.

—Thomas Merton, *No Man Is an Island*, 114

Lord Jesus, deliver me from any thought that I might be deserving of such a high calling. Bless me in my poverty and deficiency.

> [Y]ou must no longer live as the Gentiles do, in the futility of their minds; darkened in understanding, alienated from the life of God because of their ignorance, because of their hardness of heart . . . (Eph 4:17-18)

For turning prayer into a duty, or neglecting it altogether;
For being a talker and not a listener in prayer;
For talking about suffering, but being unwilling to suffer;
Lord, have mercy.
For saying "This is my Body given for you," but failing to give myself to others;
For my careless and insensitive celebration of Mass and the Sacraments;
For running away from the task of the prophet;
Lord, have mercy.
For not allowing or encouraging the laity to play their full part in the parish;
For complaining about the lack of vocations, without acknowledging
that my own life, and lack of joy and faith, may attract no one to the
priesthood;
For my laziness, lethargy and indulgence;
Lord, have mercy.
For my lack of faith, hope and love;
For allowing myself to be taken in by pagan and worldly values;
For guarding my popularity;
Lord, have mercy.
For my pettiness and parochialism;
For living by rubrics and not by the Holy Spirit;
For my lack of personal discipline,
Lord, have mercy.
For considering myself superior to others;
For my impatience with the ignorant;
For refusing to be the friend of sinners;
Lord, have mercy.

—Gerard McGinnity, *Christmen: Experience of Priesthood Today*, 34–35

Lord Jesus, I am very aware of my record of failure, and acknowledge my sins with sorrow. I beg your forgiveness. Help me to rely on your strength and your Spirit. As you forgive me, help me become a true minister of your forgiveness to others.

March 14   A Priest's Act of Repentance (Part 2)

Do not conform yourselves to this age but be transformed by the renewal of your mind, that you may discern what is the will of God, what is good and pleasing and perfect. (Rom 12:2)

For failing to love my fellow priests;
For failing to love those entrusted to me;
For failing to be humble;
> Lord, have mercy.

For failing to study Scripture;
For preaching which has been dull, unprepared and lifeless;
For scolding the people for their ignorance even when it has been caused
> by my own sins of negligence;
> Lord, have mercy.

I have been interested in practicing Catholics, with no mind for the others;
I have taught without first learning;
I have counselled many without seeking counsel for myself;
> Lord, have mercy.

I have misused my power;
I have obeyed the letter of the law without regard for the Spirit of the Gospel;
I have condemned and judged others;
> Lord, have mercy.

I have failed to be honest or cooperate with brother priests and my bishop;
I have been hypocritical;
I have presumed to be greater than my Master;
I have failed to walk with the poorest, anywhere, at any time;
> Lord, have mercy.

> —Gerard McGinnity, *Christmen: Experience of*
> *Priesthood Today*, 34–35

Lord Jesus, I am very aware of my record of failure, and acknowledge my sins with sorrow and ask for forgiveness. Help me to rely on your strength and your Spirit. As you forgive me, help me become a true minister of your forgiveness to others.

Priest as Witness to the Young

> As [Jesus] was setting out on a journey, a man ran up, knelt down before him, and asked him, "Good teacher, what must I do to inherit eternal life?" (Mark 10:17)

The priest who is in contact with youth should know how to listen and how to answer. Both of these acts should be the fruit of his interior maturity; this should be reflected in a clear consistency between life and teaching; still more, it should be the fruit of prayer, of union with Christ the Lord and of docility to the action of the Holy Spirit. Naturally an adequate training is important in this regard, but what is most important is a sense of responsibility with regard to the truth and to one's questioner. The conversation reported by the Synoptics proves first of all that the Master whom the young man questions has in the latter's eyes a special credibility and authority: moral authority. The young man expects from him the truth, and accepts his response as an expression of a truth that imposes an obligation. This truth can be demanding. We must not be afraid of demanding much from the young. It can happen that one of them may go away "saddened," when he or she seems unable to face some demand. Nevertheless, sadness of this sort can also be "salvific." Sometimes the young must make progress through such experiences of salvific sadness, so as gradually to reach the truth and that joy which truth gives.

Besides, the young know that the true good cannot be had "cheaply"; it must "cost." They possess a certain healthy instinct when it is a question of values. If the soul has not yet yielded to corruption, they react directly with this health judgment. If moral corruption has gained a hold the ground must be broken up again, and this cannot be done otherwise than by giving true answers and proposing true values.

—Saint John Paul II, Letter to Priests for
Holy Thursday, 1985

How might I make my ministry with the young more effective?

> I am the good shepherd, and I know mine and mine know me, just as the
> Father knows me and I know the Father . . . (John 10:14-15)

Here, two apparently quite different relationships are interwoven in this phrase: the relationship between Jesus and the Father and the relationship between Jesus and the people entrusted to him. . . . In our hearts we must live the relationship with Christ and, through him, with the Father; only then can we truly understand people, only in the light of God can the depths of man be understood. Then those who are listening to us realize that we are not speaking of ourselves or of some thing, but of the true Shepherd.

Jesus' words also contain the entire practical pastoral task, caring for men and women, going to seek them out, being open to their needs and questions. Obviously, practical, concrete knowledge of the people entrusted to me is fundamental, and obviously, it is important to understand this way of "knowing" others in the biblical sense: there is no true knowledge without love, without an inner relationship and deep acceptance of the other.

. . . His way of knowing his sheep must always also be knowing with the heart. However, it is only possible to do this properly if the Lord has opened our hearts; if our knowing does not bind people to our own small, private self, to our own small heart, but rather makes them aware of the Heart of Jesus, the Heart of the Lord. It must be knowing with the Heart of Jesus, oriented to him, a way of knowing that does not bind the person to me but guides him or her to Jesus, thereby making one free and open.

> —Pope Benedict XVI, Homily for the Ordination to
> the Priesthood, May 7, 2006

My heart, Lord Jesus, is too often tepid and insensitive to the needs of others. Sadly, it is at times too small. Make my heart like unto thine.

A Most Consoling Ministry of Mercy

> And all this is from God, who has reconciled us to himself through Christ and given us the ministry of reconciliation . . . (2 Cor 5:18)

Sacramental forgiveness will always require a personal encounter with the crucified Christ through the mediation of his minister. Unfortunately it is often the case that penitents do not fervently hasten to the confessional, as in the time of the Curé of Ars. [There is an] urgent need to develop a whole pastoral strategy of the Sacrament of Reconciliation. This will be done by constantly reminding Christians of the need to have a real relationship with God, to have a sense of sin when one is closed to God and to others, the need to be converted and through the Church to receive forgiveness as a free gift of God. They also need to be reminded of the conditions that enable the sacrament to be celebrated well, and in this regard to overcome prejudices, baseless fears and routine. Such a situation at the same time requires that we ourselves should remain very available for this ministry of forgiveness, ready to devote to it the necessary time and care. The faithful will then realize the value that we attach to it, as did the Curé of Ars.

This ministry presupposes on the part of the confessor great human qualities, above all an intense and sincere spiritual life; always be convinced of this, dear brother priests: this ministry of mercy is one of the most beautiful and most consoling. It enables you to enlighten consciences, to forgive them and to give them fresh vigour in the name of the Lord Jesus. . . . It enables you to be for them a spiritual physician and counsellor; it remains "the irreplaceable manifestation and the test of the priestly ministry."

—Saint John Paul II, Letter to Priests for
Holy Thursday, 1986

I am invited to consider the importance I place upon the Sacrament of Reconciliation—in my own spiritual life, and in my priestly ministry.

> In those days he departed to the mountain to pray, and he spent the night
> in prayer to God. (Luke 6:12)

Therefore to become and to continue to be a real man of prayer, seems
to me the first duty of a parish priest. What then is a real man of prayer?
He is one who deliberately wills and steadily desires that his relations
with God and other souls shall be controlled and actuated at every point
by God Himself; one who has so far developed and educated his spiritual
sense, that his supernatural environment is more real and solid to him than
his natural environment. A man of prayer is not necessarily a person who
says a number of offices, or abounds in detailed intercessions; but he is a
child of God, who is and knows himself to be in the depth of his soul attached to God, and is wholly and entirely guided by the Creative Spirit in
his prayer and his work.

This is not merely a bit of pious language. It is a description, as real and
concrete as I can make it, of the only really apostolic life. Every Christian
starts with a chance of it; but only a few develop it. The laity distinguish
in a moment the clergy who have it from the clergy who have it not: there
is nothing that you can do for God or for the souls of men, which exceeds
in importance the achievement of that spiritual temper and attitude. For the
parishes to which you are sent you are, or should be, the main links with
that supernatural world; the main channels of God's action on souls. You
are those in whom the hope of a more intense spiritual life for those parishes is centered: those in whom for this purpose God has placed His trust.

—Evelyn Underhill, *Concerning the Inner Life*, 94–95

What is there about my life that witnesses to others that I am a man of
prayer?

In Eucharist, the Whole of Reality Is Present
March 19

For in him all the fullness was pleased to dwell, / and through him to reconcile all things for him, / making peace by the blood of his cross / [through him], whether those on earth or those in heaven. (Col 1:19-20)

The Priesthood is the supreme gift, a particular calling to share in the mystery of Christ, a calling which confers on us the sublime possibility of speaking and acting in his name. Every time we offer the Eucharist, this possibility becomes a reality. *We act "in persona Christi"* when, at the moment of the consecration, we say the words: "This is my Body which will be given up for you . . . This is the cup of my Blood, the Blood of the new and everlasting covenant. It will be shed for you and for all so that sins may be forgiven. Do this in memory of me." We do precisely this: with deep humility and profound thanks. This exalted yet simple action of our daily mission as priests *opens up our humanity . . . to its furthermost limits.*

We share in the mystery of the Incarnation of the Word, "the first-born of all creation" (Col 1:15), who in the Eucharist restores to the Father the whole of creation: the world of the past and the world of the future, and above all the world of today. In this world he lives with us, he is present through us, and precisely through us he offers to the Father the Sacrifice of our Redemption. . . . In this way *the whole of reality becomes present in our Eucharistic ministry*, which . . . embraces every concrete personal need, all suffering, expectation, joy or sadness, in accordance with the intentions which the faithful present for Holy Mass. We receive these intentions in a spirit of charity, thus introducing every human problem into the dimension of universal Redemption.

—Saint John Paul II, Letter to Priests for
Holy Thursday, 1994

Lord Jesus, in my celebration of the daily Eucharist, may I be particularly aware that it is offered for the reconciliation of the whole of creation.

March 20   Confident Reliance on Christ's Promise

> Therefore, since we have this ministry through the mercy shown us, we are not discouraged. (2 Cor 4:1)

The doctrine of the *indelible character* is not a declaration that the office-bearer is superior to the lay person: it is instead the condition which makes it possible for the Church to rely confidently on Christ's promise in spite of the sins and shortcomings of office-bearers: he himself is close to his Church in the actions of those whom he has commissioned. For the office-bearer, however, the "character" conferred in ordination is a "sign of lowliness," which should be a constant reminder that he has not the power to destroy Christ's work and the existence of his Church. In fact, it is this character which first and foremost makes it possible "to undertake ecclesiastical office without presumption, but also without anxiety and embarrassment" (E. Dassmann). It is ordination, i.e. the grant of power through Christ, which gives that holiness which is required for priestly action. Looked at in this way priestly office which comes from Christ is something "objectively holy" and "objectively sanctifying" and in its official sacramental functions it represents Christ and does not depend on the personal holiness of the minister.

It was Augustine, particularly, who . . . stressed the fact that the official acts of an office-bearer derive their effectiveness from Christ, even if the office-bearer lacks personal holiness. With endless variations Augustine emphatically cites the example of Baptism: it does not matter whether John or Judas baptizes; it is always the baptism of Christ. . . . In other words: as a result of ordination it is Christ himself who is acting in the person of his minister, even when the one who has received ordination does not live in a manner which corresponds to what he does officially.

—Gisbert Greshake, *The Meaning of
Christian Priesthood*, 110–11

In what ways is my life marked by the holiness of Christ?

Our Imperishable, Missionary Joy

> May the God of hope fill you with all joy and peace in believing so that you may abound in hope by the power of the Holy Spirit. (Rom 15:13)

For me, there are three significant features of our priestly joy. It is a joy which anoints us (not one which "greases" us, making us unctuous, sumptuous and presumptuous), it is a joy which is imperishable and it is a missionary joy which spreads and attracts, starting backwards—with those farthest away from us.

A joy which anoints us. In a word: it has penetrated deep within our hearts, it has shaped them and strengthened them sacramentally. The signs of the ordination liturgy speak to us of the Church's maternal desire to pass on and share with others all that the Lord has given us: the laying on of hands, the anointing with sacred chrism, the clothing with sacred vestments, the first consecration which immediately follows . . . Grace fills us to the brim and overflows, fully, abundantly and entirely in each priest. We are anointed down to our very bones . . . and our joy, which wells up from deep within, is the echo of this anointing.

An imperishable joy. The fullness of the Gift, which no one can take away or increase, is an unfailing source of joy: an imperishable joy which the Lord has promised no one can take from us (Jn 16:22). It can lie dormant, or be clogged by sin or by life's troubles, yet deep down it remains intact, like the embers of a burnt log beneath the ashes, and it can always be renewed. Paul's exhortation to Timothy remains ever timely: I remind you to fan into flame the gift of God that is within you through the laying on of my hands (cf. 2 Tim 1:6).

A missionary joy. I would like especially to share with you and to stress this third feature: priestly joy is deeply bound up with God's holy and faithful people, for it is an eminently missionary joy. Our anointing is meant for anointing God's holy and faithful people: for baptizing and confirming them, healing and sanctifying them, blessing, comforting and evangelizing them.

—Pope Francis, Homily for the Chrism Mass,
April 17, 2014

How do those whom I serve perceive me? Do they see a priest who is happy with his life and who finds joy in his ministry? Do I have a ready smile?

[B]ear your share of hardship for the gospel with the strength that comes from God.

He saved us and called us to a holy life . . . (2 Tim 1:8-9)

St. Thomas Aquinas regards the three evangelical counsels as forming an indivisible unity: they are like three sides of a single prism—that is, of one life which is set free for God according to the example of the Gospel. Celibacy is therefore only one side of an indivisible whole. Is it then surprising if its practice as an isolated fragment cannot be convincing? Where a man does not devote himself to the whole call of the Gospel to follow Christ, his celibacy is like a foreign body in his life plan. Since, then, the Church for adequate reasons demands from the priest celibacy for the sake of God's kingdom, and that he should in this point live "according to the Gospel," this is not possible without somehow putting the other counsels into practice. If this is not done, celibacy cannot be a convincing sign or be lived in that joy which is the mark of Christ's disciples. Instead, it will be only a burden. . . .

When celibacy is integrated in a life of following Christ, it is even today a convincing and respected sign. I have, for example, never heard that anyone has found the celibacy of Mother Teresa (can anyone imagine her as a married woman?) to be a problem, or the celibacy of the Brothers of Taize. Here one can feel that celibacy has a harmonious place in the whole of their lives. For the priest also, it must be an important objective that his celibacy fits harmoniously into the whole of his life. But his effort cannot be successful except when he practices the other two forms of the imitation of Christ—obedience and poverty.

—Gisbert Greshake, *The Meaning of Christian Priesthood*, 131–32

I ponder the interconnectedness of my celibacy, obedience, and poverty. How are they interwoven in my life so as to make a seamless whole?

"For whoever does the will of my heavenly Father is my brother, and sister, and mother." (Matt 12:50)

The Church, fixing her gaze on the mystery of the Holy Family of Nazareth, is taking part in the International Year of the Family, seeing it as an exceptional opportunity to proclaim the *"gospel of the family."* Christ proclaimed this gospel by his hidden life in Nazareth in the bosom of the Holy Family. It was then *proclaimed by the apostolic Church*, as is clear from the New Testament, and it was later *witnessed to by the post-apostolic Church*, which has taught us to consider the family as the *ecclesia domestica.*

In our own century the "gospel of the family" has been taught by the Church through the voices of very many priests, pastors, confessors and Bishops, and in particular through the voice of the Successor of Peter. . . .

The 1980 Synod of Bishops inspired the Apostolic Exhortation *Familiaris Consortio*, which can be considered the *magna charta* of the apostolate to families. . . . It was necessary to develop new methods of pastoral activity in order to meet the needs of the contemporary family. In a word, it may be said that concern for the family, and particularly for married couples, children, young people and adults, requires of us, as priests and confessors, a deep appreciation and a constant promotion of the *lay apostolate* in this area. The pastoral care of the family—and I know this from personal experience—is in a way the quintessence of priestly activity at every level.

—Saint John Paul II, Letter to Priests for
Holy Thursday, 1994

Gracious Father, may I come to appreciate more fully that my pastoral care of families is at the heart of all that I do in my priestly ministry.

March 24   In Sacred Union with the Whole Church

> For in him all the fullness was pleased to dwell, / and through him to reconcile all things for him, / making peace by the blood of his cross . . . (Col 1:19-20)

It is precisely this essence of faith that liberates us from egoistic isolation and unites us in a great community, a very complete one—in parishes, in the Sunday gathering—a universal community in which I become related to everyone in the world.

It is necessary to understand this Catholic dimension of the community that gathers in the parish church every Sunday. Thus, if, on the one hand, knowing the faith is one purpose, on the other, socializing in the Church or "ecclesializing" means being introduced into the great community of the Church, a living milieu, where I know that even in the important moments of my life—especially in suffering and in death—I am not alone.

Your Excellency said that many people do not seem to need us, but that the sick and the suffering do. And this should be understood from the outset: I will never again be lonely as long as I live. Faith redeems me from loneliness. I will always be supported by a community, but at the same time, I must support the community and, from the first, also teach responsibility for the sick, the lonely, the suffering, and thereby the gift that I make is reciprocated. So it is necessary to reawaken an awareness of this great gift in the person in whom is hidden the readiness to love and to give himself or herself, and thus guarantee that I too will have brothers and sisters to support me in difficult situations, when I am in need of a community that does not leave me stranded.

—Pope Benedict XVI, *Pilgrim Fellowship of Faith*, 171

I seek to appreciate the depth of community that I find in the church. May my priestly ministry give to others that same sense of belonging.

My Mother, My Vocation

> "Honour to Mary, honour and glory, honour to the Blessed Virgin! . . .
> He who created the marvellous world honoured in her his own Mother.
> . . . He loved her as his Mother, he lived in obedience.
> Though he was God, he respected her every word."
> (from a Polish Marian hymn)

Do not be surprised if I begin this letter . . . with the words of a Polish Marian hymn. I do so because this year I wish to speak to you *about the importance of women in the life of the priest.* . . .

The hymn speaks of Christ's love for his Mother. The first and most basic relationship which any human being establishes with a woman is precisely the relationship of the child to its mother. Each of us can express his love for his earthly mother just as the Son of God did and still does for his. Our mother is *the woman to whom we owe our life.* . . . Through childbirth a special and almost sacred bond is established between a human being and his mother.

Having brought us into the world, our parents then enabled us to become in Christ . . . adopted children of God. All this further deepened the bond between us and our parents, and in particular between us and our mothers. . . . *How many of us also owe to our mothers our very vocation to the priesthood!* Very often it is the mother who nurtures in her own heart a desire for a priestly vocation for her son, and *obtains it by praying with persevering trust and deep humility.* Thus, without imposing her own will, she favours with the effectiveness typical of faith the blossoming of an aspiration to the priesthood in the soul of her son, an aspiration which will bear fruit in due season.

—Saint John Paul II, Letter to Priests for
Holy Thursday, 1995

Lord Jesus, I pause to remember my mother, and the role that both she and my father have played in my vocation to the priesthood.

Then I said, "Woe is me, I am doomed! For I am a man of unclean lips, living among a people of unclean lips, and my eyes have seen the King, the LORD of hosts!" (Isa 6:5)

This is the life of the priest: to dwell completely in the explicit nearness of God. A life at once happy and terrifying. Happy, because God alone is happiness; terrifying, because man finds it difficult to survive in the midst of this frightening splendor of God. No wonder then that the noblest plant is always the most fragile too! No wonder that the high calling conceals within it the danger of the greatest falls—the danger that the priest will think he does not need to be a man any more, the danger of being unsympathetic towards other men, of letting his human side wither away, the danger of flight away from God into the more familiar company of men, the danger of the pitiful compromise, of the attempt to meet the superhuman demands of the priestly life by cheap mediocrity.

When someone dares to take up the happy and terrifying life of a priest, then the happy occasion can strike us speechless with fear because here is the beginning of something that no human being can finish. But we comfort ourselves with the grace of God; not we but that grace will finish what it has begun. For He who called the priest is true to His word and His graces are given without repentance. But during this celebration of the holy sacrifice let us pray for the Church on earth: pray God to send workers into His harvest, for the workers are few. Pray for our priests, that they begin in the fear and joy of the Lord and persevere in faithful service up to that happy end which all aspire to, when all vocations will find one happy end in the endless sacrificial celebration of eternity, when the Son and we with Him give over everything to the Father, so that God may be all in all. Amen.

—Karl Rahner, *Meditations on the Sacraments*, 68

It would be fruitful for me to contemplate the amazing grace of God that has drawn me to priestly life and that sustains me in my great weakness.

> Then I heard the voice of the Lord saying, "Whom shall I send? Who
> will go for us?" "Here I am," I said; "send me!" (Isa 6:8)

Within the broader context of the Christian vocation, the priestly vocation is a specific call. And this tends to be borne out in our personal
experience as priests: we received Baptism and Confirmation; we took
part in catechesis, in celebrations of the Liturgy and above all in the Eucharist. Our vocation to the priesthood first appeared in the context of the
Christian life . . .

There is a typology of vocation, which I would now like to sketch
briefly. We find a first outline of this typology in the New Testament. With
the words "follow me," Christ calls widely differing people: there are fishermen like Peter and the sons of Zebedee (cf. Mt 4:19, 22), but there is
also Levi, a publican, thereafter called Matthew. In Israel, the profession of
tax-collector was considered sinful and despicable. And yet Christ calls a
publican to join the group of Apostles (cf. Mt 9:9). Even more astonishing
was the call of Saul of Tarsus (Acts 9:1-19), a known and feared persecu-
tor of Christians, who hated the name of Jesus. Yet this very Pharisee was
called on the road to Damascus: the Lord wished to make him "a chosen
instrument," destined to suffer much for his name (cf. Acts 9:15-16).

Each of us priests sees himself in the original typology of vocation
found in the Gospels. At the same time, each one knows that the story of
his vocation, the path by which Christ guides him throughout his life, is
in some sense unique.

—Saint John Paul II, Letter to Priests for
Holy Thursday, 1996

Lord Jesus, with wonder and gratitude to God for this ineffable gift, may I
often pause in prayer and meditate on the mystery of my unique vocation.

"Let your 'Yes' mean 'Yes,' and your 'No' mean 'No.'" (Matt 5:37)

On Holy Thursday *every year we renew the promises we made* in connection with the Sacrament of the Priesthood. These promises have great implications. What is at stake is the word we have given to Christ himself. *Fidelity to our vocation builds up the Church*, and every act of infidelity is a painful wound to the Mystical Body of Christ. And so, as we gather together and contemplate the mystery of the institution of the Eucharist and the Priesthood, let us implore our High Priest who, as Sacred Scripture says, showed himself to be faithful (cf. Heb 2:17), that we too may remain faithful. In the spirit of this "sacramental brotherhood" let us pray for one another—priests for priests! . . . Let us also pray for our spiritual families, for those entrusted to our ministry. Let us pray particularly for those who expect our prayers and are in need of them. May our fidelity to prayer ensure that Christ will become ever more the life of our souls.

O great Sacrament of Faith, O holy Priesthood of the Redeemer of the world! Lord Jesus Christ, how grateful we are for having brought us into communion with you, for having made us one community around you, for allowing us to celebrate your unbloody sacrifice and to be ministers of the sacred mysteries in every place: at the altar, in the confessional, the pulpit, the sickroom, prisons, the classroom, the lecture hall, the offices where we work. All praise to the Most Holy Eucharist!

—Saint John Paul II, Letter to Priests for
Holy Thursday, 1994

O Jesus, give me the grace of fidelity to my vocation. Through my daily prayer may you become ever more the life of my soul.

> Your mercy hold not back! . . . You, Lord, are our father, / our re-
> deemer you are named from of old. (Isa 63:15-16)

With that voice that you make groan in the depths of my being, I seek
the copious pouring out of yourself, like the rain that gives back life to the
arid earth, and like a breath of life that comes to animate dry bones.

Give me that Spirit that scrutinizes all, inspires all, teaches all, that
will strengthen me to support what I am not able to support. Give me that
Spirit that transformed the weak Galilean fishermen into the columns of
your church and into apostles who gave in the holocaust of their lives the
supreme testimony of their love for their brothers and sisters.

Thus, this life-giving outpouring will be like a new creation, of hearts
transformed, of a sensibility receptive to the voice of the Father, of a spontaneous fidelity to his word. Thus, you will find us again faithful and you
will not hide your face from us because you will have poured your Spirit
over us. Now I understand that in order to accomplish all this one needs a
love like that of the Father, a love that intervenes personally. "You, Lord,
are our Father. . . . Why do you let us stray from your ways? . . . Oh, that
you would tear the heavens open and come down" (Is 63:15-19).

Such was your definitive manifestation: the heavens open, a God the
Father visible, a God the Son coming down to the earth and becoming
human to save the world: "This mystery that has now been revealed through
the Spirit to his holy apostles and prophets was unknown to human beings
in past generations. . . . This, then, is what I pray, kneeling before the
Father" (Eph 3:5, 14). *Veni Sancte Spiritus!*

> —Pedro Arrupe, "Final Address of Father General to
> the Congregation of Procurators," *The Spiritual
> Legacy of Pedro Arrupe, S.J.*, 41–42

Come, Spirit most holy, transform my heart, open it wide to the voice of
the Father, that daily I might witness to God's healing love.

March 30   Celibacy: Absolute Attachment to Christ

Such is the generation that seeks [the Lord], / that seeks the face of the God of Jacob. (Ps 24:6)

The Second Vatican Council gave the reasons for the "inner consonance" of celibacy and the priesthood: "By preserving virginity or celibacy for the sake of the kingdom of heaven priests are consecrated in a new and excellent way to Christ. They more readily cling to him with undivided heart and dedicate themselves more freely in him and through him to the service of God and men. They are less encumbered in their service of his kingdom and of the task of heavenly regeneration. In this way they become better fitted for a broader acceptance of fatherhood in Christ." They "recall that mystical marriage, established by God and destined to be fully revealed in the future, by which the Church holds Christ as her only Spouse. Moreover they are made a living sign of that world to come in which the children of the resurrection shall neither be married nor take wives."

These lofty, noble spiritual reasons can be summarized in the following essential points: a more complete adherence to Christ, loved and served with an undivided heart; greater availability to serve Christ's kingdom and to carry out their own task in the Church, the most exclusive choice of a spiritual fruitfulness; leading a life more like that definitive one in the world to come, and therefore, more exemplary for life here below.

. . . It is necessary to ask for the grace to understand priestly celibacy, which doubtless includes a certain mystery: that of asking for boldness and trust in the absolute attachment to the person and redeeming work of Christ.

—Saint John Paul II, "The Church is Committed to Priestly Celibacy," General Audience, July 14, 1993

Blessed are they who receive the grace to understand celibacy and remain faithful on this journey.

> John testified to him and cried out, saying, "This was he of whom I said, 'The one who is coming after me ranks ahead of me because he existed before me.'" (John 1:15)

God's truth may slip into men's hearts without their knowing it; it may seem to be there only in a little piece, for example in silent humility of heart, in a nameless longing of the mind . . .

But tiny as it is, when it is there in the power of the Holy Spirit of God, then it is wholly there, and in it the beginning of love and eternal life. But this plain and single truth of God, in which God speaks himself into the inmost heart of man is the truth that is present in the world because it flowed out of the pierced heart of the Christ of God. And hence this truth wants to be made flesh in human words, wants to enter into all men's thoughts and words, wants to become the uninterrupted theme of an endless symphony which peals through every hall of the universe. This truth wants to be explained and preached, wants to slip through the portals of the ears into men's hearts, and out of the private chamber of their hearts, to mount up and penetrate into every area of man's activity, be preached from the rooftops, judging and purifying, redeeming and filling, and weave itself together with the whole of human truth.

And this is why this truth has its messengers, human messengers. They speak a human word. But it is filled with divine truth. And what they say is . . . the truth—which is the only thing that never fades, never wears out, never gets used up. They say God—God of eternal majesty, God of eternal life; they say that God Himself is our life; they call out that death is not the end that the world's cleverness is foolishness and shortsightedness, that there is a judgment, a justice, and an everlasting life.

—Karl Rahner, *Meditations on the Sacraments*, 62–63

Lord Jesus, bless my study of Sacred Scripture, and bless my preaching and teaching, so that I may proclaim only your Way, your Truth, your Life.

> For God is my witness, how I long for all of you with the affection of
> Christ Jesus. (Phil 1:8)

The root of charity in a priest's life is found in his identity as a "man
of God." The First Letter of John teaches us that "God is love." Since he
is a "man of God" the priest must be a man of charity. He would have no
true love for God (nor even true piety or true apostolic zeal) without love
for his neighbor.

Jesus himself showed the connection between love for God and love for
neighbor, since "loving the Lord, your God, with all your heart" cannot be
separated from "loving your neighbor." Consistently, therefore, the author
of the Letter cited above reasons: "This is the commandment we have from
him: whoever loves God must also love his brother."

Speaking of himself, Jesus describes this love as that of a "good shepherd" who does not seek his own interest, his own advantage, like a hired
hand. He notes that the Good Shepherd loves his sheep to the point of giving
his own life. Thus it is a love to the point of heroism.

We know to what extent this was realized in the life and death of Jesus.
Those who, in virtue of priestly ordination, receive the mission of *shepherds*
are called to present anew in their lives and witness to with their actions
the heroic love of the *Good Shepherd.*

. . . The mission of shepherd cannot be carried out with a superior or
authoritarian attitude, which would irritate the faithful and perhaps drive
them from the fold. In the footsteps of Christ the Good Shepherd we must
be formed in a spirit of humble service.

—Saint John Paul II, General Audience, July 7, 1993

Good Shepherd, give me the grace to love all those whom I meet with the
heroic and tender love that identifies me as your follower and friend.

> Pray without ceasing. In all circumstances give thanks, for this is the will of God for you in Christ Jesus. (1 Thess 5:17-18)

Prayer in the life of the priest must not be limited to a number of isolated, passing incidents: the minister of Christ must cultivate the spirit of prayer. What must we understand by this? An habitual disposition of soul whereby, in our troubles and discouragements, as in our joys and successes, our hearts turn towards Christ or towards our heavenly Father, as to our best friend, to the most intimate confidant of our feelings, the support of our weakness. And it is not only in the morning and in the evening that the soul should be raised to God, but always: *oculi mei semper ad Dominum* (Ps 25:15).

By virtue of our grace of adoption, we must, in our relations with God, make ourselves simple like children . . . A son treats his father with all respect, but his reverence for him does not prevent him from relying on his goodness, or from pouring out his heart to him. And so it is for the priest: God must not be for him an unapproachable lord to whom one declaims every day certain formulas to be got through as quickly as possible. No, He is the father, the counselor, the support. Even if you have the misfortune to incur His displeasure, your confidence in His goodness should not be shaken. Before every important undertaking we should formulate the desire in our heart to act for Him.

With time, this habit of raising our minds to God like this will become, as it were, natural, and our communications with the invisible world will be multiplied. Mass, the Divine Office, and meditation, instead of being isolated acts wholly unconnected with the rest of our life, will be a more intense continuation of our friendship with God. The grace of filial union will become the centre of our whole existence.

—Blessed Columba Marmion,
Christ: The Ideal of the Priest, 246

I pause to consider the efforts I make to sanctify the day by prayer.

> How hard it is for those who have wealth to enter the kingdom of God!
> For it is easier for a camel to pass through the eye of a needle than for a
> rich person to enter the kingdom of God. (Luke 18:24-25)

The humble Curé of Ars was careful to imitate the Patriarch of Assisi
in this regard, for he had accepted his rule in the Third Order of St. Francis
and he carefully observed it. He was rich in his generosity toward others
but the poorest of men in dealing with himself; he passed a life that was
almost completely detached from the changeable, perishable goods of this
world, and his spirit was free and unencumbered by impediments of this
kind, so that it could always lie open to those who suffered from any kind
of misery; and they flocked from everywhere to seek his consolation. "My
secret"—he said—"is easy to learn. It can be summed up in these few
words: give everything away and keep nothing for yourself."

This detachment from external goods enabled him to offer the most
devoted and touching care to the poor, especially those in his own parish. He was very kind and gentle toward them and embraced them "with
a sincere love, with the greatest of kindness, indeed with reverence." He
warned that the needy were never to be spurned since a disregard for them
would reach in turn to God. When beggars knocked at his door, he received
them with love and was very happy to be able to say to them: "I am living
in need myself; I am one of you." And toward the end of his life, he used
to enjoy saying things like this: "I will be happy when I go; for now I no
longer have any possessions; and so when God in his goodness sees fit to
call me, I will be ready and willing to go."

—Saint John XXIII, *Sacerdotii Nostri Primordia*, 14–15

How freely do I give to those in need? To the support of my diocese or
community? Am I a friend to the countless charities seeking my help?

Imploring the Gifts of Christ's Spirit April 4

> "As the Father has sent me, so I send you." And when he had said this, he breathed on them and said to them, "Receive the holy Spirit." (John 20:21-22)

An intimate bond unites our priesthood to the Holy Spirit and to his mission. On the day of our priestly ordination, by virtue of a unique outpouring of the Paraclete, the Risen One accomplished again in each of us what he accomplished in his disciples on the evening of Easter, and set us in the world as those who continue his mission (cf. Jn 20:21-23). This gift of the Spirit, with its mysterious sanctifying power, is the source and root of the special task of evangelization and of sanctification which is entrusted to us.

On Holy Thursday, the day when we commemorate the Lord's Supper, we contemplate Jesus, the Servant "obedient unto death" (Phil 2:8), who institutes the Eucharist and Holy Orders as the supreme sign of his love. He leaves us this extraordinary testament of love, so that always and everywhere the mystery of his Body and Blood may be perpetuated and people may approach the inexhaustible source of grace. Is there a more appropriate and evocative moment than this for us priests to contemplate the work of the Holy Spirit in us and to implore his gifts in order to conform ourselves all the more to Christ, the Priest of the New Covenant?

Veni, Creator Spiritus, Come, O Creator Spirit,

Mentes tuorum visita, visit our minds.

Imple superna gratia, Fill with your grace

Quae tu creasti pectora. the hearts you have created.

This ancient liturgical hymn reminds every priest of his Ordination day, recalling the commitment made in that unique moment to be completely open to the action of the Holy Spirit. It reminds him as well of the Paraclete's special assistance and of the many moments of grace, joy and intimacy which the Lord has granted him to enjoy on his life's journey.

—Saint John Paul II, Letter to Priests for
Holy Thursday, 1998

I reflect on the day of my ordination, and ask for the grace that stirs into a flame my complete openness to the action of the Holy Spirit.

> I urge you therefore, brothers, by the mercies of God, to offer your
> bodies as a living sacrifice, holy and pleasing to God, your spiritual
> worship. (Rom 12:1)

People find him distant, since he is outside customary conventions.
They think him indifferent, since he keeps quiet and recollected, whereas
he "considers the whole world as his parish." The ungrateful world has no
idea he is watching over it (Is 21:11). It has no concern for this guardian
protecting it in the night (Is 62:6). It derives no satisfaction from the fact
that he gives his life for it.

Here is the everlasting paradox of the priest. He carries opposites within
him. At the cost of his life he reconciles loyalty to God and man. He has
an air of poverty and helplessness, and in actual fact no one is weaker than
the priest. He disposes of neither political power nor financial resources,
nor armed strength, which others use to conquer the world. His native force
is to be disarmed and "to do all things in Him who strengthens him" (Phil
4:13). That means going, with the independence conferred on him by his
detachment, to the suffering and ignorant and falling . . .

Till the end of time, his mystery—which even for himself a sacred
enigma—will traverse events and civilizations, to serve as the greatest
witness to the unseen Kingdom. Priests know that; when they stand for
the first time at the altar they are under no illusions, knowing that till the
day of their death they are going to be the "sign of contradiction," light for
the children of the light, and darkness for the sons of night. Here we must
finally conclude, by going back to where we began. The priesthood was
founded by Love, it is Love itself, Our Lord's last great gift . . .

There is one thing [the priest] claims which no one will take from him;
one good he wants for himself, with obstinate determination; in this human
world he has chosen Love.

> —Emmanuel-Célestin Cardinal Suhard,
> *The Church Today*, 342–43

Lord Jesus, as you have chosen love, so I choose love. Yesterday, today,
forever, I choose love as the full measure of my priestly life.

> [M]y Father gives you the true bread from heaven. For the bread of
> God is that which comes down from heaven and gives life to the world.
> (John 6:32-33)

The priesthood, in its deepest reality, is *the priesthood of Christ*. It
is Christ who offers himself, his Body and Blood, in sacrifice to God the
Father, and by this sacrifice makes righteous in the Father's eyes all mankind and, indirectly, all creation. The priest, in his daily celebration of the
Eucharist, goes to the very heart of this mystery. For this reason the celebration of the Eucharist must be the most important moment of the priest's
day, the center of his life.

The words which we repeat at the end of the Preface—"Blessed is he
who comes in the name of the Lord"—take us back to the dramatic events
of Palm Sunday. Christ goes to Jerusalem to face the bloody sacrifice of
Good Friday. But the day before, at the Last Supper, he institutes the sacrament of this sacrifice. Over the bread and wine he says . . . "Do this in
memory of me."

What kind of a "memorial" is this? . . . Here we are speaking of a
"memorial" in the biblical sense, a memorial which *makes present* the event
itself. It is *memory* and *presence*. The secret of this miracle is the action
of the Holy Spirit, whom the priest invokes when he extends his hands
over the gifts of bread and wine: "Let *your Spirit* come upon these gifts
to make them holy, so that they may become for us the Body and Blood
of our Lord Jesus Christ." Thus it is not merely the priest who recalls the
events of Christ's Passion, Death, and Resurrection; it is also the Holy
Spirit who enables this event to be made present on the altar through the
ministry of the priest.

—Saint John Paul II, *Gift and Mystery*, 75–76

Come, Holy Spirit, fill me with a deeper appreciation of your sanctifying
presence in my sacramental and pastoral ministry.

> I urge you, brothers, in the name of our Lord Jesus Christ, that all of you
> agree in what you say, and that there be no divisions among you, but that
> you be united in the same mind and in the same purpose. (1 Cor 1:10)

The first mark of the church is unity. The church is one. All levels of communion in the church assume collaborative relationships whose first task is to make sure the unity of the church is tangible, palpable, and alive. This unity has always been a complex one, a unity in diversity—no surprise for those who adore a Triune God, one in Nature, three in Persons. Maintaining such unity is a paramount challenge for church ministry in all forms and for priests and bishops in particular. They function like the center of a wheel from which spokes extend in all directions. . . .

Clearly there are human and spiritual qualities that help or hinder a priest or a bishop in fulfilling such a role. Anger and hostility, for example, almost by definition, separate and divide people and are poor qualities for effective church ministers. The higher one ascends the hierarchical ladder, the more damaging such qualities become. If bishops and priests are symbols and agents of the church's unity, they themselves must be like magnets that draw people and hold them together. They must literally become *symbolon*, people who tie things together, able to call people to a wider sense of community that transcends personal self-interest. Their best efforts are devoted to calling down the *koinonia*, the communion of the Holy Spirit, the real force that joins people to one another. This communion is not a gift from above that drops down vertically and stops. Rather it becomes a circling bond of charity that joins Christians to one another as it unites them to Christ. . . .

Priests and bishops are called to be ministers who foster the unity of the church. As symbols and agents of unity, they fulfill this role by constantly balancing unity and diversity in the parish and in a diocese.

—Howard P. Bleichner, *View from the Altar*, 157–58

I reflect upon the times I have felt a great sense of family unity in the faith communities I have served. I am grateful for having been a symbol and agent of that unity.

"Yes, It Is Worth It!"

[We are] always carrying about in the body the dying of Jesus, so that the life of Jesus may also be manifested in our body. (2 Cor 4:10)

"Is it really worth it?" you ask. When the dust has settled and the clouds have disappeared, if only for a moment, we see more clearly the truly important difference that priests make in the lives of their people. And then we can say, "Yes, it is worth it!" This is why I cherish my priesthood.

Priests often have a special awareness of being the instruments of God's healing, reconciling grace. It is an awesome thing to be so used by God—but it is not without its share of suffering. On [Good] Friday we will recall in a vivid way that Jesus was both priest and victim—for the salvation and new life of others.

My brothers, our recommitment today is an expression of our willingness to participate in Jesus' mission with renewed fidelity and enthusiasm. The oils have long since dried since our ordination day. We have known periods of questioning and doubt. We know the pain of loss as some of our friends have chosen to leave the active ministry. We have walked through the valley of darkness with our people—the dark valley of moral dilemmas, of physical and spiritual sickness, of injustice and oppressive structures. So, the question, "Is it worth it?" may still haunt us.

In all this, the Church asks us today to keep our eyes fixed on Jesus as he comes upon the clouds of darkness, suffering, and doubt. We are to watch him with great hope and love as he embraces all who need his care. The transformation that our eyes behold in this Eucharist—the transformation we see and experience each day in our ministry—evokes a promise that we will sing forever of the goodness of God.

—Joseph Cardinal Bernardin, Homily for
the Chrism Mass, April 14, 1987

Can I remember asking, or perhaps feeling, in times of discouragement, "Is it worth it?" Where have I found the strength to go on?

Priestly Vocations Rooted in the Family

> Honor your father and your mother, that you may have a long life in the land the LORD your God is giving you. (Exod 20:12)

The call to pray with families and for families, dear Brothers, concerns each one of you in a very personal way. We owe our life to our parents and we owe them a permanent debt of gratitude. Whether they are still alive or have already passed into eternity, we are united with them by a close bond which time does not destroy. While we owe our vocation to God, a significant role in it is also to be attributed to our parents. The decision of a son to dedicate himself to the priestly ministry, particularly in mission lands, is no small sacrifice for his parents. This was true also in the case of our own dear ones, yet they offered their feelings to God, letting themselves be guided by a deep faith. They then followed us with their prayer, just as Mary did with Jesus when he left the home at Nazareth in order to carry out his Messianic mission.

What an experience it was for each of us, and, at the same time, for our parents, our brothers and sisters and those dear to us, when we celebrated our first Holy Mass! What a great thing that celebration was for our parishes and the places where we grew up! Every new vocation makes the parish aware of the fruitfulness of its spiritual motherhood: the more often it happens, the greater the encouragement that results for others! Every priest can say of himself: "I am indebted to God and to others." There are many people who have accompanied us with their thoughts and prayers, just as there are many who by their thoughts and prayers accompany my own ministry in the See of Peter.

—Saint John Paul II, Letter to Priests for
Holy Thursday, 1994

In what ways in my ministry do I continue to honor my father, my mother, my family?

Clothed in Christ Jesus

> [B]e renewed in the spirit of your minds, and put on the new self, created in God's way in righteousness and holiness of truth. (Eph 4:23-24)

Leo Tolstoy, the Russian writer, tells in a short story of a harsh sovereign who asked his priests and sages to show him God so that he might see him. The wise men were unable to satisfy his desire. Then a shepherd, who was just coming in from the fields, volunteered to take on the task of the priests and sages. From him the king learned that his eyes were not good enough to see God. Then, however, he wanted to know at least what God does. "To be able to answer your question," the shepherd said to the king, "we must exchange our clothes."

Somewhat hesitant but impelled by curiosity about the information he was expecting, the king consented; he gave the shepherd his royal robes and had himself dressed in the simple clothes of the poor man. Then came the answer: "This is what God does." Indeed, the Son of God, true God from true God, shed his divine splendour: "he emptied himself, taking the form of a servant, being born in the likeness of men; and being found in human form he humbled himself . . . , even unto death on a cross" (Phil 2: 6ff.). . . .

With regard to what happens in Baptism, St. Paul explicitly uses the image of clothing: "For as many of you as were baptized into Christ have put on Christ" (Gal 3: 27). This is what is fulfilled in Baptism: we put on Christ, he gives us his garments and these are not something external. It means that we enter into an existential communion with him, that his being and our being merge, penetrate one another.

This theology of Baptism returns in a new way and with a new insistence in priestly Ordination. Just as in Baptism an "exchange of clothing" is given, an exchanged destination, a new existential communion with Christ, so also in priesthood . . .

—Pope Benedict XVI, Homily for the Chrism Mass,
April 5, 2007

I am invited to reflect upon the royal robes that I donned at baptism, and the richer texture of those robes that I discovered at ordination.

"If anyone wishes to come after me, he must deny himself and take up his cross daily and follow me. For whoever wishes to save his life will lose it, but whoever loses his life for my sake will save it." (Luke 9:23-24)

We need to "go out," then, in order to experience our own anointing, its power and its redemptive efficacy: to the "outskirts" where there is suffering, bloodshed, blindness that longs for sight, and prisoners in thrall to many evil masters. . . . Grace comes alive and flourishes to the extent that we, in faith, go out and give ourselves and the Gospel to others, giving what little ointment we have to those who have nothing, nothing at all.

The priest who seldom goes out of himself, who anoints little—I won't say "not at all" because, thank God, the people take the oil from us anyway—misses out on the best of our people, on what can stir the depths of his priestly heart. Those who do not go out of themselves, instead of being mediators, gradually become intermediaries, managers. We know the difference: the intermediary, the manager, "has already received his reward," and since he doesn't put his own skin and his own heart on the line, he never hears a warm, heartfelt word of thanks. This is precisely the reason for the dissatisfaction of some, who end up sad—sad priests—in some sense becoming collectors of antiques or novelties, instead of being shepherds living with "the odour of the sheep." This I ask you: be shepherds, with the "odour of the sheep," make it real, as shepherds among your flock, fishers of men. True enough, the so-called crisis of priestly identity threatens us all and adds to the broader cultural crisis; but if we can resist its onslaught, we will be able to put out in the name of the Lord and cast our nets. It is not a bad thing that reality itself forces us to "put out into the deep," where what we are by grace is clearly seen as pure grace, out into the deep of the contemporary world, where the only thing that counts is "unction"—not function—and the nets which overflow with fish are those cast solely in the name of the One in whom we have put our trust: Jesus.

—Pope Francis, Homily for the Chrism Mass,
March 28, 2013

I read and reread these words of Pope Francis. In his words I hear the challenge to beware of the lethargy and mediocrity that can inhabit my heart. I hear his call to embody the joy of the gospel.

Esteeming the Priesthood

Whoever listens to you listens to me. (Luke 10:16)

There are . . . situations which can never be sufficiently deplored where the Church herself suffers as a consequence of infidelity on the part of some of her ministers. Then it is the world which finds grounds for scandal and rejection. What is most helpful to the Church in such cases is not only a frank and complete acknowledgement of the weaknesses of her ministers, but also a joyful and renewed realization of the greatness of God's gift, embodied in the splendid example of generous pastors, religious afire with love for God and for souls, and insightful, patient spiritual guides.

Here the teaching and example of St. John Mary Vianney can serve as a significant point of reference for us all. The Curé of Ars was quite humble, yet as a priest he was conscious of being an immense gift to his people: "A good shepherd, a pastor after God's heart, is the greatest treasure which the good Lord can grant to a parish, and one of the most precious gifts of divine mercy." He spoke of the priesthood as if incapable of fathoming the grandeur of the gift and task entrusted to a human creature . . .

Explaining to his parishioners the importance of the Sacraments, he would say: "Without the Sacrament of Holy Orders, we would not have the Lord. Who put Him there in that tabernacle? The priest. Who welcomed your soul at the beginning of your life? The priest. Who feeds your soul and gives it strength for its journey? The priest. Who will prepare it to appear before God, bathing it one last time in the blood of Jesus Christ? The priest, always the priest. And if this soul should happen to die [as a result of sin], who will raise it up, who will restore its calm and peace? Again, the priest."

—Pope Benedict XVI, Letter Proclaiming
a Year for Priests, June 16, 2009

I am continually in awe that God would choose me for a share in the priesthood of his Son.

[M]ay I never boast except in the cross of our Lord Jesus Christ . . .
(Gal 6:14)

I have been a bishop for twenty months. As I clearly foresaw, my
ministry has brought me many trials, but, and this is strange, these are not
caused by the Bulgarians for whom I work but by the central organs of
ecclesiastical administration. This is a form of mortification and humiliation
I did not expect and which hurts me deeply, "Lord, you know all." I must,
I will accustom myself to bearing this cross with more patience, calm and
inner peace than I have so far shown. I shall be particularly careful in what
I say to anyone about this. Every time I speak my mind about it I take away
from the merit of my patience, "Set a guard over my mouth, O Lord." I shall
make this silence, which must be, according to the teaching of St. Francis
de Sales, meek and without bitterness, an object of my self-examinations.

The time I give to active work must be in proportion to what I give
to the work of God, that is, to prayer. I need more fervent and continual
prayer to give character to my life. So I must give more time to meditation,
and stay longer in the Lord's company, sometimes reading or saying my
prayers aloud or just keeping silent. . . .

The brief experience of these months as Bishop convinces me that for
me, in this life, there is nothing better than bearing my cross, as Jesus sets
it on my shoulders and on my heart. I must think of myself as the man
bearing the cross, and love the cross that God sends me without thinking
of any other. All that is not to the honour of God, the service of the Church
and the welfare of souls is extraneous to me, and of no importance.

—Saint John XXIII, *Journal of a Soul*, 267–68

Lord Jesus, I am so often prone to complaining and whining in times of
difficulty. Give me wisdom to recognize and embrace your cross in my life.

The Priest as Spouse to the Community

> Tell me, you whom my soul loves, / where you shepherd, where you give rest at midday. (Song 1:7)

Christ's gift of himself to his Church, the fruit of his love, is described in terms of that unique gift of self made by the bridegroom to the bride. Christ stands before the Church and nourishes and cherishes her (Eph. 5:29), giving his life for her.

The priest is called to be the living image of Jesus Christ, the spouse of the Church. Of course, he will always remain a member of the community as a believer alongside his other brothers and sisters who have been called by the spirit. In virtue of his configuration to Christ, the head and shepherd, however, the priest stands in this spousal relationship in regard to the community. "Inasmuch as he represents Christ, the head, shepherd and spouse of the Church, the priest is placed not only in the Church but also in the forefront of the Church." In his spiritual life, then, he is called to live out Christ's spousal love toward the Church, his bride. Therefore, the priest's life ought to radiate this spousal character, which demands that he be a witness to Christ's spousal love and thus be capable of loving people with a heart which is new, generous, and pure—with genuine self-detachment, with full, constant and faithful dedication and at the same time with a kind of "divine jealousy" (cf. 2 Cor.11:2)—and even with a kind of maternal tenderness, capable of bearing "the pangs of birth" until Christ be formed in the faithful (cf. Gal.4:19).

—Saint John Paul II, *Pastores Dabo Vobis*, 22

How is my priestly heart new and generous and pure?

> Like fine oil on the head, / running down upon the beard, / Upon the beard of Aaron, / upon the collar of his robe. (Ps 133:2)

A good priest can be recognized by the way his people are anointed. This is a clear test. When our people are anointed with the oil of gladness, it is obvious: for example, when they leave Mass looking as if they have heard good news. Our people like to hear the Gospel preached with "unction", they like it when the Gospel we preach touches their daily lives, when it runs down like the oil of Aaron to the edges of reality, when it brings light to moments of extreme darkness, to the "outskirts" where people of faith are most exposed to the onslaught of those who want to tear down their faith. People thank us because they feel that we have prayed over the realities of their everyday lives, their troubles, their joys, their burdens and their hopes. And when they feel that the fragrance of the Anointed One, of Christ, has come to them through us, they feel encouraged to entrust to us everything they want to bring before the Lord: "Pray for me, Father, because I have this problem", "Bless me", "Pray for me"—these words are the sign that the anointing has flowed down to the edges of the robe, for it has turned into prayer. What I want to emphasize is that we need constantly to stir up God's grace and perceive in every request, even those requests that are inconvenient and at times purely material or downright banal—but only apparently so—the desire of our people to be anointed with fragrant oil, since they know that we have it.

To perceive and to sense, even as the Lord sensed the hope-filled anguish of the woman suffering from hemorrhages when she touched the hem of his garment. At that moment, Jesus, surrounded by people on every side, embodies all the beauty of Aaron vested in priestly raiment, with the oil running down upon his robes. It is a hidden beauty, one which shines forth only for those faith-filled eyes of the woman troubled with an issue of blood. But not even the disciples—future priests—see or understand: on the "existential outskirts", they see only what is on the surface: the crowd pressing in on Jesus from all sides (cf. Lk 8:42). The Lord, on the other hand, feels the power of the divine anointing which runs down to the edge of his cloak.

—Pope Francis, Homily for the Chrism Mass,
March 28, 2013

In what ways is my priestly ministry a fragrant anointing of the people whom I serve?

Celibacy Sustained by a Life of Prayer

> It was not you who chose me, but I who chose you and appointed you to go and bear fruit that will remain, so that whatever you ask the Father in my name he may give you. (John 15:16)

Every Christian who receives the sacrament of Orders commits himself to celibacy with full awareness and freedom. . . . He decides upon a life of celibacy only after he has reached a firm conviction that Christ is giving him this "gift" for the good of the Church and the service of others. Only then does he commit himself to observe celibacy for his entire life. It is obvious that such a decision obliges not only by virtue of a law laid down by the Church but also by virtue of personal responsibility. It is a matter here of keeping one's word to Christ and the Church. Keeping one's word is, at one and the same time, a duty and a proof of the priest's inner maturity; it is the expression of his personal dignity. It is shown in all its clarity when this keeping one's promise to Christ, made through a conscious and free commitment to celibacy for the whole of one's life, encounters difficulties, is put to the test, or is exposed to temptation—all things that do not spare the priest, any more than they spare any other Christian. At such a moment, the individual must seek support in more fervent prayer. Through prayer, he must find within himself that attitude of humility and sincerity before God and his own conscience; prayer is indeed the source of strength for sustaining what is wavering. Then it is that there is born a confidence like the confidence expressed by St. Paul in the words: "There is nothing that I cannot master with the help of the One who gives me strength." These truths are confirmed by the experience of many priests and proved by the reality of life.

—Saint John Paul II, Letter to Priests for
Holy Thursday, 1979

I can only truly appreciate the gift of celibacy if I am fully committed to daily prayer, which is a total reliance on the faithful companionship of Jesus.

> [W]e all attain to the unity of faith and knowledge of the Son of God, to
> mature manhood, to the extent of the full stature of Christ . . . (Eph 4:13)

However busy we may be, however mature and efficient we may seem, our spiritual growth, if we are real Christians, must go on. Even the greatest teachers, such as St. Paul and St. Augustine, could never afford to relax the tension of their own spiritual lives; they never seem to stand still, are never afraid of conflict and change. Their souls too were growing entities, with a potential capacity for love, adoration and creative service; in other words for holiness, the achievement of the stature of Christ.

A saint is simply a human being whose soul has thus grown up to its full stature, by full and generous response to its environment, God. He has achieved a deeper, bigger life than the rest of us, a more wonderful contact with the mysteries of the Universe; a life of infinite possibility, the term of which he never feels that he has reached.

That desire and willingness for growth at all costs, that sense of great un-reached possibilities which await the fully-expanded human soul, is important for us all; but surely specially important for priests?

Prayer and mortification are hard words; but after all that which they involve is simply communion with God and discipline of self. They are the names of those two fundamental and inseparable activities which temper the natural resources of man to his supernatural work; and every Christian worker must have in his life the bracing and humbling influences of such continuous self-surrender and self-conquest. They involve a ceaseless gentle discipline; but being a disciple means living a disciplined life, and it is not very likely that you will get other disciples, unless you are one first.

—Evelyn Underhill, *Concerning the Inner Life*, 105–6

I ponder the place of daily prayer and mortification in my life. What positive effect does it have for my pastoral ministry?

> But when you fast, anoint your head and wash your face, so that you may not appear to others to be fasting, except to your Father who is hidden. And your Father who sees what is hidden will repay you. (Matt 6:17-18)

The ascetic discipline of the priest is not to be set alongside the pastoral activity, as an additional burden and an extra program that overloads my day still further. In my work itself, I am learning to overcome myself, to let my life go and give it up to others; in disappointment and failure, I am learning renunciation and the acceptance of pain, letting go of myself. In the joy of succeeding, I am learning thankfulness. When I celebrate the sacraments, I am inwardly receiving them along with the recipients; I am indeed not doing some outward work or other; I am talking with Christ and, through Christ, with God the Trinity, and thus I am praying with others and for them. There is no doubt that this asceticism of service or ministry, seeing ministry itself as the actual ascetic discipline in my life, is a most important theme, which does of course demand repeated and conscious practice, an inner ordering of my activity on the basis of who I am.

. . . Even if I am trying to live the ministry as a form of asceticism, and the sacramental actions as a personal encounter with Christ, I still need moments in which to catch my breath, so that this inner orientation can be put into effect at all. All this—the Council's decree says—can be achieved only if priests, through the lives they live, penetrate ever more profoundly into the mystery of Christ.

—Pope Benedict XVI, *Pilgrim Fellowship of Faith*, 170

How frequently I need to remind myself that I must surrender my ego and allow Christ to live his life in me!

For God did not give us a spirit of cowardice but rather of power and love and self-control. (2 Tim 1:7)

Lord Jesus, we thank You for having had confidence in us, in spite of our weakness and human frailty, infusing into us at Baptism the vocation and grace of perfection to be acquired day by day. We ask that we may always be able to carry out our sacred duties according to the measure of a pure heart and an upright conscience. May we be faithful "to the end" to You, who loved us "to the end."

When on Holy Thursday, as You instituted the Eucharist and the Priest-hood, You were leaving those whom You had loved to the end, You promised them the new "Counselor." May this Counselor, the "Spirit of Truth," be with us through His holy gifts! May there be with us wisdom and under-standing, knowledge and counsel, fortitude, piety and the holy fear of God. . . ."

Save us from "grieving your Spirit": by our lack of faith and lack of readiness to witness to Your Gospel "in deed and in truth"; by secularism and by wishing at all costs to conform to the mentality of this world; by a lack of that love which is "patient and kind . . . "

Save us from "grieving" Your Spirit: by everything that brings inward sadness and is an obstacle for the soul; by whatever makes us a fertile soil for all temptations; by whatever shows itself as a desire to hide one's Priesthood before men . . . ; by whatever can in the end bring one to the temptation to run away, under the pretext of the "right to freedom."

Save us from demeaning the fullness and richness of our freedom, which we have ennobled and realized by giving ourselves to You and ac-cepting the gift of the Priesthood.

—Saint John Paul II, Letter to Priests for
Holy Thursday, 1982

Save me, Lord, from anything that conceals or diminishes the sacred gift of the priesthood.

Not I, but Christ

> For we do not preach ourselves but Jesus Christ as Lord, and ourselves as your slaves for the sake of Jesus. (2 Cor 4:5)

The power to exercise the official ministry comes from God himself, according to what Paul says: "Not that we are sufficient to think anything of ourselves, as if we could attribute anything to ourselves: our sufficiency comes from God, who has made us fit ministers of the New Testament, not of the letter, but of the spirit" (2 Cor 3:5f). Consequently, human sins and failures cannot frustrate and destroy this power. The "character," therefore, does not establish an "undue preferential position of the priest before the community, but means in the first place that his official actions do not ultimately depend on his personal situation before God with regard to his own salvation" (Letter of the German Bishops, 1969). E. Dassmann points out that already in the early Church, the great lay theologians had noticed and spoken about the discrepancy between the deficiency of personal spiritual qualities in the bishop or priest and their spiritual ministry. Thus, he says that in the opinion of Origen "arrogance and pride . . . [are] typical qualities of clerics, as well as their failure themselves to practice what they preach to the faithful according to the Gospel. People of modest position and no culture often have a perfection which is wanting in bishops and priests." It is just in this way that it becomes abundantly clear that the spiritual ministries of the office-bearers are far beyond their human capacity, and simply "cannot be carried out unless the Church by conferring the office in ordination is able to guarantee the assistance of the Holy Spirit."

If the ministry of salvation depended upon personal holiness, not only would the priest be completely overstretched, but the eschatological and final offer of salvation, made by God in Jesus Christ, would be limited by the sin and weakness of men, and its ultimate validity would be open to question.

—Gisbert Greshake, *The Meaning of Christian Priesthood*, 109–10

Lord Jesus, deliver me from any trace of arrogance or pride in my priestly ministry.

> [The young man] replied and said to him, "Teacher, all of these I have observed from my youth." Jesus, looking at him, loved him and said to him, "You are lacking in one thing. Go, sell what you have, and give to [the] poor and you will have treasure in heaven; then come, follow me." (Mark 10:20-21)

In the Gospel account of Christ's conversation with the young man there is an expression that we must assimilate in a particular way. The Evangelist says that Jesus "looked at him and loved him." We touch here the truly crucial point. If we were to question those among the generations of priests who have done the most for young lives, for boys and girls—those who have borne the most lasting fruit in work with the young—we would realize that the first and most profound source of their effectiveness has been that "loving look" of Christ.

We must clearly identify this love in our hearts as priests. It is simply love "of neighbour": love of man in Christ, directed to every individual, including every single one. With regard to young people, this love is not something exclusive, as if it did not also concern others, such as adults, the old, the sick. Indeed, love for the young has a specifically evangelical character only when it flows from love for every single person and for all. . . . At the same time, as love it has its own specific and one might say charismatic quality. It flows from a particular concern for what being young means in human life. Young people undoubtedly have a great attraction, proper to their age; but sometimes they also have not a few weaknesses and defects. The young man in the Gospel with whom Christ speaks appears on the one hand as an Israelite faithful to God's commandments, but then he appears as one who is too conditioned by his wealth and too attached to his possessions.

—Saint John Paul II, Letter to Priests for
Holy Thursday, 1985

Are there obstacles I see in myself that prevent me from being more engaged in ministry with the young? If so, what are they? How do I proceed?

The Wanderer between Two Worlds April 22

> [E]verything of mine is yours and everything of yours is mine, and I have been glorified in them. And now I will no longer be in the world, but they are in the world, while I am coming to you. (John 17:10-11)

Graced with Christ's efficacious word, the priest confers Christ's mysteries, the sacraments. Men usually want something else from him: bread, the solution of the social question, recipes for being happy on this earth. They are irritated and bored when they hear over and over only words that have to be believed, that only produce results in God's eternity, that have no value in the traffic of the markets of the world. The priest, however, goes on speaking his word, the word of the sacraments. What they produce cannot be tested in the laboratories of men, who want to recognize as real only what they find there. But it works. And so at his word the fortunes of the children of God take their beginning, sins are forgiven, the banquet of everlasting life is celebrated, there wells up out of the murky depths of death the light that is never extinguished.

With the gifts, I should say the offer, of God's mysteries, the priest, like a man from another world, stands on the street corners while the endless procession of men and their histories hurries by, speeding towards death or towards life, one cannot say which. Whoever pauses, whoever accepts the offer of this wanderer between two worlds who is the priest, that man receives the secrets of God; in time he finds eternity, in death life, in darkness light and the pure presence of God. And the man who is authorized to speak into the ever unique situation of the individual these words of the living God's sacramental presence and efficaciousness in the holy Church, that man we call the priest.

—Karl Rahner, *Meditations on the Sacraments*, 64–65

Surround me, Lord, in your mystery, that in time I may find eternity, in death I may find life, and in darkness, the radiance of your light.

[Solomon stood and addressed the whole community of Israel], saying in a loud voice: . . . "May these words of mine, the petition I have offered before the LORD, our God, be present to the LORD our God day and night, that he may uphold the cause of his servant and the cause of his people Israel as each day requires . . . " (1 Kgs 8:55, 59)

We call you "Father" and we are your "family." We need you desperately. We need you where God has placed you, at the head of our family, just as he has placed human fathers in the midst of their families to nurture and love them.

I would like to suggest, dear Fathers, that you meditate often on the state and plight of the laity you serve. We are young, middle-aged, or elderly. Some of us are married, some single. We are both well-educated and illiterate. We are rich and poor. However, all of us are like the grass, here today and gone tomorrow. Nevertheless, you can learn from us. Consider for a moment the situation of the father of a family. He works hard for his family to fulfill their needs. At times he dreams of greener fields opening up to him. However, if he loves his family he will not follow those dreams if they conflict with the real needs of his loved ones. As monotonous, unsatisfying and painful as this may be, loving fathers demonstrate their responsiveness to the needs of others by sticking to the task at hand. Yet, in spite of the two thousand problems that assail the family, things work out. They work out because of love and because of God.

. . . Always keep in mind that you were ordained to serve us, to feed us with the Eucharist, to heal us with anointing, to reconcile us to God and one another in penance, to witness our unions of love in marriage, to preach God's word. . . . We need to be taught by your patience, your kindness, your understanding and your fortitude, what it is to be a Christian.

—Catherine de Hueck Doherty, *Dear Father*, 14–15

As Jesus was faithful to his people, like Solomon before him, may I seek always to serve others with prayerful compassion.

[Jesus] unrolled the scroll and found the passage where it was written: / "The Spirit of the Lord is upon me, / because he has anointed me / to bring glad tidings to the poor." (Luke 4:17-18)

By the sacramental anointing of holy orders, the Holy Spirit configures priests in a new and special way to Jesus Christ the head and shepherd; he forms and strengthens them with his pastoral charity; and he gives them an authoritative role in the Church as servants of the proclamation of the Gospel to every people and of the fullness of Christian life of all the baptized.

The truth of the priest as it emerges from the Word of God, that is, from Jesus Christ himself and from his constitutive plan for the Church, is thus proclaimed with joyful gratitude by the Preface of the liturgy of the Chrism Mass: *"By your Holy Spirit you anointed your only Son high priest of the new and eternal covenant. With wisdom and love you have planned that this one priesthood should continue in the Church. Christ gives the dignity of a royal priesthood to the people he has made his own. From these, with a brother's love, he chooses men to share his sacred ministry by the laying on of hands. He appointed them to renew in his name the sacrifice of redemption as they set before your family his paschal meal. He calls them to lead your holy people in love, nourish them by your word and strengthen them through the sacraments. Father, they are to give their lives in your service and for the salvation of your people as they strive to grow in the likeness of Christ and honor you by their courageous witness of faith and love."*

—Saint John Paul II, *Pastores Dabo Vobis*, 15–16

I reflect today upon the annual celebration of the chrism Mass with my bishop, and allow the words of the liturgy to again stir into a burning flame my commitment to priestly service.

> [T]hough he was in the form of God, / [Christ] did not regard equality
> with God something to be grasped. / Rather, he emptied himself, / tak-
> ing the form of a slave . . . (Phil 2:6-7)

God is himself eternal, loving, self-emptying, and groundlessly free.
He reveals Himself in the self-giving obedience of the Son on the Cross.
The obedience of Jesus is an obedience of total cooperation with sinners,
representing the totally unique transference of his eternal love as the Son
towards the ever greater Father.

. . . This divine self-giving love, while shattering all human forms of
love and service, at the same time becomes the ground of a new and radical
experience of what Christian agape is called to become. In the context of
ministerial priesthood, this more clearly delineates the distinctive form of
pastoral love.

. . . We glimpse the Christian mystery of God who, without leaving
His own side, comes over to ours. This crossing over towards humankind
and the surrender of all the richness of divine love into our hands takes on
the "form" of the Son who, allowing himself to be delivered over by the
Father to sinners, "lays bare the heart of the Father" and the extent of His
love for the world.

Only in His "holding on to nothing" for himself is God the Father of
all: He pours forth his substance and generates the Son, and only in the
"holding on to nothing" for himself of what has been received does the
Son show himself to be of the same essence of the Father. In the shared
"holding on to nothing" are they one in the Spirit . . .

The Son lays bare the heart of the Father as he becomes the servant
of all and breathes into the world his Spirit of service and of taking the
last place.

—Dermot Power, *A Spiritual Theology of
the Priesthood*, 29–30

What is it that I hold on to that prevents my being of total service to Christ?

One with the Apostles

> As he passed by the Sea of Galilee, he saw Simon and his brother Andrew casting their nets into the sea; they were fishermen. Jesus said to them, "Come after me, and I will make you fishers of men." (Mark 1:16-17)

The image of vocation handed down to us by the Gospels is particularly linked to the figure of the fisherman. Jesus called to himself some fishermen of Galilee, and defined the apostolic mission by speaking of their trade. After the miraculous draught of fishes, . . . Christ replied: "Do not be afraid; henceforth you will be catching men" (Lk 5:8, 10). . . . Peter and the other Apostles lived and traveled with Jesus. . . . They heard his words, marveled at his works and were astonished at his miracles.

However, it was during that Paschal event that Christ revealed to them that their vocation was to become priests like him and in him. This took place when, in the Upper Room, he took bread and then the cup of wine, and spoke over them the words of consecration. The bread and the wine became his Body and Blood, given up in sacrifice for all mankind. Jesus concluded by commanding the Apostles: "Do this . . . in memory of me" (1 Cor 11:25). With these words he entrusted to them his own sacrifice and, through their hands, communicated it to the Church for all time. By entrusting to the Apostles the memorial of his sacrifice, Christ made them sharers in his priesthood. For there is a close and inseparable bond between the offering and the priest: the one who offers the sacrifice of Christ must have a share in the priesthood of Christ. Consequently, the vocation to the priesthood is a vocation to offer *in persona Christi* his own sacrifice, by virtue of sharing in his priesthood.

—Saint John Paul II, Letter to Priests for
Holy Thursday, 1996

Jesus, Son of Man, strengthen me in following in the footsteps of the apostles, so that the whole of my life might be offered in sacrifice.

> Therefore, we are not discouraged; rather, although our outer self is wasting away, our inner self is being renewed day by day. (2 Cor 4:16)

A renewal of ordination is the *yes of our good will*. If God's grace ordains anew—if his charism which is the Spirit of God himself, wants to become a new living fire in us—then our, alas, otherwise so problematic "good will" may also find the courage for a new "yes." Then, and for this reason, this day may also be a day of new "resolutions," since all of them need only be a believing "yes" to God's action in our life. Such personal new beginnings are therefore no romantic dream which, in a festive hour, forgets what we have experienced, how we have failed, what we have suffered and what we have become since our priestly ordination; they are no flight into illusion. No, we summon up the whole of our past life into this hour and add the unknown, dark future into it, and yet say our "yes" which gathers together everything past and to come in order to give it to God, so that He may make it a priestly life. No matter what has already happened in our life: deep down, everything is still open and can be fashioned into a priestly existence.

Are we concerned about the fruitlessness of our often so laborious efforts? In our "yes," it becomes a participation in the Gethsemane-anguish of the High Priest who redeemed the world. Are we perturbed by the grey sameness of our everyday life? In our "yes," it becomes a part of the everyday life of the one who was found like a man in everything.

—Karl Rahner,
"The Renewal of Priestly Ordination," 175

What parts of my life have I not yet surrendered to Christ, the High Priest, who wishes to fashion the whole of my life in his service?

"I am the vine, you are the branches. Whoever remains in me and I in him will bear much fruit, because without me you can do nothing" (John 15:5)

Jesus established a close relationship between the ministry entrusted to the apostles and his own mission: "He who receives you receives me, and he who receives me receives him who sent me" (Mt. 10:40); "He who hears you hears me, and he who rejects you rejects me, and he who rejects me rejects him who sent me" (Lk. 10:16). Indeed, in the light of the paschal event of the death and resurrection, the fourth Gospel affirms this with great force and clarity: "As the Father has sent me, even so I send you." Just as Jesus has a mission which comes to him directly from God and makes present the very authority of God, so too the apostles have a mission which comes to them from Jesus. And just as "the Son can do nothing of his own accord" (Jn. 5:19) such that his teaching is not his own but the teaching of the One who sent him (cf. Jn. 7:16), so Jesus says to the apostles: "Apart from me you can do nothing" (Jn. 15:5). Their mission is not theirs but is the same mission of Jesus. All this is possible not as a result of human abilities, but only with the "gift" of Christ and his Spirit, with the "sacrament": "Receive the Holy Spirit. If you forgive the sins of any, they are forgiven; if you retain the sins of any, they are retained" (Jn. 20:22-23). And so the apostles, not by any special merit of their own, but only through a gratuitous participation in the grace of Christ, prolong throughout history to the end of time the same mission of Jesus on behalf of humanity.

—Saint John Paul II, *Pastores Dabo Vobis*, 14

Lord Jesus, may I never claim priestly ministry as my own, but be ever conscious that it is you who walks the earth again in me.

With the Fragrance of Christ's Charity

> Owe nothing to anyone, except to love one another; for the one who loves another has fulfilled the law. (Rom 13:8)

The Second Vatican Council presents priestly consecration as a source of pastoral charity: "The priests of the New Testament are, it is true, by their vocation to ordination, set apart in some way in the midst of the people of God, but this is not in order that they should be separated from that people or from anyone, but that they should be completely consecrated to the task for which God chooses them. They could not be servants of Christ unless they were witnesses and dispensers of a life other than that of this earth. On the other hand, they would be powerless to serve men if they remained aloof from their life and circumstances. . . . their very ministry makes a special claim on them not to conform themselves to this world; still it requires at the same time that they should live among men in this world and that as good shepherds they should know their sheep and should also seek to lead back those who do not belong to this fold, so that they too may hear the voice of Christ and they may be one fold and one Shepherd."

The presbyter is to cultivate and practice those "virtues which are rightly held in high esteem in human relations: goodness of heart, sincerity, strength and constancy of mind, careful attention to justice and courtesy," as well as patience, readiness to forgive quickly and generously, kindness, affability, the capacity to be obliging and helpful without playing the benefactor. There are a myriad of human and pastoral virtues which the fragrance of Christ's charity can and must determine in the priest's conduct.

—Saint John Paul II, General Audience,
July 7, 1993

Lord Jesus, may my daily interactions with your people be marked by the virtues that you so clearly radiated in your life of loving service.

Being Human in a Christian Way

> May the God of peace . . . furnish you with all that is good, that you may do his will. May he carry out in you what is pleasing to him through Jesus Christ, to whom be glory forever [and ever]. Amen. (Heb 13:20-21)

A priest today must be utterly and genuinely human. He must be able to win people, to meet them as man to man. He must make some effort to be convincing also when as an individual he comes up against the critical attitude of another person. He cannot always simply feel that the armies of God and the church are behind him, that he is the great herald of the church of the masses, 300 or 500 million strong, ready to sound the trumpet and cry: "Here we come!" In our non-Christian mass-age he will not get at people this way. Small and insignificant, he comes before the individual and can effectively win over the other person only by showing in the light of his own Christianity that it is worth while to be a Christian. In this situation he must be convincing also as a human being.

. . . The genuine, mature, pure, modest, joyous human reality is itself a testimony to the fact that Christ's grace is in the world. This at any rate is what modern man expects. Saints who seem to reach the point at which they are stunted, humanly speaking, may perhaps be very holy, but their realization of this laudable holiness in their lives is not very effective for the apostolate. To be human in a Christian way does not simply mean to be "conformed to this world" (Rom 12:2), but implies that a person who meets us has a chance to see that being a Christian is not something contrary to his basic feelings.

—Karl Rahner, *Meditations on Priestly Life*, 150–51

Lord Jesus, Love Incarnate, help me to understand that as you revealed the face of God in your humanity, so I may be fully human in revealing your love to all others.

> Whoever serves me must follow me, and where I am, there also will
> my servant be. The Father will honor whoever serves me. (John 12:26)

Priests are called to prolong the presence of Christ, the one high priest, embodying his way of life and making him visible in the midst of the flock entrusted to their care. We find this clearly and precisely stated in the first letter of Peter: "I exhort the elders among you, as a fellow elder and a witness of the sufferings of Christ as well as a partaker in the glory that is to be revealed. Tend the flock of God that is your charge, not by constraint but willingly, not for shameful gain but eagerly, not as domineering over those in your charge but being examples to the flock. And when the chief Shepherd is manifested you will obtain the unfading crown of glory" (1 Pt. 5:1-4).

In the Church and on behalf of the Church, priests are a sacramental representation of Jesus Christ—the head and shepherd—authoritatively proclaiming his word, repeating his acts of forgiveness and his offer of salvation—particularly in baptism, penance and the Eucharist, showing his loving concern to the point of a total gift of self for the flock, which they gather into unity and lead to the Father through Christ and in the Spirit. In a word, priests exist and act in order to proclaim the Gospel to the world and to build up the Church in the name and person of Christ the head and shepherd.

This is the ordinary and proper way in which ordained ministers share in the one priesthood of Christ.

—Saint John Paul II, *Pastores Dabo Vobis*, 15

Lord Jesus, it is humbling that you wish to prolong your presence in the world through my life. It is only by your amazing grace that I can embody your way of life.

> For Love is strong as Death, / longing is fierce as Sheol. / Its arrows are arrows of fire . . . (Song 8:6)

We need to have a great love of God to remain faithful to our mission and to the self-denial which it involves. Our heart was made for love; we have an immense need to love; we cannot live without it. So powerful is the force of love that it can raise our poor nature to the point of overcoming monotony, suffering and even death: *Aquae multae non potuerunt exstinguere caritatem* [Deep waters cannot quench love] (Song 8:7).

The richer a nature is and the more capable of great things, the more it feels the need of a higher love. If we do not turn generously towards God we shall inevitably be drawn towards creatures. There can be no doubt about it: there can be nothing so fine, so potent and so profitable on this earth as a priestly heart completely dominated by the love of God. . . .

It requires great virtue to live up to this vocation. To help us to do so, we must try to establish a loyal friendship with the divine Master and we may be assured that, if we love Him, He will be the most excellent of friends to us. Our defects are no obstacle to this. A true friend will not withdraw his friendship because he knows our defects, if he knows also that we regret them, and that we are seeking his help to fight against them.

Friendship consists in harmony between hearts; it is concord: *concordes*. That is what Our Lord asks of us: love, the union of our heart with His. Not to seek this intimacy constitutes for us priests a certain measure of infidelity, and this negligence will leave a great void in our souls.

—Blessed Columba Marmion,
Christ: The Ideal of the Priest, 141

I contemplate the story of my friendship with Christ. I remember feeling very close, and feeling at a distance. I notice the present state of our friendship.

Be imitators of me, as I am of Christ. (1 Cor 11:1)

Thanks be to you, priests, who like a lantern illumine those who come to you, and for whom, like salt, you give life its savor. Thank you for what you do and above all for what you are. With deep feeling, I would like to thank all those priests who, in fidelity to their own identity and mission, continue to suffer in the most varied situations. Thank you for your toil, thank you for your efforts, thank you for your strength, thank you for your tears, thank you for your smile. Thank God for your being there!

And thank you, priests of the past 2,000 years who, faithful to your identity and mission even unto martyrdom, like precious grains of incense were consumed in the burning fire of pastoral charity and are now our intercessors in the splendour of the heavenly Church without spot or blemish. Thank you for such an admirable example!

However, my thanks above all become a "Te Deum" for the gift of the priesthood and an exhortation to you to be more and more in the world but less and less of the world, so that you can always show yourselves for what you are to everyone, with humble pride and the proper external sign: it is the sign of an unceasing, ageless service, because it is inscribed in your "being."

With tender affection I entrust each of you to the Virgin, given to us in an extraordinary way as Mother of the Eternal Priest. For each of you I place in her clasped hands a humble request for perseverance and for the commitment to leave as a legacy to your brethren at least one who will continue that unique priesthood that lives and springs from love within us.

I bless you all, together with the souls that the Eternal High Priest has entrusted to your care and still places on your path.

—Saint John Paul II, Message to the Participants in the
Fourth International Meeting of Priests, June 19, 1999

In what ways has my priestly example inspired at least one other to consider entering the seminary?

> Of this I became a minister by the gift of God's grace that was granted me in accord with the exercise of his power. To me, the very least of all the holy ones, this grace was given, to preach to the Gentiles the inscrutable riches of Christ . . . (Eph 3:7-8)

Draw near, O Lord, holy Father, almighty and eternal God, author of human dignity: it is you who apportion all graces, through you everything progresses; through you all things are made to stand firm. To form a priestly people you appoint ministers of Christ your Son by the power of the Holy Spirit, arranging them in different orders.

Already in the earlier covenant offices arose, established through mystical rites: when you set Moses and Aaron over your people to govern and sanctify them, you chose men next in rank and dignity to accompany them and assist them in their task.

So too in the desert you implanted the spirit of Moses in the hearts of seventy wise men; and with their help he ruled your people with greater ease. So also upon the sons of Aaron you poured an abundant share of their father's plenty, that the number of the priests prescribed by the Law might be sufficient for the sacrifices of the tabernacle, which were a shadow of the good things to come.

But in these last days, holy Father, you sent your Son into the world, Jesus, who is Apostle and High Priest of our confession. Through the Holy Spirit he offered himself to you as a spotless victim; and he made his Apostles, consecrated in the truth, sharers in his mission.

—Rite of Ordination of Priests, 131

I barely remember them, but I now meditate upon the words prayed by the bishop on the day of my ordination.

I give thanks to my God always, remembering you in my prayers, as I hear of the love and the faith you have in the Lord Jesus and for all the holy ones, so that your partnership in the faith may become effective in recognizing every good there is in us that leads to Christ. (Phlm 4-6)

You provided [your apostles] with companions to proclaim and carry out the work of salvation throughout the whole world. And now we beseech you, Lord, in our weakness, to grant us this helper that we need to exercise the priesthood that comes from the Apostles.

Grant, we pray, Almighty Father, to this, your servant, the dignity of the priesthood; renew deep within him the Spirit of holiness; may he henceforth possess this office which comes from you, O God, and is next in rank to the office of Bishop; and by the example of his manner of life, may he instill right conduct.

May he be a worthy co-worker with our Order, so that by his preaching and through the grace of the Holy Spirit the words of the Gospel may bear fruit in human hearts and reach even to the ends of the earth.

Together with us, may he be a faithful steward of your mysteries, so that your people may be renewed in the waters of rebirth and nourished from your altar; so that sinners may be reconciled and the sick raised up. May he be joined with us, Lord, in imploring your mercy for the people entrusted to his care and for all the world.

And so may the full number of the nations, gathered together in Christ, be transformed into your one people and made perfect in your Kingdom. Through our Lord Jesus Christ, your Son, who lives and reigns with you in the unity of the Holy Spirit, God for ever and ever. Amen.

—Rite of Ordination of Priests, 131

I prayerfully ask that the graces of my ordination to the priesthood be renewed within me.

> Such confidence we have through Christ toward God. Not that of our-selves we are qualified to take credit for anything as coming from us; rather, our qualification comes from God . . . (2 Cor 3:4-5)

Since priestly office is a sign and instrument of the Lord, present and effectively acting in his Church, it has the same centre and aim as Christ's own person and work—the kingdom of God. This is true in the first place of priestly office only in its objective sacramental essence—that is, insofar as its action is something institutional and more than individual, a sign which points to and mediates Christ's work of salvation, and which does not attach to the priest as an individual, to his achievements, his talents, his personality . . . It is precisely the objective nature of the office that brings about the union of the community not with the office-bearer but with the Lord. Just as the glass windows in a house are not an intrusion between the sunlight and the room, but are a transparent medium making possible a meeting of the brightness of the day and the darkness inside, so also the priest is not a sort of "relay" interposed between God and his people: on the contrary, his mediating office brings about an immediate mutual relationship. But this is possible only because the office-bearer has received a power from Christ, which enables him to act on Christ's behalf and to represent him sacramentally. This power is not attached to the personal action of the priest, but to his office, to his calling, his ordination, his mission.

In the Church, this power given in ordination is traditionally called a *character indelebilis*—an indelible stamp. It is indelible because it is ef-fected by the unbreakable promise and unchanging will of Christ to transmit his work of salvation through the ministry of the ordained.

—Gisbert Greshake, *The Meaning of*
Christian Priesthood, 108–9

Can I recall times when I have "gotten in the way" of Christ's ministry?

> I pleaded and the spirit of Wisdom came to me. / I preferred her to scepter and throne, / And deemed riches nothing in comparison with her . . . (Wis 7:7-8)

Therefore it is necessary that the priest, even among the absorbing tasks of his charge, and ever with a view to it, should continue his theological studies with unremitting zeal. The knowledge acquired at the seminary is indeed a sufficient foundation with which to begin; but it must be grasped more thoroughly, and perfected by an ever-increasing knowledge and understanding of the sacred sciences. Herein is the source of effective preaching and of influence over the souls of others. Yet even more is required. The dignity of the office he holds and the maintenance of a suitable respect and esteem among the people, which helps so much in his pastoral work, demand more than purely ecclesiastical learning. The priest must be graced by no less knowledge and culture than is usual among well-bred and well-educated people of his day. This is to say that he must be healthily modern, as is the Church, which is at home in all times and all places, and adapts itself to all; which blesses and furthers all healthy initiative and has no fear of the progress, even the most daring progress, of science; if only it be true science.

. . . Wise encouragement and help should be given to those members of the clergy, who, by taste and special gifts, feel a call to devote themselves to study and research, in this or that branch of science, in this or that art; they do not thereby deny their clerical profession; for all this, undertaken within just limits and under the guidance of the Church, redounds to the good estate of the Church and to the glory of her divine Head, Jesus Christ.

—Pope Pius XI, *Ad Catholici Sacerdotii*, 58–60

I am invited to reflect upon the seriousness with which I have embraced continuing study in the course of my ministry.

> But Moses said to God, "Who am I that I should go to Pharaoh and bring the Israelites out of Egypt?" (Exod 3:11)

As we go through life we may become increasingly puzzled about why the call to priesthood was made to someone like us. We come to see more clearly what is expected of a priest and the sublime nature of our calling while at the same time becoming more conscious of our own shortcomings. Life opens up a dismaying gap between what we know ourselves to be and what the priesthood demands of us. Dwelling on that, however, can easily disconcert. It would be unhealthy to allow the sense of our inadequacy to paralyze us in our priestly work.

I take comfort from two texts. The call of Levi in Matthew chapter 9 is one of my great standbys. The unexpected choice of a public enemy and traitor to his people is an encouragement in moments of personal despondency. It is a reminder that every saint has a past and every sinner a future. God's chosen instrument may well have many personal failings; the chief requirement however is a willingness to let God work through us.

I also take comfort from Our Lord's words at the Last Supper as reported in St. John's Gospel. Addressed in the first instance to the apostles, they have a profound message for every Christian and inspiration for the priest. Jesus' words assure us that we are not servants but friends, that we did not choose him but he us and that we are sent out to the world of our time on the same mission which he had received from the Father.

—Basil Hume, Light in the Lord, 25

Lord Jesus, may I never allow my human weaknesses to prevent me from serving you with loving and joyful confidence.

> For he has clothed me with garments of salvation, / and wrapped me in
> a robe of justice . . . (Isa 61:10)

With the garment of light which the Lord gave us in Baptism and in a new way in priestly Ordination, we can also think of the wedding apparel which he tells us about in the parable of God's banquet.

In the homilies of Gregory the Great, I found in this regard a noteworthy reflection. Gregory distinguishes between Luke's version of the parable and Matthew's. He is convinced that the Lucan parable speaks of the eschatological marriage feast, whereas—in his opinion—the version handed down by Matthew anticipates this nuptial banquet in the liturgy and life of the Church. In Matthew, in fact, and only in Matthew, the king comes into the crowded room to see his guests. And here in this multitude he also finds a guest who was not wearing wedding clothes, who is then thrown outside into the darkness.

Then Gregory asks himself: "But what kind of clothes ought he to have been wearing? All those who are gathered in the Church have received the new garment of baptism and the faith; otherwise, they would not be in the Church. So what was it that was still lacking? What wedding clothes must there be in addition?"

The Pope responds: "the clothes of love." And unfortunately, among his guests to whom he had given new clothes, the white clothes of rebirth, the king found some who were not wearing the purple clothes of twofold love, for God and for neighbor . . .

Now that we are preparing for the celebration of Holy Mass, we must ask ourselves whether we are wearing these clothes of love. Let us ask the Lord to keep all hostility away from our hearts, to remove from us every feeling of self-sufficiency and truly to clothe ourselves with the vestment of love, so that we may be luminous persons. . . .

> —Pope Benedict XVI, Homily for the Chrism Mass,
> April 5, 2007

As I vest for Mass, I will call to mind that I am to see my vestments as garments of love.

> I came so that they might have life and have it more abundantly.
> (John 10:10)

When, some years ago I heard these words I was utterly perplexed. Can that be true? . . . Hitherto I had thought of priests as pitiable creatures with whom one must have compassion, for they have been forced by the Church to live a restricted life in as far as it is denied them to find happiness in the arms of a woman. So they have to look for compensation. This could take the form of material benefits, unless they would work for people to the point of self-abandonment. In any case, their personal development was bound to be stunted.

Hence the words "I am a happy priest" penetrated me to the marrow. I felt that they were true. I wanted to discover this man's secret. His sermons attracted me. . . . His way of celebrating the Eucharist gave me a longing for what he possessed, but I did not. This experience led to the discovery that he was entirely immersed in the love of God. His heart was on fire and inflamed others, mine too. Since God has opened my eyes by this experience I have met many such priests.

. . . I wanted to find living proof that priests, who renounce what the world thinks impossible to relinquish, enjoy the promise of Jesus: "I came, that they may have life and have it abundantly" (Jn 10:10).

What is this life in abundance? How is it to be gained? Everyone who wants to lay claim to the promises of Jesus has this question on his mind. In the Apocalypse, St. John gives us an important pointer . . . "But I have this against you, that you have abandoned the love you had at first. Remember from what you have fallen" (Rev 2:4-5). . . . Holding fast with one's whole heart to the first love; that seems to me to be the key to the power of attraction that priests possess as fishers of men.

—Gertrude Resseguier, *The First Love*, 5–6

Am I seen by those whom I serve, and by my brother priests, as a genuinely happy person?

> Then the word of the LORD came to me: Can I not do to you, house of Israel, as this potter has done?—oracle of the LORD. Indeed, like clay in the hand of the potter, so are you in my hand, house of Israel. (Jer 18:5-6)

Bearing the burdens of the day and the oppressive heat which saps our spiritual energies—the withering cynicism, the scorching apathy, the blistering materialism—we can only keep fresh in our dedication by relying on the healing and strengthening resources of the sacrament of reconciliation.

It is the prophet Jeremiah who offers a powerful message of hope to the dispirited priest who is overcome by failure and hopelessness. His message of hope comes by the symbol of the potter shaping clay. It would be difficult to find a more apt picture of the positive side of the sacrament of reconciliation in a priest's life. Jeremiah found himself faced with a frighteningly difficult mission. He happened to be leading God's people at a particularly awkward and depressing time in their history. Although they had been singled out by God to be shining light to the nations, they had become defeated and quarrelsome. On the point of giving up, Jeremiah was directed by God to the potter's house, and there he saw that the potter did not discard the warped vessel even when its appearance disappointed him, but reshaped it and remade it into something new and attractive. Jeremiah was reassured that God had the power to do the same with him and so with the people he served, when they had become broken on the turning wheels of life.

Our reconciliation is more than confession. It is redesigning; like Jeremiah we must hear God's word of hope: we must believe that he can redesign. Misshapen by sin or grooved by sinful habit, the vessel of our lives does not defeat his power. His image may have become deformed in us. The disfigurement may have settled in the clay, but his image is never too misshapen to be remade. God, the all-powerful potter, can still envisage what the clay might be and his skilled hands can realize his vision. With God our priestly lives are always a possibility, an opportunity, a new creation.

—Gerard McGinnity, *Christmen: Experience of Priesthood Today*, 27

I am all too aware that my stubbornness and hardness of heart prevent God's reshaping of my priestly life. Lord, make my life supple in your hands. Refashion me into a more faithful servant.

Whoever has my commandments and observes them is the one who loves me. And whoever loves me will be loved by my Father, and I will love him and reveal myself to him. (John 14:21)

St. John Mary Vianney arrived in Ars, a village of 230 souls, warned by his bishop beforehand that there he would find religious practice in a sorry state: "There is little love of God in that parish; you will be the one to put it there." As a result, he was deeply aware that he needed to go there to embody Christ's presence and to bear witness to His saving mercy: "[Lord,] grant me the conversion of my parish; I am willing to suffer whatever you wish, for my entire life!" With this prayer he entered upon his mission. The Curé devoted himself completely to his parish's conversion, setting before all else the Christian education of the people in his care. Dear brother priests, let us ask the Lord Jesus for the grace to learn for ourselves something of the pastoral plan of St. John Mary Vianney!

The first thing we need to learn is the complete identification of the man with his ministry. In Jesus, person and mission tend to coincide: all Christ's saving activity was, and is, an expression of His "filial consciousness" which from all eternity stands before the Father in an attitude of loving submission to His will. In a humble yet genuine way, every priest must aim for a similar identification. Certainly this is not to forget that the efficacy of the ministry is independent of the holiness of the minister; but neither can we overlook the extraordinary fruitfulness of the encounter between the ministry's objective holiness and the subjective holiness of the minister. The Curé of Ars immediately set about this patient and humble task of harmonizing his life as a minister with the holiness of the ministry he had received . . .

—Pope Benedict XVI, Letter Proclaiming
a Year for Priests, June 16, 2009

In a humble yet genuine way, I seek an attitude of loving submission to the Father's will, in all aspects of my priestly ministry.

God, you have taught me from my youth; / to this day I proclaim your wondrous deeds. (Ps 71:17)

I wish to invite you, dear Brothers in the priesthood, to share in my *Te Deum* of thanksgiving for the gift of my vocation. Jubilees are important moments in a priest's life: they represent as it were milestones along the road of our calling. In the Biblical tradition, a jubilee is a time of joy and thanksgiving. The farmer gives thanks to the Creator for the harvest; on the occasion of our jubilees, we wish to thank the Eternal Shepherd for the fruits of our priestly life, for the service we have rendered to the Church and to humanity in the different parts of the world, in the most varied conditions and in the different working situations to which Divine Providence has led us and wished us to be. We know that we are "unworthy servants" (Lk 17:10), but we are grateful to the Lord for having wished to make us his ministers.

We are grateful also to those who helped us to reach the priesthood, and to those whom Divine Providence has placed on the path of our vocation. We thank them all, beginning with our parents, who in so many ways have been a gift of God for us!

As we give thanks, we also ask pardon of God, and of our brothers and sisters, for our negligence and failures, the results of human weakness. The jubilee, according to Sacred Scripture, could not be just thanksgiving for the harvest: it also involved the cancellation of debts. Let us therefore beg our merciful God to forgive the debts which we have accumulated in the exercise of our priestly ministry.

—Saint John Paul II, Letter to Priests for
Holy Thursday, 1996

Lord Jesus, I use this occasion to reflect upon my own ministry, with gratitude for your countless blessings, and with sorrow for the times I have failed to serve you in others.

> [O]ur qualification comes from God, who has indeed qualified us as ministers of a new covenant, not of letter but of spirit; for the letter brings death, but the Spirit gives life. (2 Cor 3:5-6)

What is mysticism? It is in its widest sense the reaching out of the soul to contact with those eternal realities which are the subject matter of religion. And the mystical life is the complete life of love and prayer which transmutes those objects of belief into living realities: love and prayer directed to God for Himself, and not for any gain for ourselves. Therefore there should surely be some mystical element in the inner life of every real priest.

All our external religious activities, services, communions, formal devotions, good works—these are either the expressions or the support of this inward life of loving adherence. We must have such outward expressions and supports, because we are not pure spirits but human beings, receiving through our senses the messages of Reality. But all their beauty is from within; and the degree in which we can either exhibit or apprehend that beauty depends on our own inward state. I think that if this were more fully realized, a great deal of the hostility which is now shown to institutional religion by good and earnest people would break down. It is your part, isn't it? to show them that it is true: to transmute by your love those dead forms of which they are always complaining, and make of them the chalice of the Spirit of Life.

In one of the Apocryphal Gospels of the Infancy there is a story of how the child Jesus, picking up the clay sparrows with which the other boys were playing, threw them into the air, where they became living birds. As a legend, we may regard this as an absurdity. As a spiritual parable it is profoundly true.

—Evelyn Underhill, *Concerning the Inner Life*, 108

When my ministry is marked by measures of boredom or monotony, I know that I may be neglecting the refreshing fountain of life that is prayer.

They went out of the town and came to him. Meanwhile, the disciples urged him, "Rabbi, eat." But he said to them, "I have food to eat of which you do not know." (John 4:30-32)

We know how radically Charles Borromeo gave of himself to people, dying at the age of forty-six, having been entirely consumed by his sacrificial service. This man, of all others, who truly wore himself out for Christ and on behalf of Christ for other people, teaches us that without the discipline and the refuge of a true inner dimension of faith, such self-sacrifice is not possible.

This is a point we have to learn anew. The inward dimension has in the last few decades been widely regarded as promoting and indulging intimacy and privacy and has thus been suspect. Yet ministry without an inner dimension becomes mere activism. The breakdown and failure of not a few priests, who had approached their work with great idealism, ultimately results from this suspicion of the inner dimension. Making time for God ourselves, for inwardly standing before him, is a pastoral priority that is equal to all other priorities has, indeed, in a certain sense precedence over the others. This is not an additional burden but space for the soul to draw breath, without which we necessarily become breathless—we lose that spiritual breath, the breath of the Holy Spirit within us. Other kinds of rest are important and make good sense, but the most fundamental way of resting from our work and learning how to love it again is that of inwardly seeking God's face, which always restores to us our joy in God. One of the very humble parish priests of this century—Dom Didimo Mantiero (1912–1992) of Bassano del Grappa, noted in his spiritual journal: "Converts were, and still are, acquired through the prayer and sacrifice of the unknown faithful. Christ won, not by the power of his marvelous speeches, but rather by the power of his constant prayer. He preached by day, but by night he prayed."

—Pope Benedict XVI, *Pilgrim Fellowship of Faith*, 171

How often in my ministry do I lose my spiritual breath, the breath of the Holy Spirit, because of my endless busyness?

> So do not be ashamed of your testimony to our Lord . . . but bear your
> share of hardship for the gospel with the strength that comes from God.
> (2 Tim 1:8)

Every Christian who receives the sacrament of Orders . . . decides upon a life of celibacy only after he has reached a firm conviction that Christ is giving him this "gift" for the good of the Church and the service of others. Only then does he commit himself to observe celibacy for his entire life. . . .

One should add at this point that the commitment to married fidelity, which derives from the sacrament of Matrimony, creates similar obligations in its own sphere; this married commitment sometimes becomes a source of similar trials and experiences for husbands and wives, who also have a way of proving the value of their love in these "trials by fire." Love, in fact, in all its dimensions, is not only a call but also a duty. Finally, we should add that our brothers and sisters joined by the marriage bond have the right to expect from us, priests and pastors, good example and the witness of fidelity to one's vocation until death, a fidelity to the vocation that we choose through the sacrament of Orders just as they choose it through the sacrament of Matrimony. Also in this sphere and in this sense we should understand our ministerial Priesthood as "subordination" to the common Priesthood of all the faithful, of the laity, especially of those who live in marriage and form a family. In this way, we serve in "building up the body of Christ"; otherwise, instead of cooperating in the building up of that body we weaken its spiritual structure. Closely linked to this building up of the body of Christ is the authentic development of the human personality of each Christian—as also of each priest—a development that takes place according to the measure of the gift of Christ.

—Saint John Paul II, Letter to Priests for
Holy Thursday, 1979

Lord Jesus, strengthen my commitment to priestly celibacy, so the laity might see in my life a fidelity that gives them inspiration and hope.

> "As the Father has sent me, so I send you." And when he had said this,
> he breathed on them and said to them, "Receive the holy Spirit. Whose
> sins you forgive are forgiven them, and whose sins you retain are re-
> tained." (John 20:21-23)

The word that God put in the mouth of the priest is not just a word-
in-general. . . . It is God's word; hence it ought to find its mark in the
individual in his uniqueness and in his unique place in time. It ought to be
said to the individual—in the morning hours of his life, when he begins
to create an eternity in time; on the many everydays of his pilgrimage,
during which he has to pick his way laboriously through all the valleys
and meanderings of a human life; in the dead despair of guilt; in that holy
moment, the moment of death, when it looks as though the fruits of time
will issue once and for all into the inescapable grasp of death and eternity.
In such moments must the priest speak the word of God, the mighty and
creative word, the word that does not talk but acts, the sacramental word.
I baptize thee, I absolve thee from thy sins, this is my body—such are the
words, spoken in the person of Christ, which the priest speaks into man's
concrete situation.

. . . In virtue of these [sacramental] words the priest is completely
stripped of power and completely powerful, because they are not his words
any more at all, and they are wholly the words of Christ. But he is allowed
to say them. To say them over and over. To say them patiently, believingly,
indefatigably. All other words that he uses, what he says in preaching and
instructions, are only an echo, an explanation, a commentary added to these
basic words of his priestly existence which he speaks in the administration
of the sacraments, where he accompanies them with holy actions that use
the poor elements of earth to hide the bliss of heaven, fecundating them
with Christ's word.

—Karl Rahner, *Meditations on the Sacraments*, 64–65

Lord Jesus, deliver me from the routine celebration of the sacraments.

[Jesus] was praying in a certain place, and when he had finished, one of his disciples said to him, "Lord, teach us to pray just as John taught his disciples." (Luke 11:1)

Dear Father, have mercy on us, your ordinary and monotonous flock! Teach us how to love. Teach us how to pray. Inflame our hearts with the desire to wash the feet of our poor brethren, to feed them love, and to preach the Gospel with our lives. Send us forth into the world everywhere in the world of poverty, hunger, misery, so that we may change it because we heard your voice "sending us there," the Shepherd's voice. Come with us if God appoints you to do so. Lead us, wherever he tells you. But do not desert us in order to fulfill personal ambition or your own immediate needs. Always seek to do God's will and you will fulfill your deepest needs and longings.

. . . If you follow the voice of the Shepherd and pursue his values you will find peace. True, there will be turmoil in your life, just as there was turmoil in the life of every prophet and in the life of the Divine Master himself. Nevertheless, there will be that unshakeable tranquility that comes from knowing that you are doing God's will and not your own.

The prophets of old were seized with the desire to preach God's word, to teach his people. They emptied themselves for the sake of the people. They spent themselves in God's service meeting the needs of others.

. . . I would like to tell you clearly, dear Father, that any overpowering urge to fulfill your own needs at the expense of the needs of your flock, your spiritual family, does not come from God.

—Catherine de Hueck Doherty, *Dear Father*, 15–16

In what ways have I taught my people to pray and to love? What have they learned by observing how I love and pray?

No one has greater love than this, to lay down one's life for one's friends. You are my friends if you do what I command you. (John 15:13-14)

Wherever vocations are scarce, the Church must be attentive. And she is indeed attentive, very attentive. This concern is shared also by the laity in the Church. At the 1987 synod we heard touching words in this regard not only from the bishops and priests, but also from the lay people who were there.

This concern shows in the best possible way who the priest is for the laity: It testifies to his identity, and here we are talking of a community testimony, a social testimony, for the Priesthood is a "social" sacrament: the priest "chosen from among men is appointed to act on behalf of men in relation to God."

Jesus washed the feet of the apostles at the Last Supper on the day before his passion and death on the Cross, and he did this to stress the fact that he came "not to be served but to serve." All that Christ did and taught was at the service of our redemption. The ultimate and most complete expression of this messianic service was to be the Cross on Calvary. The Cross confirmed in the fullest possible way that the Son of God became man "for us men and for our salvation" (*Credo of the Mass*). And this salvific service, which embraces the whole universe, is "inscribed" forever in the Priesthood of Christ. The Eucharist the sacrament of Christ's redeeming sacrifice contains in itself this "inscription." Christ, who came to serve, is sacramentally present in the Eucharist precisely in order to serve. At the same time this service is the fullness of salvific mediation: Christ has entered an eternal sanctuary, "into heaven itself, now to appear in the presence of God on our behalf." In truth, he was "appointed to act on behalf of men in relation to God."

—Saint John Paul II, Letter to Priests for
Holy Thursday, 1989

May I never forget that I am called to a life of generous self-giving and joyful service, always in the spirit of Christ Jesus.

My child, when you come to serve the Lord, / prepare yourself for trials. / Be sincere of heart and steadfast, / and do not be impetuous in time of adversity. / Cling to him, do not leave him, / that you may prosper in your last days. (Sir 2:1-3)

What we wish to say to you today is this: never doubt your priesthood. This we say for several reasons.

By your ordination you have been endowed with the sacramental mystery which has conferred upon you powers that liken you to Christ: the power to celebrate the Holy Eucharist, to administer the sacrament of Penance, and so on. Through the priestly ministry that is now yours you are likened to the Apostles, you have been made ministers of the Gospel. To you are now applied in a special way the words that Christ spoke to his disciples: "As the Father has sent me, even so I send you" (Jn 20:21). Those words are addressed personally to each one of you.

Never doubt your priesthood. Your task is now to serve the Church and the world with all your strength. What a noble task, and how varied are the forms that it will take! How lofty too are the obligations that you have undertaken, that of holiness, of charity to all men, of sacrifice. It is the Cross that you have willingly accepted, the Cross which will give your lives a serious character, but which will make them strong.

Whatever difficulties and trials you may encounter, you are assured of never-failing help and support: the assistance of God's grace, the communion of the Church, the esteem—and the good example—of the People of God.

Therefore we repeat: never doubt your priesthood. Go forward with confidence. The Lord be with you, and may the Mother of God ever assist you.

—Blessed Pope Paul VI, Address to the Newly
Ordained Priests, March 20, 1972

When I find myself discouraged in my priestly ministry, I pray for the grace to find my strength in the cross of Christ.

We know that all things work for good for those who love God, who are called according to his purpose. (Rom 8:28)

Twenty-five years a priest! I think of all the ordinary and special graces I have received, of my preservation from grave sins, innumerable opportunities of doing good, sound bodily health, undisturbed tranquility of mind, good reputation among men, immensely superior to what I deserve, and the successful outcome of the various undertakings entrusted to me under obedience. Later on have come ecclesiastical honours, and finally the episcopate, not merely above but in contrast to what I deserve . . . all these graces, O God! This thought must keep me habitually in a loving frame of mind, full of humility and awe.

In twenty-five years of priesthood what innumerable failings and deficiencies! My spiritual organism still feels healthy and robust, thanks to God, but what weaknesses! What frequent little indulgences in sloth and in satisfying my preferences for one thing rather than another! What inner impatience with all that demands effort and toil! What countless distractions in public and private prayers! What haste, at times, to get these over! And what a waste of time spent in reading or in matters that had little to do with the performance of my immediate duty! So many petty attachments to places, to things, to details, amidst all of which I ought rather to have passed as a pilgrim and exile.

How easily I have offended against charity towards my fellows, even if in a correct and pious form. In my imagination and in the trend of my thought, what a mixture still remains of the human and worldly with the sacred, supernatural and divine, of the spirit of this world with the spirit of the Cross of Jesus Christ.

Therefore I must always see myself as . . . deserving none but the lowest place: truly the servant of all . . .

—Saint John XXIII, *Journal of a Soul*, 270–71

As conscious as I am of my countless failings in my years of priestly ministry, I continue to rejoice in God's call to service.

How good and how pleasant it is, / when brothers dwell together as one!
(Ps 133:1)

In the context of a spirituality nourished by the practice of the evangelical counsels, I would like to invite all priests, during this Year dedicated to them, to welcome the new springtime which the Spirit is now bringing about in the Church, not least through the ecclesial movements and the new communities. "In his gifts the Spirit is multifaceted. . . . He breathes where He wills. He does so unexpectedly, in unexpected places, and in ways previously unheard of, . . . but he also shows us that He works with a view to the one body and in the unity of the one body." In this regard, the statement of the Decree "*Presbyterorum Ordinis*" continues to be timely: "While testing the spirits to discover if they be of God, priests must discover with faith, recognize with joy and foster diligently the many and varied charismatic gifts of the laity, whether these be of a humble or more exalted kind." These gifts, which awaken in many people the desire for a deeper spiritual life, can benefit not only the lay faithful but the clergy as well. The communion between ordained and charismatic ministries can provide "a helpful impulse to a renewed commitment by the Church in proclaiming and bearing witness to the Gospel of hope and charity in every corner of the world."

I would also like to add, echoing the Apostolic Exhortation *Pastores Dabo Vobis* of Pope John Paul II, that the ordained ministry has a radical "communitarian form" and can be exercised only in the communion of priests with their bishop. This communion between priests and their bishop, grounded in the Sacrament of Holy Orders and made manifest in Eucharistic con-celebration, needs to be translated into various concrete expressions of an effective and affective priestly fraternity.

—Pope Benedict XVI, Letter Proclaiming
a Year for Priests, June 16, 2009

Lord Jesus, deliver me from a "Lone Ranger" mentality that isolates me from my people and my brother priests.

> Whoever causes one of these little ones who believe in me to sin, it would be better for him to have a great millstone hung around his neck and to be drowned in the depths of the sea. (Matt 18:6)

One often hears objections today to the fact that the world in general and the faithful in particular expect a higher degree of morality from the priest than they do from others and that this puts unjustifiable pressures and demands on the priest. After all, we are told, he is a man like any other, suffering from all the same weaknesses and temptations as any other man suffers. All this is true, of course. And all are called to the same degree of personal sanctity, priests and laity alike. But it is also true that those who have assumed a public ministry, . . . those who have been publicly and sacramentally configured to the priestly life of Christ, are expected to manifest that life in a publicly more intense way.

The laity are those Christians hidden in the world transforming it from within. The priests are those who conspicuously manifest Christ in our midst. This is one reason that, in imitation of Christ, priests do not marry, they do not have families, they do not have a home, they do not do their own will but rather that of the One who sends them to one assignment after another. . . . This is one of the prices that they pay for making of their lives an oblation offered up for the salvation of the world. Thus, when they fail the sacred trust, when they betray their sacral character as a total offering to God, the price exacted is often excruciating, not only for the priest but for the faithful as well.

—John M. Haas, "The Sacral Character
of the Priest as the Foundation for his
Moral Life and Teaching," 138–39

Forgive me, Lord, for the times that I have violated my sacred promises. Give healing to all whom I have in any way scandalized.

"The teacher is here and is asking for you." (John 11:28)

These words can be read with reference to the priestly vocation. God's call is at the origin of the journey which every person must make in life: it is the primary and fundamental aspect of vocation, but it is not the only one. Priestly ordination is in fact the beginning of a journey which continues until death, a journey which is "vocational" at every step. The Lord calls priests to a number of tasks and ministries deriving from this vocation. But there is a still deeper level. Over and above the tasks which are the expression of priestly ministry, there always remains the underlying reality of "being a priest." The situations and circumstances of life constantly call upon the priest to confirm his original choice, to respond ever anew to God's call. Our priestly life, like every authentic form of Christian existence, is a succession of responses to God who calls.

Emblematic in this regard is the parable of the servants who await their master's return. Because the master delays, they must stay awake in order to be found vigilant at his coming (cf. Lk 12:35-40). Could not this evangelical watchfulness be another way of defining the response to a vocation? For a vocation is lived out thanks to a vigilant sense of responsibility. Christ emphasizes this: "Blessed are those servants whom the master finds awake when he comes . . . And if he comes in the second watch, or in the third, and finds them so, blessed are those servants!" (Lk 12:37-38).

—Saint John Paul II, Letter to Priests for
Holy Thursday, 1996

Lord Jesus, may I remain ever vigilant to Your voice, always ready to respond with priestly charity and generous obedience.

Tell me, you whom my soul loves, / where you shepherd, where you give rest at midday. (Song 1:7)

In the weeks following Hitler's invasion of Poland in September 1939, Maximilian Kolbe had been ordered to close his monastery of over six hundred friars. As he bade farewell he gave last-minute instructions, practical advice for what was to come, spiritual advice to keep up their spirits. And from the doorstep he gave them one last bit of advice: "Do not forget love." "Do not forget love," he said, as his brothers left the monastery for an uncertain future.

Do not forget love! If we pray, our love will grow. If we celebrate the sacraments with devotion, our love will grow. If we put others first, our love will grow. If we forgive, our love will grow. If we learn to give ourselves in sacrifice, bitterness will flee and love will grow. If we listen to our people, our love will grow. If we keep our hearts open to their suffering and their yearning, our love will grow. If we hold fast to the Lord Jesus, our love will grow. If we love, our love will grow. Do not forget love!

I could easily make a list of the many things I have left undone. . . . Sometimes I think of them, but the Lord reminds me to let go. Though we move or retire, the Lord remains and abides steadfastly, loving his people with his own heart and through the hearts, words, and deeds of those who come after us. He asked us to be his servants at a certain time and place, and made use of us beyond our capacity to recognize just how. Because he is at work, we can move in peace. The good news is that we can move on in peace not just when our assignment changes, or when it's time to retire; we can move forward in peace every day. We are unprofitable servants, instruments of God whose power to love, hear, forgive, reconcile, and nourish is greater than we could possibly imagine.

—Archbishop J. Peter Sartain,
Strengthen Your Brothers, 79

Because I have committed the whole of my life to Christ, I must never forget love.

> I will appoint for you shepherds after my own heart, / who will shepherd you wisely and prudently. (Jer 3:15)

The presbyter-pastor [i.e., shepherd] must exercise this authority by modeling himself on Christ the Good Shepherd, who did not impose it with external coercion but by forming the community through the interior action of his Spirit.

He wanted to share his burning love with the group of disciples and with all those who accepted his message, in order to give life to a "community of love," which at the right moment he also established visibly as the Church. As co-workers with the bishops, the successors of the Apostles, presbyters too fulfill their mission in the visible community by enlivening it with charity so that it may live in the Spirit of Christ . . .

The community dimension of pastoral care, however, cannot overlook *the needs of the individual faithful*. As we read in the Council: "It is the priests' part as instructors in the faith to see to it either personally or through others that each member of the faithful shall be led in the Holy Spirit to the full development of his own vocation in accordance with the Gospel teaching, to sincere and active charity and to the liberty with which Christ has set us free."

The Council stresses the need to help each member of the faithful to discover his specific vocation as a proper, characteristic task of the pastor who wants to respect and promote each one's personality. One could say that by his own example Jesus himself, the Good Shepherd who "calls his own sheep by name," has set the standard of individual pastoral care; knowledge and a relationship of friendship with individual persons.

—Saint John Paul II, General Audience,
May 19, 1993

How in my ministry do I not only form community but also nurture individuals?

> Whomever you forgive anything, so do I. For indeed what I have for-
> given, if I have forgiven anything, has been for you in the presence of
> Christ . . . (2 Cor 2:10)

[In the complex work of pastoral relationships], after we have explained ourselves and may or may not have sorted things out, the moment comes when there is always the last resort, gratuitous forgiveness, which is the unique character of our God and religion.

Because forgiveness as the Gospel understands it is not found anywhere else: forgiveness as pure gift, absolutely free without anything in return, is something that belongs to Christ, to Christ alone and those who are his. It is something that challenges all human cultures, civilizations, traditions; none of them knows forgiveness like this. With forgiveness the Gospel shows itself to be above every culture, because none of them, however noble, reaches this level . . . The Gospel gives us Jesus forgiving from the cross, it gives us a standard by which to judge all others and the whole of human history with its enmity and strife.

We have the gift of being able to forgive; we can say "Now I am at the heart of the Gospel, now I am—as St. Ignatius of Antioch said—beginning to be a Christian."

. . . The root of our ministry is understanding and compassion. It is a ministry of peace. A ministry of peace because it tries to understand the depth of the human heart, its sufferings, its ignorance, its resistance, and tries to sympathize so that people can go forward.

—Carlo Maria Cardinal Martini,
In the Thick of His Ministry, 35–36, 57

In matters large and small, Lord Jesus, may understanding and compassion be the roots of my ministry.

> And it happened that, while he was with them at table, he took bread, said the blessing, broke it, and gave it to them. With that their eyes were opened and they recognized him, but he vanished from their sight. (Luke 24:30-31)

The 1971 Synod of Bishops took up the conciliar doctrine, declaring: "Even if the Eucharist should be celebrated without the participation of the faithful, it nevertheless remains the center of the life of the entire Church and the heart of priestly existence."

This is a wonderful expression: "The center of the life of the entire Church." *The Eucharist makes the Church, just as the Church makes the Eucharist.* The presbyter, having been given the charge of building up the Church, performs this task essentially through the Eucharist. . . .

The Synod speaks further of the Eucharist as the "heart of priestly existence." This means that the presbyter, desiring to be and remain personally and profoundly attached to Christ, finds him first in the Eucharist, the sacrament which brings about this intimate union, open to a growth which can reach the heights of mystical identification.

At this level, too, which is that of so many holy priests, the priestly soul is not closed in on itself, because in a particular way in the Eucharist it draws on the "charity of him who gives himself as food to the faithful." Thus he feels led to give himself to the faithful to whom he distributes the Body of Christ. It is precisely in being nourished by the Body that he is impelled to help the faithful to open themselves in turn to that same presence, drawing nourishment from his infinite charity, in order to draw ever richer fruit from the sacrament.

—Saint John Paul II, General Audience, June 9, 1993

Heavenly Father, in the celebration of the Eucharist as the heart of my life and ministry, help me to remain personally and profoundly attached to your Son, Jesus Christ.

> And the Word became flesh / and made his dwelling among us, / and we saw his glory, / the glory as of the Father's only Son, / full of grace and truth. (John 1:14)

The whole identity of the pastor in Catholic tradition is connected to a fundamental incarnational grasp of ecclesial life, in which the statement "God is with us" is first a proclamation of a living experience of God and the communion of life that shapes and sustains this experience. The pastor proclaims in his own life and in his ministry within the community of faith the Incarnation of God.

The presence, therefore, of the priest in his parish is as a witness to the fundamental presence of God's care: God's "dwelling beside or near" the "ordinary and commonplace household" of His people is witnessed to in the pastoral vocation of the diocesan priest who is called to live near the community entrusted to his care. The sense of "living beside" and sharing life with the people of God roots the servant priesthood in the most radical and concrete experience of incarnational and redemptive mission. The radical witness, therefore, of the priest of the parish rests in Christ's call to root priestly presence in the very fabric of the commonplace, everyday life of the people.

The parish priest has a unique calling to live an incarnational life, to remain near the people, yet to be continually open to a mission that is beyond simple maintenance of community life and order. Living beside or near his people, the priest lives out of the whole mission of the Son: he is called to walk on the way the Son has already gone.

—Dermot Power, *A Spiritual Theology of
the Priesthood*, 114–15

How do I understand my "priestly presence" among God's people?

> If I, therefore, the master and teacher, have washed your feet, you ought
> to wash one another's feet. I have given you a model to follow, so that
> as I have done for you, you should also do. (John 13:14-15)

It would therefore be a perversion, a reversal in the truest sense, to be
an official sacramentally representing Christ, and perhaps to claim this as
much as possible on the strength of being ordained, while on the other hand
regarding personal representation (i.e. the formation of one's own life after
the model of Christ), as something possibly pious and edifying, but still an
optional extra. No: without a corresponding personal practice the ordained
priesthood becomes a religious bureaucracy, fruitless, abstract, lifeless,
which is not surprising: an office-bearer who does no more than the bare
discharge of his official duties is a *monstrum*, an "impossible possibility."

For example: when the priest at every Mass says "This is my Body,
which will be given up for you," he is speaking these words *in persona
Christi*, in place of Christ, or, more correctly, Christ speaks them through
him. And yet it is the priest who utters these words. Christ's word is transmitted through the word of the priest. Can this word be no more than a ritual,
an official sacramental utterance? This might suffice for objective salvific
validity. Yet Christ wishes to be seen in his completeness as a person. And
consequently the words "This is my Body which will be given up for you"
must also become the personal words of the priest, in the sense "Here is
my body, i.e., my person, my life, which I give up with and in Christ for
you, brethren, as your priest and pastor."

When the words of consecration are not spoken in this sense also,
there is a grating contradiction between official sacramental action and
personal life.

—Gisbert Greshake, *The Meaning of
Christian Priesthood*, 113

In what ways does my pastoral ministry find expression in the Eucharist,
and vice versa?

May 31   The Presence of Mary at the Eucharist

> On the third day there was a wedding in Cana in Galilee, and the mother of Jesus was there. (John 2:1)

Even though the Holy Thursday liturgy does not speak of Mary—rather we find her on Good Friday at the foot of the Cross with the Apostle John— *it is difficult not to sense her presence at the institution of the Eucharist*, the anticipation of the Passion and Death of the Body of Christ, that Body which the Son of God had received from the Virgin Mother at the moment of the Annunciation.

For us, as priests, the Last Supper is an especially holy moment. Christ, who says to the Apostles: "Do this in remembrance of me" (1 Cor 11:24), institutes the Sacrament of Holy Orders. With respect to our lives as priests, this is *an eminently Christocentric moment:* for we receive the priesthood from Christ the Priest, the one Priest of the New Covenant. But as we think of the sacrifice of the Body and Blood, which we offer *in persona Christi, we find it difficult not to recognize therein the presence of the Mother.* Mary gave life to the Son of God so that he might offer himself, even as our mothers gave us life, that we too, through the priestly ministry, might offer ourselves in sacrifice together with him. Behind this mission there is the vocation received from God, but there is also hidden the great love of our mothers, just as behind the sacrifice of Christ in the Upper Room there was hidden the ineffable love of his Mother. *O how truly and yet how discreetly is motherhood and thus womanhood present in the Sacrament of Holy Orders* which we celebrate anew each year on Holy Thursday!

—Saint John Paul II, Letter to Priests for
Holy Thursday, 1995

Jesus, give me the grace to recognize in the Most Holy Eucharist the presence also of your Loving Mother.

The Ordained Priest, a Gift to the Faithful   June 1

> [I]t was not Christ who glorified himself in becoming high priest, but rather the one who said to him: / "You are my son: / this day I have begotten you . . . " (Heb 5:5)

This sacrament, dear brothers, which is specific for us, which is the fruit of the special grace of vocation and the basis of our identity, by virtue of its very nature and of everything that it produces in our life and activity, serves to make the faithful aware of their common Priesthood and to activate it: the sacrament reminds them that they are the People of God and enables them "to offer spiritual sacrifices," through which Christ Himself makes us an everlasting gift to the Father. This takes place, above all, when the priest "by the sacred power that he has . . . in the person of Christ *(in persona Christi)* effects the Eucharistic Sacrifice and offers it to God in the name of all the people," as we read in the conciliar text quoted above.

Our sacramental Priesthood . . . constitutes a special *ministerium*, that is to say "service," in relation to the community of believers. It does not, however, take its origin from that community, as though it were the community that "called" or "delegated." The sacramental Priesthood is truly a gift for this community and comes from Christ Himself, from the fullness of His Priesthood. This fullness finds its expression in the fact that Christ, while making everyone capable of offering the spiritual sacrifice, calls some and enables them to be ministers of His own sacramental Sacrifice, the Eucharist—in the offering of which all the faithful share—in which are taken up all the spiritual sacrifices of the People of God.

—Saint John Paul II, Letter to Priests for
Holy Thursday, 1979

Lord Jesus, Eternal High Priest, may my ministry as priest be a model and incentive for the laity to live their priestly vocation with dignity and generosity.

My eyes are ever upon the LORD . . . (Ps 25:15)

Many people think that sanctity consists in spending long hours in prayer. Others conceive it as a series of renouncements and sufferings endured for love's sake: to their mind the function of sanctity is to mortify all tendencies of nature in man.

As against these one-sided points of view, St. Benedict has laid down his ascetic principle: "At all times we must serve God by means of those gifts which He Himself has placed in us." This is a very healthy standard in the spiritual life. Its aim is to produce in us submission to God and a harmony between the human and the divine. Progress is achieved by the exercise of our human faculties in the accomplishment of our duties in the state in which Providence has placed us.

Many of you have your days crowded with diverse occupations, and these seem to combine to impede any effort to achieve an interior life. All the same you must not lose heart: you can sanctify yourself by all your activities, even the most commonplace. . . .

Certain conditions are necessary to ensure the sanctifying effect of these actions: they must be—true—inspired by the idea of supernatural love—united to the merits of the actions of Jesus—and through them our priestly sanctification must be dedicated to the good of the Church.

It is not necessary that we should have these conditions always in mind; it is sufficient if we think of them from time to time in order to revive our faith and to help us to refer all the glory to the Lord. You may be quite sure that the spiritual life should be a life, not of anxiety or rush, but of peace.

—Blessed Columba Marmion,
Christ: The Ideal of the Priest, 276

Lord Jesus, may my daily ministry be sanctified by my awareness of your abiding and loving presence.

In Union with Christ the Head and Shepherd   June 3

I am the good shepherd, and I know mine and mine know me. (John 10:14)

Jesus Christ has revealed in himself the perfect and definitive features of the priesthood of the new Covenant. He did this throughout his earthly life, but especially in the central event of his passion, death and resurrection.

As the author of the letter to the Hebrews writes, Jesus, being a man like us and at the same time the only begotten Son of God, is in his very being the perfect mediator between the Father and humanity (cf. Heb. 8-9). Thanks to the gift of his Holy Spirit he gives us immediate access to God: "God has sent the Spirit of his Son into our hearts, crying, 'Abba! Father!'" (Gal. 4:6; cf. Rom. 8:15).

Jesus brought his role as mediator to complete fulfillment when he offered himself on the cross, thereby opening to us, once and for all, access to the heavenly sanctuary, to the Father's house (cf. Heb. 9:24-28). Compared with Jesus, Moses and all other "mediators" between God and his people in the Old Testament—kings, priests and prophets—are no more than "figures" and "shadows of the good things to come" instead of "the true form of these realities" (cf. Heb. 10:1).

Jesus is the promised good shepherd (cf. Ez. 34), who knows each one of his sheep, who offers his life for them and who wishes to gather them together as one flock with one shepherd (cf. Jn. 10:11-16). He is the shepherd who has come "not to be served but to serve" (Mt. 20:28).

—Saint John Paul II, *Pastores Dabo Vobis*, 13

Lord Jesus, Good Shepherd, it is you and you alone whom I seek to imitate in my priestly life. When I stray, as I too often do, lead me safely back into your fold.

June 4 Commissioned to Proclaim the Kingdom

> After John had been arrested, Jesus came to Galilee proclaiming the gospel of God: "This is the time of fulfillment. The kingdom of God is at hand. Repent, and believe in the gospel." (Mark 1:14-15)

The death of Jesus on the cross bears the signature of the coming kingdom: as the "suffering servant" he takes the place which we on account of our sins should occupy, and takes us up into his attitude of radical obedience, unprotesting self-surrender and total trust in the love of the Father. Therefore, nothing can again "separate us from the love of God" (Rom 8:39), which was promised to us in his Resurrection and which allows us to have a sure hope of the ultimate and definitive coming of the kingdom. . . .

This mission of Jesus, to prepare and open up to the world for the coming kingdom of God, must be continued in the Church: in fact, the Church as a whole is charged with continuing the mission of Jesus by following in his footsteps. Therefore, . . . there is a need for men who, representing him and with a commission from him, are willing to be sent in his name to proclaim the word of the kingdom and the message of God's "foolish" love. By a sacramental rite they are to pass on the reconciliation which has been accomplished in him, and the irrevocable alliance of God with men founded on the death and Resurrection of Jesus. As pastors they are to issue a call to follow him, to gather and lead a community: . . . there is a need of men who will "equip the rest of the faithful to fulfill their service, for the building up of the body of Christ" (Eph 4:12). But the purpose of all their ministry is to free the world from the self-satisfaction and narrowness of sin, and to prepare it for, to open it up to, and unite it into the kingdom of God.

—Gisbert Greshake, *The Meaning of Christian Priesthood*, 107

How does Christ bring freedom to his people through my ministry?

What is man that you are mindful of him, / and a son of man that you care for him? / Yet you have made him little less than a god, / crowned him with glory and honor. (Ps 8:5-6)

Gloria Dei vivens homo (St. Irenaeus). Love for God's glory does not distance the priest from life and all that life entails; on the contrary, his vocation brings him to discover its full meaning.

What does *vivens homo* mean? It means man in the fullness of his truth: man created by God in his own image and likeness; . . . freed from sin and raised to the dignity of an adopted child of God.

. . . This is the man and the humanity which the priest has before him when he celebrates the divine mysteries: from the newborn infant brought for Baptism, to the children and youngsters he meets for religious instruction. And then there are the young people who in that most delicate period of life choose their path, their own vocation, and set out to form new families or to consecrate themselves to the Kingdom of God by entering the Seminary or the Consecrated Life. The priest must be very close to young people. At this stage of life they often turn to him for the support of his advice, for the help of his prayer, for wise vocational guidance. In this way the priest experiences how open and dedicated to people his vocation is. In coming close to young people he is meeting future fathers and mothers of families, future professionals or, at any event, people who will be able to contribute their own abilities to the building of tomorrow's society. Each of these many different vocations is close to his priestly heart and he sees each one as a particular path along which God guides people and leads them to himself.

—Saint John Paul II, Letter to Priests for
Holy Thursday, 1996

Lord Jesus, truly God and truly man, bless me with a deepening reverence for the dignity of all persons, especially the young.

> Moses, however, said to the LORD, "If you please, my Lord, I have never been eloquent, neither in the past nor now that you have spoken to your servant; but I am slow of speech and tongue." (Exod 4:10)

We are still God's apprentices. God bids us to speak about what we ourselves have only half grasped. Yet we begin. We stutter, we are embarrassed, we realize that everything we have to say sounds so odd and improbable on the lips of a mere man.

But we go and deliver the message. And the miracle happens: We actually find men who hear the word of God in this odd talk, men into whose heart the word penetrates, judging, redeeming, and making happy, consoling and dispensing strength in weakness, even though we say it, even though we deliver the message badly. But God is with us. With us in spite of our misery and sinfulness. We preach not ourselves but Jesus Christ, We preach in His name. To the marrow of our bones we are ashamed that He said, "Whoever hears you, hears me; whoever despises you, despises me." But He said it. And so we go and deliver the message. We know that it is possible to be sounding brass and tinkling cymbal and to be ourselves lost after having preached to others. But we have not chosen ourselves. We were called and sent. And so we have to go and preach. In season and out. We traverse the fields of the world and scatter the seed of God. We are thankful when a little of it grows. And we implore the mercy of God for ourselves, so that not too much of it remains unfruitful through our fault. We sow in tears. And usually it is someone else who reaps what we have sowed. But we know this: the word of God must run and bring fruit; for it is God's blessed truth, heart's light, comfort in death, and hope of eternal life.

—Karl Rahner, *Meditations on the Sacraments*, 63–64

How much room do I give the Holy Spirit in my preaching? How much does prayer permeate my preparation for preaching?

Priesthood, a Life of Glory and Praise

I will bless the LORD at all times; / his praise shall be always in my mouth. / My soul will glory in the LORD; / let the poor hear and be glad. (Ps 34:2-3)

Gloria Dei vivens homo. These words of Saint Irenaeus profoundly link the glory of God and man's self-realization. "Not to us, O Lord, not to us, but to your name give glory" (Ps 115:1): repeating often these words of the Psalmist, we come to understand that "realizing" ourselves in life has a point of reference and an end which are transcendent, both of them included in the concept of the "glory of God": we are called to make our life an *officium laudis.*

The priestly vocation is a special call to this "*officium laudis.*" When the priest celebrates the Eucharist, when he grants God's pardon in Penance or administers the other sacraments, always he is giving praise to God. The priest must therefore love the glory of the living God and proclaim, together with the community of believers, the divine glory which shines forth in creation and in redemption . . .

Officium laudis includes not only the words of the Psalter, liturgical hymns, the songs of God's people lifted up in the sight of the Creator in all the different languages; *officium laudis* is above all the unceasing discovery of what is true, good and beautiful, which the world receives as a gift from the Creator. Along with that, it is the discovery of the meaning of human existence. The mystery of the Redemption has fully accomplished and revealed this meaning, bringing human life closer to the life of God.

Redemption, definitively achieved in the Paschal Mystery . . . reveals not only the transcendent holiness of God but also, as the Council teaches, reveals "man to man himself."

> —Saint John Paul II, Letter to Priests for
> Holy Thursday, 1996

Heavenly Father, may my daily ministry give you glory, as I seek to discover all that is true and good and beautiful in this world.

> I made known to them your name and I will make it known, that the love
> with which you loved me may be in them and I in them. (John 17:26)

To put off idle hopes of earthly good, to be sick of flattery and the
world's praise, to see the emptiness of temporal greatness, and to be watchful against self-indulgence—these are but the beginnings of religion; these
are but the preparation of heart, which religious earnestness implies; without
a good share of them, how can a Christian move a step?

But to love our brethren with a resolution which no obstacles can overcome, so as almost to consent to an anathema on ourselves, if so, we may
save those who hate us—to labour in God's cause against hope, and in
the midst of sufferings—to read the events of life, as they occur, by the
interpretation which Scripture gives them, and that, not as if the language
were strange to us, but to do it promptly—to perform all our relative daily
duties most watchfully—to check every evil thought, and bring the whole
mind into captivity to the law of Christ,—to be patient, cheerful, forgiving,
meek, honest, and true—to persevere in this good work till death, making fresh and fresh advances towards perfection—and after all, even to
the end, to confess ourselves unprofitable servants, nay, to feel ourselves
corrupt and sinful creatures, who (with all our proficiency) would still be
lost unless God bestowed on us His mercy in Christ: these are some of the
difficult realities of religious obedience which we must pursue, and which
the Apostles in high measure attained, and which we may well bless God's
holy name, if He enables us to make our own.

—Blessed John Henry Newman,
Parochial and Plain Sermons, 1:343–44

I must daily work on the fundamentals of the Christian life, for only then
will I be able to live a priestly life.

For a priest's lips preserve knowledge, / and instruction is to be sought from his mouth, / because he is the messenger of the LORD of hosts. (Mal 2:7)

We are not asked to be flawless, but to keep growing and wanting to grow as we advance along the path of the Gospel; our arms must never grow slack. What is essential is that the preacher be certain that God loves him, that Jesus Christ has saved him and that his love always has the last word. Encountering such beauty, he will often feel that his life does not glorify God as it should, and he will sincerely desire to respond more fully to so great a love. Yet if he does not take time to hear God's word with an open heart, if he does not allow it to touch his life, to challenge him, to impel him, and if he does not devote time to pray with that word, then he will indeed be a false prophet, a fraud, a shallow impostor. But by acknowledging his poverty and desiring to grow in his commitment, he will always be able to abandon himself to Christ, saying in the words of Peter: "I have no silver and gold, but what I have I give you" (*Acts* 3:6). The Lord wants to make use of us as living, free and creative beings who let his word enter their own hearts before then passing it on to others. Christ's message must truly penetrate and possess the preacher, not just intellectually but in his entire being. The Holy Spirit, who inspired the word, "today, just as at the beginning of the Church, acts in every evangelizer who allows himself to be possessed and led by him. The Holy Spirit places on his lips the words which he could not find by himself."

—Pope Francis, *Evangelii Gaudium*, 151

Lord Jesus, strengthen me in times of doubt and discouragement. Possess my life so completely that it is your word of love which is ever on my lips and in my heart.

A great sign appeared in the sky, a woman clothed with the sun, with the moon under her feet, and on her head a crown of twelve stars. (Rev 12:1)

The Blessed Virgin Mary, though numbered among the laity, can nonetheless provide the model for the moral life of the priest. This is because the priest's life is based on the paschal mystery of Jesus Christ, i.e., on our Lord's entire life of sacrificial service, which is imprinted on the priest in his sacral character. No one has patterned the paschal mystery more perfectly than our Blessed Mother herself, who totally joined her life to that of her Son in his sacrifice. She did this from the first moment she declared, "Be it done unto me according to your word." Her sacrifice unfolded throughout her life with his own sacrifice. It can be seen when she presented her Son in the Temple. The true offering she made on that occasion was not the two young turtledoves but her acceptance of the sufferings that would accompany her Son's ministry as foretold by Simeon. The Jesuit Jean Galot describes its significance beautifully: "We have here a first offering of the sacrifice that redeems, a mother's sacrifice which precedes and already implies Jesus' own priestly offering of himself still to come. This consecration transcends ritual formalism; it bespeaks a personal commitment" (*Theology of the Priesthood*, 39). This consecration was a surrender to a life of sacrificial service in imitation of her Divine Son. As Saint Augustine said, "Because there is a sacrifice, there is a priesthood" (Confessions, X, 43,69).

> —John M. Haas, "The Sacral Character of the Priest as
> the Foundation for his Moral Life and Teaching," 147

Jesus, Son of Mary, may I embrace the spirit of sacrificial obedience that you learned from your beloved Mother.

Visits to the Blessed Sacrament June 11

The LORD spoke to Moses: . . . They are to make a sanctuary for me, that I may dwell in their midst. (Exod 25:1, 8)

To Priests the Council also recommends, in addition to the daily celebration of the Mass, "personal devotion" to the Holy Eucharist, and particularly that "daily talk with Christ the Lord in their visit to the Blessed Sacrament." Faith in and love for the Eucharist cannot allow Christ's presence in the tabernacle to remain alone. Already in the Old Testament we read that God dwelt in a "tent" (or "tabernacle"), which was called the "meeting tent." The meeting was desired by God. It can be said that in the tabernacle of the Eucharist too Christ is present in view of a dialogue with his people and with individual believers. The presbyter is the first one called to enter this meeting tent, to visit Christ in the tabernacle for a "daily talk."

More than any other, the presbyter is called to share the fundamental disposition of Christ in this sacrament, that is, the "thanksgiving" from which it takes its name. Uniting himself with Christ the Priest and Victim, the presbyter shares not only his offering, but also his feelings, his disposition of gratitude to the Father for the benefits He has given to humanity, to every soul, to the priest himself, to all those who in heaven and on earth have been allowed to share in the glory of God. *Gratias agimus tibi propter magnam gloriam tuam. . . .*

Thus, the priest offers the chorus of praise and blessing, which is raised up by those who are able to recognize in man and in the world the signs of an infinite goodness.

—Saint John Paul II, General Audience, June 9, 1993

Lord Jesus, present in the most Blessed Sacrament, so fill me with a spirit of gratitude that I am drawn to spend prayerful time each day in your most sacred presence.

> [Love] bears all things, believes all things, hopes all things, endures all things. (1 Cor 13:7)

The choice of celibacy does not connote ignorance of or contempt for the sexual instinct and man's capacity for giving himself in love. That would certainly do damage to his physical and psychological balance. On the contrary, it demands clear understanding, careful self-control and a wise elevation of the mind to higher realities. In this way celibacy sets the whole man on a higher level and makes an effective contribution to his perfection.

We readily grant that the natural and lawful desire a man has to love a woman and to raise a family is renounced by the celibate in sacred orders; but it cannot be said that marriage and the family are the only way for fully developing the human person. In the priest's heart love is by no means extinct. His charity is drawn from the purest source, practiced in the imitation of God and Christ, and is no less demanding and real than any other genuine love. It gives the priest a limitless horizon, deepens and gives breadth to his sense of responsibility—a mark of mature personality—and inculcates in him, as a sign of a higher and greater fatherhood, a generosity and refinement of heart which offer a superlative enrichment.

All the People of God must give testimony to the mystery of Christ and His kingdom, but this witnessing does not take the same form for all. The Church leaves to her married children the function of giving the necessary testimony of a genuinely and fully Christian married and family life. She entrusts to her priests the testimony of a life wholly dedicated to pondering and seeking the new and delightful realities of God's kingdom.

—Blessed Pope Paul VI,
Sacerdotalis Caelibatus, 55–57

Lord Jesus, help me to see the whole of my life as one of faithful and enduring love.

Priests: Ordained to Celebrate Mass

I am the bread of life; whoever comes to me will never hunger, and whoever believes in me will never thirst. (John 6:35)

"The priestly ministry reaches its summit in the celebration of the Eucharist, which is the source and center of the Church's unity." The Dogmatic Constitution on the Church asserts, "It is in the Eucharistic cult or in the Eucharistic assembly of the faithful that they exercise in a supreme degree their sacred functions; there, acting in the person of Christ and proclaiming his mystery they unite the votive offerings of the faithful to the sacrifice of Christ their head, and in the sacrifice of the Mass they make present again and apply, until the coming of the Lord, the unique sacrifice of the New Testament, that namely of Christ offering himself once for all a spotless victim to the Father."

The community is gathered by the proclamation of the Gospel so that all can make a spiritual offering of themselves; the spiritual sacrifice of the faithful is made perfect through union with the Christ's sacrifice, offered in an unbloody, sacramental manner by the hands of the priests. Their whole priestly ministry draws its force from this one sacrifice.

This shows the connection between the ministerial priesthood and the common priesthood of the faithful. It also shows how the priest, among all the faithful, is especially called to identify himself mystically—as well as sacramentally—with Christ, in order to be himself in some way *Sacerdos et Hostia*, according to the beautiful expression of St. Thomas Aquinas.

—Saint John Paul II, General Audience, May 12, 1993

In what way is the whole of my priestly life "eucharistic"?

Strive eagerly for the greatest spiritual gifts. (1 Cor 12:31)

Lord, I need your Spirit, that divine force that has transformed so many human personalities, making them capable of extraordinary deeds and extraordinary lives. Give me that Spirit which, coming from you and going to you, infinite holiness, is a Holy Spirit.

The judges of Israel, without expecting it, without inclination, without being able to resist, simple sons of villagers, Samson, Gideon, Saul . . . were changed by you, abruptly and completely. Not only did they become capable of tremendous acts of boldness and strength, but they took on new personalities and felt themselves capable of performing a mission as difficult as liberating a whole people. . . .

Feeling the difficulty of my mission, I desire your profound action in my soul, not only that you descend but that you repose in me, and give me those wondrous gifts that you lavish on your elect: wisdom and intelligence, as to Bezalel and Solomon; counsel and strength, as to David; knowledge and fear of God, which was the ideal of so many holy souls of Israel.

Give me what you gave the Prophets: The word that came to them was not their own word but yours, of your Spirit, sent to them not only to create a new personality for service but also to explain its sense and secrets, of your Spirit that is not only intelligence and strength but also knowledge of God and God's ways. Give me, then, the strength with which you not only opened up to the Prophets your word to the point of revealing to them your glory, but also that strength that kept them standing as they spoke to the people.

—Pedro Arrupe, "Final Address of Father General
to the Congregation of Procurators," *The Spiritual
Legacy of Pedro Arrupe, S.J.*, 40–41

I find it difficult to believe that *all* the abundant gifts of the Spirit are already given to me, and that the Lord is but waiting patiently for my generous response.

The Fascinating Humanity of Jesus   June 15

The LORD let his face shine upon you, and be gracious to you! (Num 6:25)

On the Feast of the Sacred Heart of Jesus let us fix the eyes of our minds and hearts with a constant loving gaze on Christ, the one Savior of our lives and of the world. Focusing on Christ means focusing on that Face which every human being, consciously or not, seeks as a satisfying response to his own insuppressible thirst for happiness.

We have encountered this Face and on that day, at that moment, his Love so deeply wounded our hearts that we could no longer refrain from asking ceaselessly to be in his Presence. "In the morning you hear my voice; in the morning I prepare a sacrifice for you and watch" (Ps 5).

Only by looking again at the perfect and fascinating humanity of Jesus Christ—alive and active now—who revealed himself to us and still today bends down to each one of us with his special love of total predilection, can we let him illumine and fill the abyss of need which is our humanity, certain of Hope encountered and sure of Mercy that embraces our limitations and teaches us to forgive what we ourselves do not even manage to discern. "Deep calls to deep at the thunder of your cataracts" (Ps 42[41]).

. . . On the occasion of the traditional World Day of Prayer for the Sanctification of Priests that is celebrated on the Feast of the Sacred Heart, I would like to recall the priority of prayer over action since it is on prayer that the effectiveness of action depends. The Church's mission largely depends on each person's personal relationship with the Lord Jesus and must therefore be nourished by prayer.

—Pope Benedict XVI, Letter on the Occasion of the
World Day of Prayer for the Sanctification of Priests

It is only when I meditate daily on the fascinating humanity of Jesus Christ that I can begin to understand how to live a fully human priestly life.

Strive eagerly for the greatest spiritual gifts. (1 Cor 12:31)

There are many qualities which a priest ought to have, and which I lack. And the first of all is that he must purify his soul entirely of ambition for the office. For if he is strongly attracted to this office, when he gets it he will add fuel to the fire, and, being mastered by ambition, he will tolerate all kinds of evil to secure his hold upon it, even resorting to flattery, . . . or to spending lavishly.

. . . I think a man must rid his mind of this ambition with all possible care, and not for a moment let it be governed by it, in order that he may always act with freedom. For if he does not want to achieve fame in this position of authority, he will not dread its loss either. And if he does not fear this, he can always act with the freedom which befits Christian men.

. . . So we must be thoroughly on guard against ambition and examine ourselves carefully to prevent a spark of it from smoldering anywhere unseen. It is much to be desired that those who at first were free from this infection should be able to keep clear of it when they have entered office. But if anyone nurtures within himself this terrible, savage beast before attaining office, there is no telling what a furnace he will fling himself into, after he has attained it.

—Saint John Chrysostom, *On the Priesthood*, III

How have I nurtured ambition? How has it affected my relations with my brother priests?

He said to them, "Today this scripture passage is fulfilled in your hearing." (Luke 4:21)

Every time the liturgical assembly gathers to celebrate the Eucharist, this "today" is actualized. The mystery of Christ, the single and supreme High Priest of the new and eternal Covenant, is made present and efficacious.

In this light, we understand better the value of our priestly ministry. The Apostle invites us to revive ceaselessly the gift of God received through the imposition of hands (cf. 2 Tm 1:6), sustained by the comforting certainty that the One who has begun this work in us will bring it to completion until the day of Jesus Christ (cf. Phil 1:6).

Today, with the Holy Chrism Mass, we commemorate this great truth that directly concerns us. Christ has called us, in a special way, to share in his Priesthood. Every vocation to the priestly ministry is an extraordinary gift of God's love and, at the same time, a profound mystery which concerns the inscrutable divine designs and the depths of the human conscience.

"Forever I will sing the goodness of the Lord" (Responsorial Psalm). With hearts filled with gratitude, we will shortly be renewing our priestly promises. This rite takes our minds and hearts back to the unforgettable day on which we made the commitment to be closely united to Christ, the model of our priesthood, and to be faithful stewards of God's mysteries, not allowing human interest to guide us, but only love for God and our neighbour.

Dear Brothers in the priesthood, have we remained faithful to these promises? Never let the spiritual enthusiasm of priestly Ordination be extinguished within us. And you, beloved faithful, pray for priests so that they may be attentive stewards of the gifts of divine grace, especially of God's mercy in the sacrament of Confession and of the Bread of life in the Eucharist, the living memorial of the death and Resurrection of Christ.

—Saint John Paul II, Homily for the Chrism Mass,
April 17, 2003

Lord Jesus, may I always renew my priestly promises with the utmost seriousness. May I never take for granted my call to servanthood in the love of your people.

> [I]n him we have put our hope [that] he will also rescue us again, as you help us with prayer, so that thanks may be given by many on our behalf for the gift granted us through the prayers of many. (2 Cor 1:10-11)

Have I ever had such a relationship of trust with the community? Have I ever reached the point of saying: Pray for me because I am in a very difficult situation? Look, I was in a very difficult situation and I got over it thanks to your prayers and support?

When we succeed in having this kind of relationship, the community reacts very strongly and it shakes their idea of the ministry in which the minister is either unreachable and infallible or criticized as faithless and incompetent.

The community is restored to a more human relationship. The ordained minister, the servant of God, has his grace but also his weakness and needs prayer. He needs to feel that people are united in his struggles and efforts.

Of course, it is hard to find the right words, especially because the community is not used to such confession and may be scandalized. Should not the community be comforted and reassured by the bishop, and the priest? People's image of the bishop or the priest is of someone who never wavers, never doubts, never has problems, who should reassure others. If he has problems he must turn to God.

The opposite image is also mistaken, of a man showing weakness and demanding pity. The right one lies somewhere between the two: that the community should share in the priest's sufferings, just as the priest shares in the community's.

—Carlo Maria Cardinal Martini,
In the Thick of His Ministry, 22–23

How vulnerable have I been with my parishioners?

> But because he wished to justify himself, he said to Jesus, "And who is
> my neighbor?" (Luke 10:29)

Christ, true man and yet Eternal and Only-Begotten Son of the Heavenly Father, has, on the spiritual plane, a countless number of brothers and sisters. For the family of God includes everyone: not just those who through Baptism become God's adopted children, but in a certain sense all mankind, since Christ has redeemed all men and all women and offered them the possibility of becoming adopted sons and daughters of the Eternal Father. Thus we have all become brothers and sisters in Christ.

At this point in our reflection on the relationship between priests and women, beside the figure of the mother there emerges the figure of the sister. Thanks to the Redemption, the priest shares in a special way in the relationship of brotherhood offered by Christ to all the redeemed.

Many of us priests have sisters in our families. In any event, every priest from childhood onwards has met girls, if not in his own family at least in the neighbourhood, in childhood games or at school. A type of mixed community has enormous importance for the formation of the personalities of boys and girls.

Here we encounter the original plan of the Creator, who in the beginning created man "male and female" (cf. Gen 1:27). This divine creative act continues from generation to generation. The Book of Genesis speaks of it in the context of the vocation to marriage: "Therefore a man leaves his father and his mother and cleaves to his wife" (Gen 2:24). The vocation to marriage obviously assumes and requires that the environment in which one lives is made up of both men and women.

—Saint John Paul II, Letter to Priests for
Holy Thursday, 1995

Loving Father, instill within my heart the conviction that every woman I meet is my sister in Christ.

Here is my servant whom I uphold, / my chosen one with whom I am pleased. / Upon him I have put my spirit . . . (Isa 42:1)

The unity of office and personal life, of "objective" and "subjective" holiness, is the fundamental reason why priestly office must set its mark on the whole of the priest's life, not merely in all its aspects, but also throughout its whole length. G. Bachl says rightly that "if we are speaking about sacrifice and commitment, what other more important thing can one sacrifice and commit than one's time? . . . Undoubtedly it is in this aspect of his life that a man is challenged when he is called upon to offer his life by Christian preaching: the sacrifice is essentially a sacrifice of his time."

How can radicalism in time show itself otherwise than by a radical sacrifice of time? In this connection J. B. Metz's assertions are valid for every radical commitment, for every decision about life: "A decision cannot be changeable as often as one pleases, if it is not to reveal itself once again as temporary and trivial, if it is not once again to be submerged in that ceaseless vacillation which is supposed to be ended by a responsible decision. For this reason a decision essentially tends to be once and for all, irreplaceable and irrevocable." This is true of every real decision about life: but it is especially true when it is a decision about a mission from God and readiness to serve him. Already in the time of the Old Testament prophets, God "takes over" the life of the one he calls, so that the one called cannot escape from his vocation (cf. Jer 20:7ff). This is particularly true of the priestly ministry which has to make present the self-sacrifice of Jesus for mankind; this can credibly happen only when the priest realizes that he has been chosen and called to sacrifice all his strength and the whole time of his life. Thus, a priest's vocation is essentially a lifetime vocation.

—Gisbert Greshake, *The Meaning of Christian Priesthood*, 117–18

Lord Jesus, I have made an irrevocable decision to live the whole of my life in your service. Strengthen me when I am tempted to place limits on the energy and time required of me.

True Friendship with Christ June 21

I no longer call you slaves . . . I have called you friends . . . (John 15:15)

Anyone who exercises the priestly ministry exercises it not for himself alone, but for others. For every high priest taken from among men is appointed for men in the things that pertain to God (Heb 5:1). Christ himself taught that lesson when he compared the priest to salt and to light, in order to show the nature of the priestly ministry. The priest then is the light of the world and the salt of the earth. Everyone knows that he fulfills this function chiefly by the teaching of Christian truth; and who can be unaware that this ministry of teaching is practically useless if the priest fails to confirm by the example of his life the truths which he teaches? Those who hear him might say, insultingly it is true, but not without justification: They profess that they know God but in their works they deny him (Ti 1:16); they will refuse to accept his teaching and will derive no benefit from the light of the priest.

. . . A priest who neglects his own sanctification can never be the salt of the earth; what is corrupt and contaminated is utterly incapable of preserving from corruption; where sanctity is lacking, there corruption will inevitably find its way. Hence Christ, continuing this comparison, calls such priests salt that has lost its savor, which is good for nothing any more, but to be cast out and to be trodden on by men (Mt. 5:13).

. . . True friendship consists in unity of mind and will, identity of likes and dislikes; therefore, as friends of Jesus Christ, we are bound to have that mind in us which was in Jesus Christ who is holy, innocent, undefiled (Heb 7:26).

—Saint Pius X, *Haerent Animo*

Bless our friendship, Lord Jesus, so that you and I might be of one mind and heart in our service of your people.

> And now I commend you to God and to that gracious word of his that
> can build you up and give you the inheritance among all who are con-
> secrated. (Acts 20:32)

The second mark of the church is holiness. Priests are called to be symbols and agents of the church's holiness. Since God alone is holy, the goal is to make the church transparent to the presence of God, to let the sacramental nature of the church shine forth. Just as Christ is the sacrament of encounter with God, so the church must be the sacrament of Christ's presence within the human family.

What fosters the holiness of the church? This is a special challenge for Catholics who have a deep and abiding faith in the sacramentality of material objects, churches, statues, paintings, relics, vestments, and sacred vessels. But at times those objects no longer point to Christ's presence but obscure it. Old buildings, for example, quickly point to big dollars, to problems of deferred maintenance, to earthly baggage accumulated along the way that is best discarded. The same question can be asked about church organization. When does middle-management lose a sense of transparency to the church's mission and instead become an end in itself?

The largest obstacle to holiness is sin, and though the church may be holy, its members often are not. But by the same token, because they are sinners, the church's holiness does not remain an abstraction to them. They encounter it in the forgiveness of their sins. They also can see it on occasion in the holiness of others. How much difference one holy person makes, one person who seems transparent to God's presence! Is there any more adequate sacramental vessel, a monstrance of God's presence, than a human personality suffused with the love of God? Is there anything more riveting, more justifying of the church's existence than a single person in whom holiness of life has found a home? When such a person appears, everyone thinks, "This is the reason the church exists." Isn't this true of a priest as well? And isn't the absence of such holiness also notable?

—Howard P. Bleichner, *View from the Altar*, 159–60

Lord Jesus, I desire a holiness that extends beyond the sanctuary, and transforms the whole of my pastoral life.

The Ministry of Preaching and Catechesis

> Let the word of Christ dwell in you richly, as in all wisdom you teach and admonish one another . . . (Col 3:16)

The Curé of Ars was also careful never to neglect in any way the ministry of the Word, which is absolutely necessary in predisposing people to faith and conversion. He even said: "Our Lord, who is truth itself, considers his Word no less important than his Body." We know how long he spent, especially at the beginning, in laboriously composing his Sunday sermons. Later on he came to express himself more spontaneously, always with lively and clear conviction, with images and comparisons taken from daily life and easily grasped by his flock. His catechetical instructions to the children also formed an important part of his ministry, and the adults gladly joined the children so as to profit from this matchless testimony which flowed from his heart.

He had the courage to denounce evil in all its forms; he did not keep silent, for it was a question of the eternal salvation of his faithful people: "If a pastor remains silent when he sees God insulted and souls going astray, woe to him! If he does not want to be damned, and if there is some disorder in his parish, he must trample upon human respect and the fear of being despised or hated." This responsibility was his anguish as parish priest. But as a rule, "he preferred to show the attractive side of virtue rather than the ugliness of vice," and if he spoke sometimes in tears about sin and the danger for salvation, he insisted on the tenderness of God who has been offended, and the happiness of being loved by God, united to God, living in his presence and for him.

—Saint John Paul II, Letter to Priests for
Holy Thursday, 1986

In what ways can I strengthen my ministry of preaching as a preeminent responsibility in my priestly life?

> Rejoice always. Pray without ceasing. In all circumstances give thanks, for this is the will of God for you in Christ Jesus. (1 Thess 5:16-18)

With an unquenchable thirst and longing for Christ, the most authentic dimension of our Priesthood is mendicancy, simple and continuous prayer that is learned in silent oration. It has always characterized the life of Saints and should be asked for insistently. This awareness of our relationship with him is subjected to the purification of daily testing. Every day we realize again and again that not even we Ministers who act *in Persona Christi Capitis* are spared this drama. We cannot live a single moment in his Presence without a gentle longing to know him and to continue to adhere to him. Let us not give in to the temptation to see being priests as a burden, inevitable and impossible to delegate, henceforth assumed, which can perhaps be carried out "mechanically" with a structured and coherent pastoral programme. Priesthood is the vocation, the path and the manner through which Christ saves us, has called us and is calling us now to abide with him.

The one adequate measure, with regard to our Holy Vocation, is radicalism. This total dedication with awareness of our infidelity can only be brought into being as a renewed and prayerful decision which Christ subsequently implements, day after day. The actual gift of priestly celibacy must be accepted and lived in this dimension of radicalism and full configuration to Christ. Any other approach to the reality of the relationship with him risks becoming ideological. Even the great mass of work that the contemporary conditions of the ministry sometimes impose on us, far from discouraging us must spur us to care with even greater attention for our priestly identity which has an incontrovertibly divine root.

> —Pope Benedict XVI, Letter on the Occasion of the
> World Day of Prayer for the Sanctification of Priests

Lord Jesus, I beg the grace to be always grateful, to live continually in your presence.

> For our gospel did not come to you in word alone, but also in power and in the holy Spirit and [with] much conviction. (1 Thess 1:5)

Once I was asked how I prepare to preach. After thinking for a long time, I answered that I try to pay attention. That is, I said, if I am to be the preacher of the day, I attend to the texts that are going to be read, to the people who are going to gather and to the purpose of their gathering, and to the world in which they gather. I will be responsible, once again, to say what these texts might mean, who the people are, what the significance of their gathering is, and how we might see the world. I will be responsible to say these things together, believing that—in the mercy and presence of God—they belong together.

It sounds simple. It is not. Paying attention is not easy. I have found that years of familiarity or common presuppositions may have left me with a prematurely narrowed sense of what this scripture passage may mean or who these people are. Attention requires me to see again the strangeness of the texts and the mystery of each person. . . .

Because these texts are to be read at the Eucharist and because these people are constituted as church as they gather to do the Eucharist, the task of preparing to preach is deeper still. I am not going to give a public lecture on the possible significances of ancient texts for modern people. I am not going to expound my own interpretation of current events. I am to arise in the assembly to articulate the meaning of the meeting as an encounter with one another in God's present grace, believing that this assembly casts a searing, gracious light on all the world . . . it is the faith of the Church that is to be brought to expression in my speech. So I must attend to the mystery of Christ in the texts, to the mystery of the Spirit constituting this people as church, and to the mystery of the world as it is held in the endless mercy of the triune God.

—Gordon W. Lathrop, *The Pastor: A Spirituality*, 55

I consider how often I have procrastinated in preparing to preach, and have relied far too much on what others have said and not on my own prayer and reflection. I pray for a true spirit of homiletic attentiveness.

Be imitators of me, as I am of Christ. (1 Cor 11:1)

The example of the Curé of Ars naturally leads me to point out that there are sectors of co-operation which need to be opened ever more fully to the lay faithful. Priests and laity together make up the one priestly people and in virtue of their ministry priests live in the midst of the lay faithful, "that they may lead everyone to the unity of charity, 'loving one another with mutual affection; and outdoing one another in sharing honour.'" Here we ought to recall the Vatican Council II's hearty encouragement to priests "to be sincere in their appreciation and promotion of the dignity of the laity and of the special role they have to play in the Church's mission. . . . They should be willing to listen to lay people, give brotherly consideration to their wishes, and acknowledge their experience and competence in the different fields of human activity. In this way they will be able together with them to discern the signs of the times."

St. John Mary Vianney taught his parishioners primarily by the witness of his life. It was from his example that they learned to pray, halting frequently before the tabernacle for a visit to Jesus in the Blessed Sacrament. "One need not say much to pray well"—the Curé explained to them—"We know that Jesus is there in the tabernacle: let us open our hearts to Him, let us rejoice in His sacred presence. That is the best prayer." And he would urge them: "Come to communion, my brothers and sisters, come to Jesus. Come to live from Him in order to live with Him. . . . Of course you are not worthy of him, but you need him!"

—Pope Benedict XVI, Letter Proclaiming
a Year for Priests, June 16, 2009

What do those whom I serve learn from witnessing my priestly life?

> If I, therefore, the master and teacher, have washed your feet, you ought to wash one another's feet. (John 13:14)

My dear brothers: You know how some people in positions of leadership and authority try at times to make their importance felt: fancy cars, the best tailor-made suits, high-power, high-profile lifestyles, the finest in material comfort. They climb the academic, corporate, or ecclesial ladders of success and assume the trappings which announce, "I've made it. . . . I'm successful. . . . I'm a leader. . . . I'm important."

It cannot be that way with you, my brothers, who are about to be ordained. As priests, you are certainly going to assume high-profile positions of leadership in the communities where you are assigned to serve. The Church needs you; it wants you to exercise wise and competent leadership. But beware. Leadership and authority—even religious leadership and authority—can be a seductive, slippery slope. It is easy to lose perspective, to lose balance. It is easy to fall into the trap of self-centeredness.

I know that you have been blessed with many gifts for leadership. You are bright, articulate, skillful men. But keep your gifts in perspective. As St. Paul reminds us in today's second reading, your gifts, manifestations of the Spirit, have been given, not for your own self-aggrandizement, but for the common good, to build up the body of Christ.

I truly hope that, as priests, you will experience a profound sense of your giftedness and efficacy; I pray that you will be creative, vigorous preachers of the gospel; I pray that your people will be able to trust you and turn to you for direction, wisdom, and counsel.

. . . The most effective, satisfied priests I know are those who carry their authority gracefully, without trying to lord it over people. They realize from their own prayerful reflection, that, if they have any authority at all, it is the authority of love, Christ's love.

—Joseph Cardinal Bernardin, Homily for
Priesthood Ordination, May 18, 1991

Where are the traces of self-interest and clericalism in my ministry? Might there be a subtle sense of entitlement in my life?

> With such affection for you, we were determined to share with you not only the gospel of God, but our very selves as well, so dearly beloved had you become to us. (1 Thess 2:8)

It is interesting to note that Providence has brought me back to where I began to exercise my priestly vocation, that is, to pastoral work. Now I am ministering directly to souls. To tell the truth, I have always believed that for an ecclesiastic, diplomacy (so-called!) must be imbued with the pastoral spirit; otherwise it is of no use and makes a sacred mission look ridiculous. Now I am confronted with the Church's real interests, relating to her final purpose, which is to save souls and guide them to heaven. This is enough for me and I thank the Lord for it. I said so in St. Mark's in Venice on 15 March, the day of my solemn entry. I desire and think of nothing else but to live and die for the souls entrusted to me. "The good shepherd gives his life for his sheep . . . I am come that they may have life, and may have it more abundantly" (John 10).

I am beginning my direct ministry at an age—seventy-two years—when others end theirs. So, *I find myself on the threshold of eternity*. O Jesus, chief Shepherd and Bishop of our souls, the mystery of my life and death is in your hands, close to your heart. On the one hand I tremble at the approach of my last hour; on the other hand I trust in you and only look one day ahead. I feel I am in the same condition as St. Aloysius Gonzaga, that is, I must go on with what I have to do, always striving after perfection but thinking still more of God's mercy. In the few years that I have still to live, I want to be a holy pastor, in the full sense of the word.

—Saint John XXIII, *Journal of a Soul*, 338

What is it that so clutters my life? What distractions draw me away from whole-hearted pastoral service to God's people?

Celibate Loneliness

> It is right that I should think this way about all of you, because I hold you in my heart, you who are all partners with me in grace . . . (Phil 1:7)

[There is] loneliness involved in the celibate life of a priest; but there is loneliness in every life, as each one of us has to let go of and grieve over the realization that I will never find a particular "someone" out there who will be everything for me. Authentic priestly celibacy is a gift that aspires to have no one in particular for the sake of being more available to love and to minister to many others. The particular vulnerability in which a priest finds himself, without any particular "other" of his own, is greatly exacerbated by the fact that by his priesthood he is in a position in which people can expect him to be everything for them. The aura of transcendent omnipotence that can surround a priest may complicate even more the entanglement of power with sexual feeling. A "spiritual intimacy" can soon appear to take on a privileged quality beyond space and time, making this spiritual relationship seem uniquely special and singular, an exception to every rule and every limit. On whichever side these feelings of omnipotence arise, it can be very tempting for a priest to try to exercise that power with which someone has endowed him or with which he would like to be endowed.

Ultimately, as a celibate, the priest is in a privileged position to love many, to love selflessly, and to witness to the totally, infinitely self-giving love of God, who alone can be everything for us. The kenosis of Christ must predominate how a priest loves and ministers, especially in any exercise of power in his priestly office. Ultimately, the priest must cultivate this disposition in all honesty, so as to be open to receive the grace of his vocation and office.

—Thomas Acklin,
The Unchanging Heart of the Priesthood, 22

In what ways can I grow in understanding that celibacy is a personal invitation to imitate Christ for the sake of God's kingdom?

For I have experienced much joy and encouragement from your love, because the hearts of the holy ones have been refreshed by you, brother. (Phlm 1:7)

Priestly joy is a joy which is sister to obedience. An obedience to the Church in the hierarchy which gives us, as it were, not simply the external framework for our obedience: the parish to which I am sent, my ministerial assignments, my particular work . . . but also union with God the Father, the source of all fatherhood. It is likewise an obedience to the Church in service: in availability and readiness to serve everyone, always and as best I can, following the example of "Our Lady of Promptness" (cf. Lk 1:39, *meta spoudes*), who hastens to serve Elizabeth her kinswoman and is concerned for the kitchen of Cana when the wine runs out. The availability of her priests makes the Church a house with open doors, a refuge for sinners, a home for people living on the streets, a place of loving care for the sick, a camp for the young, a classroom for catechizing children about to make their First Communion . . . Wherever God's people have desires or needs, there is the priest, who knows how to listen (*ob-audire*) and feels a loving mandate from Christ who sends him to relieve that need with mercy or to encourage those good desires with resourceful charity.

All who are called should know that genuine and complete joy does exist in this world: it is the joy of being taken from the people we love and then being sent back to them as dispensers of the gifts and counsels of Jesus, the one Good Shepherd who, with deep compassion for all the little ones and the outcasts of this earth, wearied and oppressed like sheep without a shepherd, wants to associate many others to his ministry, so as himself to remain with us and to work, in the person of his priests, for the good of his people.

On this priestly Thursday I ask the Lord Jesus to enable many young people to discover that burning zeal which joy kindles in our hearts as soon as we have the stroke of boldness needed to respond willingly to his call.

—Pope Francis, Homily for the Chrism Mass,
April 17, 2014

I consider whether there is a spirit of generosity in my availability in service of God's people, and how promptly I respond to others.

"I Saw God in a Man"   July 1

> And the Word became flesh / and made his dwelling among us, / and we saw his glory, / the glory as of the Father's only Son, / full of grace and truth. (John 1:14)

"To master inclinations" is discipline. The phrase "a little at a time" indicates discipline, which requires a continued, long, and difficult effort. Even the angels that Jacob saw in a dream were not flying, but climbing one step at a time; you can just imagine us, poor men without wings.

The "great" discipline requires a suitable atmosphere; and, in the first place, meditation. At Milan station I once saw a porter, who, with his head resting on a sack of coal propped against a pillar, was sound asleep . . . Trains left whistling and arrived with clanking wheels the loudspeakers continually boomed out announcements; people came and went in confusion and noise, but he—sleeping on—seemed to be saying: "Do what you like, but I need to be quiet." We priests should do something similar: around us there is continual movement and talking, of persons, newspapers, radio and television. With priestly moderation and discipline we must say: "Beyond certain limits, for me, who am a priest of the Lord, you do not exist. I must take a little silence for my soul. I detach myself from you to be united with my God."

And today it is the desire of many good faithful to feel their priest habitually united with God. They reason like the lawyer of Lyons on his return from a visit to the Curé d'Ars. "What did you see at Ars?" he was asked. Answer: "I saw God in a man." St. Gregory the Great reasons in a similar way. He hopes that the pastor of souls will dialogue with God without forgetting men, and dialogue with men without forgetting God.

—Pope John Paul I, Address to a Meeting of
the Roman Clergy, September 7, 1978

Would my parishioners say the same of me as did the lawyer from Lyons of the Curé of Ars?

July 2   The Eucharist: Strength in Difficult Times

Can you drink the cup that I drink or be baptized with the baptism with which I am baptized? (Mark 10:38)

For several years I was involved as a priest in pastorally responding to victims, their families, and the accused priests. In later years, as a bishop, I have had the responsibility to help all members of the diocese deal with their upset, embarrassment, and sometimes their disillusionment with the Church and with me concerning these horrific events. I was singled out in the media as someone particularly to blame. This was very painful. As time passed, I wondered how I could ever help others, or even myself, find the strength needed.

As I emptied my heart to Christ in prayer before the Blessed Sacrament, I became more aware that he would lead the faithful and me through this. I felt comforted and strengthened by his Eucharistic presence. The Eucharist reminds me of how suffering is transformed by love. Christ was made perfect through his suffering on the cross. Like the grain of wheat, Jesus died so that we might be nourished and live in his love. Through the love I experienced in the Eucharist, I knew he was helping me die to self and live for others.

I know that I would not have been able to keep moving forward in my life and ministry without personally knowing his love for me and for everyone. Praying to Christ present in the Blessed Sacrament, especially during these difficult times, has drawn me closer to him. His Eucharistic presence has given me strength.

Through the cross of these days, I have tasted the humility of our crucified Lord and his compassionate love for his people. Coming to believe more fully in His presence in the Eucharist and in other people, whether faithful friends or constant critics, has truly become a joy for me. It has been a time of great suffering for many, and for me, but I have found it also to be a unique time of grace.

—John B. McCormack, "The Eucharist Strengthens
Us in Difficult Times," 63–64

Lord Jesus, teach me to turn to you in my holy hours of suffering and abandonment, in those hours when I am drained of strength.

> If I, therefore, the master and teacher, have washed your feet, you ought to wash one another's feet. (John 13:14)

"Without priests who are able to call upon the laity to play their role in the Church and in the world, and who can assist in the laity's formation for the apostolate, supporting them in their difficult vocation, an essential witness in the life of the Church would be lacking." With these words a highly regarded and expert representative of the laity commented on [the need for priests]. Nor was this a solitary voice. The same need is felt by the People of God both in the countries where Christianity and the Church have existed for many centuries and in the mission countries where the Church and Christianity are beginning to take root. Although in the first years after the Council a certain disorientation was felt in this area, both by the laity and by pastors of souls, nowadays the need for priests has become obvious and urgent for everyone.

Also implicit in this entire issue is the need for a careful re-reading of the Council's teaching concerning the relationship between the "Priesthood and the faithful," which results from their basic insertion through Baptism into the reality of the priestly mission of Christ, and the "ministerial Priesthood," shared in different degrees by bishops, priests and deacons. This relationship corresponds to the structure of the Church as a community. The Priesthood is not an institution that exists "alongside" the laity, or "above" it. The Priesthood of bishops and priests, as well as the ministry of deacons, is "for" the laity, and precisely for this reason it possesses a "ministerial" character, that is to say one "of service." Moreover, it highlights the "baptismal Priesthood," the Priesthood common to all the faithful.

—Saint John Paul II, Letter to Priests for
Holy Thursday, 1990

How might my collaboration with the laity be strengthened? What about my openness to their concerns, suggestions, and insights?

July 4   Craftsman of Universal Reconciliation

God looked at everything he had made, and found it very good. (Gen 1:31)

In the Church he [the priest] is responsible for the universal reconciliation of creation. It does not happen immediately or without effort, but progressively, commencing with the lowliest realities. One has only to open this wonderful book [The Ritual, the official collection of sacramental rites and blessings] to be convinced. Nothing else in the Church shows more plainly her touching and maternal love for the passing companions of our earthly journey. The liturgy forgets nothing. It blesses houses, bread, eggs, fruits. It thinks of fountains, ships, stables, fields, sick animals, it remembers bees, wax, working tools. It hallows water, light, fire, and incense. Everything is greeted with sympathy, even tenderness. The latest discoveries do not surprise it: machinery, railways, cars, planes, telegraph, seismograph, and now television. It includes everything, admits everything, hallows everything, both for man's good use, and also, as related to his eternal end for which these mysterious elements serve (as the Liturgy emphasizes), by way of symbolism.

Like the Church, the priest rejects nothing in the temporal order. Known as a man who rejects the world, and rightly so in a certain sense, he is also the man who accepts and welcomes it. He is accused of withdrawal, yet he remains minister of universal integration. Thanks to him, "all is good that God has made; nothing is to be rejected; only we must be thankful to Him when we partake of it, then it is hallowed for our use by God's blessing and the prayer which brings it" (1 Tim 4, 4-5). . . .

The Church has composed this blessing as a wonderful indication of her great magnanimity and of her complete confidence in the grace of Christ the King, the blessing *ad omnia*: "O God, whose word hallows all things, pour forth on these creatures Thy Blessing . . . through Christ Our Lord."

—Emmanuel-Célestin Cardinal Suhard,
The Church Today, 301–2

Christ Jesus, through you all things were made. Give to me a deepening reverence for all of your creation, and a gracious humility for all that it reveals to me.

> Rejoice always. Pray without ceasing. In all circumstances give thanks, for this is the will of God for you in Christ Jesus. (1 Thess 5:16-18)

As sharers in the Priesthood of Christ, which is inseparably connected with his sacrifice, we too must place at the foundation of our priestly existence the cornerstone of prayer. It will enable us to harmonize our lives with our priestly service, preserving intact the identity and authenticity of this vocation which has become our special inheritance in the Church as the community of the People of God.

Priestly prayer, in particular that of the Liturgy of the Hours and of Eucharistic Adoration, will help us first of all to preserve the profound awareness that, as "servants of Christ," we are in a special and exceptional way "stewards of the mysteries of God." Whatever our actual task may be, whatever the type of work by which we carry out our pastoral service, prayer will ensure our awareness of those divine mysteries of which we are "stewards," and will cause that awareness to express itself in everything that we do. In this way too we shall be for people a clear sign of Christ and his Gospel.

Dear brothers! We need prayer, profound and in a sense "organic" prayer, in order to be able to be such a sign. "By this all men will know that you are my disciples, if you have love for one another." Yes! In a word, this is a question of love, love "for others"; in fact "to be," as priests, "stewards of the mysteries of God" means to place oneself at the disposal of others, and in this way to bear witness to that supreme love which is in Christ, that love which is God himself.

—Saint John Paul II, Letter to Priests for
Holy Thursday, 1987

I review my priestly life of prayer, observing both the quantity and quality of the time I spend with Christ.

The earth is the LORD's and all it holds, / the world and those who dwell in it. (Ps 24:1)

At the Offertory . . . we see all humanity on the paten and in the chalice. As Our Lord obtained the first elements of His own human Body from a woman, so for the Eucharist He takes bread and wine from the earth. The bread and wine are thus representative of mankind. Two of the substances that have most widely nourished man are bread and wine. Bread has been called the marrow of the earth; wine, its very blood. In giving what has traditionally made our flesh and blood, we are equivalently offering all mankind on the paten and in the chalice.

The people no longer bring bread and wine, as they did in the early Church, but their contributions to the Offertory collection permit the purchase of the bread and wine. There would be less resistance to the collection basket if we made more effort to present it as a symbol of the incorporation of the entire congregation into the Sacrifice of the Mass. Similarly, we could simultaneously edify and win the Lord's blessing if we ourselves gave generously to every collection to which we ask the people to contribute. Why should we be exempt from a sacrifice for the Propagation of the Faith on Mission Sunday? "Be as generous as possible" is idle talk if the generosity of the pastor has not preceded the generosity of his flock.

. . . At the Offertory we gather up the whole world into the narrow compass of a plate and a cup. Every drop of sweat, every day of labor; the decisions of the economist, the financier, the draftsman and the engineer; every exertion and invention that went into the preparation of the elements of the Offertory is symbolically redeemed, justified and sanctified by our act. We bring not only redeemed man, but unredeemed creation, to the steps of Calvary and the threshold of Redemption.

—Fulton J. Sheen, *The Priest Is Not His Own*, 42

Deliver me, Lord, from all that prevents me from recognizing the cosmic nature of the Eucharist. As all the world is placed upon the altar, expand my heart in a humble embrace of all that you have created.

Simply "God's Man"   July 7

The LORD has sought out a man after his own heart . . . (1 Sam 13:14)

Since according to Scripture and Tradition the priest is a representative, deputy and outward form of Jesus Christ, and since his office is founded on a special mission from the Lord of the Church, this office-bearer must also set his course towards Jesus Christ and take him as a standard. Christ is the prototype of all priesthood.

. . . When asked, "What exactly are you? What exactly is your work?" the priest would like to be able to point to something socially plausible, something accepted and relevant. He would like people to realize that the priesthood of the Church is something of the greatest importance for mankind. But the priest of today may perhaps have to accept that his calling no longer holds, as once it did, a definite, recognizable and generally accepted place in our society, and a corresponding social prestige. Did Jesus then have a definite, recognizable and generally accepted position? Did his mission not involve his being homeless, his not receiving universal recognition, but instead meeting with opposition and not fitting in with the social structure of the time (cf. Mt 8:20)?

If Jesus Christ is the standard and prototype of priestly office, it is necessary to inquire into the central feature of his life and mission. He was the "Man for others"—an expression of Dietrich Bonhoeffer which is often and rightly used today. He was totally the "man for others" surrendering himself in the service of his brethren. But this he was in such a way that he was simply "God's man"—to use a biblical expression. He was there for men, because he was there for God, and obediently accepted his mission from God to save mankind.

—Gisbert Greshake, *The Meaning of Christian Priesthood*, 105–6

In what ways am I "God's man," "a man after his own heart"?

> [The Eleven] went forth and preached everywhere, while the Lord worked with them and confirmed the word through accompanying signs. (Mark 16:20)

My brothers, I am confident that you will find much joy and fulfillment in your priestly ministry. I certainly have. But I also know that there will be moments when things will not be so joyful or fulfilling. You can count on it.

There will be times when, perhaps due to the stress of ministry or the challenge of celibacy, or some other personal difficulty, you will ask yourself, "Why in the world did I ever become a priest?" Let me assure you, those kinds of questions are normal, even healthy. I can assure you that I have had to face the questions and challenges many times during the nearly four decades I have been a priest and bishop. Talk to any married couple, and they will assure you that they sometimes ask themselves similar questions.

It is precisely during those difficult times that you will need to rely on your commitment to carry you through. You will be able to do this because commitment is a two-way street; there is an element of mutuality in it. Not only do you make a commitment to give your life to the risen Lord by serving his people as a priest, but Christ affirms what you do, and makes a commitment to give his life to you through his body, the Church. Through his Church, in which both his word and sacrament are celebrated, he will offer you the sustenance and strength you need.

To put it another way: the Church lays claim on you in the commitment you make today. But you also lay claim on the Church in order to receive the support and nourishment you will need to exercise your ministry effectively.

—Joseph Cardinal Bernardin, Homily for
Priesthood Ordination, May 18, 1991

Lord Jesus, help me recognize the blessing of your support, generously shown to me through the love and care of your people.

"Brothers, We Are Debtors!"

> It was not you who chose me, but I who chose you and appointed you
> to go and bear fruit that will remain . . . (John 15:16)

Besides all those whom we know and whom we can personally identify along the road of our own vocation, there are still others who remain
unknown. We are never able to say with certainty to whom we owe this
grace, to whose prayers and sacrifices we are indebted, in the mystery of
the divine plan.

In any case, the words "a priest chosen from among men" have a broad
application. If we meditate today on the birth of Christ's Priesthood, first
of all in our own hearts (even before we received it through the imposition
of hands by the bishop), we must live this day as debtors. Yes, brothers, we
are debtors! It is as debtors to God's inscrutable grace that we are born to
the Priesthood, both from the heart of the Redeemer himself in the midst of
his sacrifice and from the womb of the Church, the priestly people. For this
people are, as it were, the spiritual seedbed of vocations. The earth tilled
by the Holy Spirit, who is the Church's Paraclete for all time.

The people of God rejoices in the priestly vocation of its sons. In this
vocation it finds the confirmation of its own vitality in the Holy Spirit, the
confirmation of the royal Priesthood, by means of which Christ, the "high
priest of the good things that have come," is present in every generation of
individuals and in Christian communities. He too was "chosen from among
men." He is "the Son of Man," the son of Mary.

—Saint John Paul II, Letter to Priests for
Holy Thursday, 1989

Lord Jesus, bless me with the daily consciousness of your personal call to
priesthood, your infinitely beautiful gift for which I am certainly not worthy.

July 10 Heralds of Hope, Reconciliation, and Peace

[God] chose us in [Christ], before the foundation of the world, to be holy and without blemish before him. (Eph 1:4)

Dear brother priests, the celebration of the 150th anniversary of the death of St. John Mary Vianney (1859) follows upon the celebration of the 150th anniversary of the apparitions of Lourdes (1858). In 1959 Blessed Pope John XXIII noted that "shortly before the Curé of Ars completed his long and admirable life, the Immaculate Virgin appeared in another part of France to an innocent and humble girl, and entrusted to her a message of prayer and penance which continues, even a century later, to yield immense spiritual fruits. The life of this holy priest whose centenary we are commemorating in a real way anticipated the great supernatural truths taught to the seer of Massabielle. He was greatly devoted to the Immaculate Conception of the Blessed Virgin; in 1836 he had dedicated his parish church to Our Lady Conceived without Sin and he greeted the dogmatic definition of this truth in 1854 with deep faith and great joy." The Curé would always remind his faithful that "after giving us all he could, Jesus Christ wishes in addition to bequeath us His most precious possession, His Blessed Mother."

To the Most Holy Virgin I entrust this Year for Priests. I ask her to awaken in the heart of every priest a generous and renewed commitment to the ideal of complete self-oblation to Christ and the Church which inspired the thoughts and actions of the saintly Curé of Ars. It was his fervent prayer life and his impassioned love of Christ Crucified that enabled John Mary Vianney to grow daily in his total self-oblation to God and the Church. May his example lead all priests to offer that witness of unity with their bishop, with one another and with the lay faithful, which today, as ever, is so necessary.

—Pope Benedict XVI, Letter Proclaiming
a Year for Priests, July 16, 2009

Lord Jesus, I beg the grace of daily, ongoing conversion of life, so that I might more radiantly reveal your love to the world.

I will sing of your mercy forever, LORD / proclaim your faithfulness through all ages. (Ps 89:2)

Our vocation is precisely this. In this consists the specific nature, the originality of the priestly vocation. It is in a special way rooted in the mission of Christ Himself, Christ the Messiah. "The Spirit of the Lord God is upon me, because the Lord has anointed me to bring good news to the afflicted; he has sent me to bind up the brokenhearted, to proclaim liberty to the captives, and the opening of the prison to those who are bound . . . to comfort all who mourn."

In the very heart of this messianic mission of Christ the Priest is rooted our vocation and mission too: the vocation and mission of the priests of the new and eternal Covenant. It is the vocation and mission of the proclaimers of the Good News; of those who must bind up the wounds of human hearts; of those who must proclaim liberation in the midst of all the many afflictions, in the midst of the evil that in so many ways "holds" man prisoner; of those who must console.

This is our vocation and mission as servants. Our vocation, dear brothers, includes a great and fundamental service to be offered to every human being! Nobody can take our place. With the Sacrament of the new and eternal Covenant we must go to the very roots of human existence on earth. Day by day, we must bring into that existence the dimension of the Redemption and the Eucharist. We must strengthen awareness of divine filiation through grace. And what higher prospect, what finer destiny could there be for man than this?

—Saint John Paul II, Homily for Priests at
the Jubilee of Redemption, April 24, 1984

Lord Jesus, grace me with a daily awareness of your deep desire to live your life of reconciling love and peace.

> But you, be self-possessed in all circumstances; put up with hardship;
> perform the work of an evangelist; fulfill your ministry. (2 Tim 4:5)

Today my heart is full of a sense of joyful contentment and at the
same time full of shame. I have received from God so many ordinary and
special graces during these ten years! In the sacraments, received and
administered, and in the many and varied duties of my ministry, in words
and works, in public and in private, in prayer, in study, amidst the little
difficulties and disappointments, successes and failures—my experience
growing richer and stronger every day, in my contacts with my Superiors,
with the clergy and with people of all ages and all social conditions. The
Lord has indeed been faithful to the promise made me on the day of my
ordination in Rome, in the Church of Santa Maria in Monte Santo, when
he said to me: "No longer do I call you a servant, . . . but a friend." Jesus
has been a real friend to me, allowing me to share in all the sacred intima-
cies of his Heart. When I think of all that he knows about me and has seen
in me, I should be lacking in sincerity if I did not admit to feeling a great
satisfaction in my soul. In the field which I sowed, and in which I have
worked, there are in fact a few ears of corn, enough perhaps to make up a
small sheaf. I bless you, Lord, for this, because it is all due to your love.

But for my own part, I can only feel ashamed that I have not done more,
that I have reaped so little. I have been like barren waste ground. With all
the grace I have received, or even with much less, so many others would
already be holy. I have had so many good impulses which have not yet
borne fruit. My Lord, I acknowledge my failings, my total worthlessness;
be generous in forgiveness and mercy.

—Saint John XXIII, *Journal of a Soul*, 248–49

Can I rejoice in all that God has done through my ministry, and yet feel the
call to even greater service?

So we are ambassadors for Christ, as if God were appealing through us. We implore you on behalf of Christ, be reconciled to God. (2 Cor 5:20)

For our own part, we have rediscovered, better than during the last century, the community aspect of penance, preparation for forgiveness and thanksgiving after forgiveness. But sacramental forgiveness will always require a personal encounter with the crucified Christ through the mediation of his minister. Unfortunately it is often the case that penitents do not fervently hasten to the confessional, as in the time of the Curé of Ars. Now, just when a great number seem to stay away from confession completely, for various reasons, it is a sign of the urgent need to develop a whole pastoral strategy of the Sacrament of Reconciliation. This will be done by constantly reminding Christians of the need to have a real relationship with God, to have a sense of sin when one is closed to God and to others, the need to be converted and through the Church to receive forgiveness as a free gift of God. They also need to be reminded of the conditions that enable the sacrament to be celebrated well, and in this regard to overcome prejudices, baseless fears and routine. Such a situation at the same time requires that we ourselves should remain very available for this ministry of forgiveness, ready to devote to it the necessary time and care, and I would even say giving it priority over other activities. The faithful will then realize the value that we attach to it, as did the Curé of Ars.

—Saint John Paul II, Letter to Priests for
Holy Thursday, 1986

When I preach about the sacrament of penance, in what ways do I share my own love for the sacrament, and its meaning in my own spiritual life?

> You are lacking in one thing. Go, sell what you have, and give to [the] poor
> and you will have treasure in heaven; then come, follow me. (Mark 10:21)

There is a triple motive for the poverty of the disciples: In the preacher who is poor, needy, and unpretentious, the claim of the message itself can appear unadulterated and without distortion. . . . St. Paul says that many who are preaching Christ are motivated by self-interest. Although such preaching is not without value, it runs contrary to sincerity and grieves the Apostle. On the contrary, Paul's glory is to have accepted nothing from anyone. . . . The poverty of the preacher helps the unhindered exposition of the Gospel, and his own credibility.

In the poverty of the disciple and the Apostle, the content of their message comes visibly to the hearers. Their poverty is like a "sacrament" which makes it possible to see the Gospel and the one who has been influenced by it. Not with words alone, but through his life, the Apostle must proclaim the central point of the "glad news," that the kingdom of God is approaching and the structure of this world is passing away, that the crucified Lord is the risen Lord, that death means life and true life cannot be won without dying. . . . The message of cross and resurrection become visible in the poverty of the Apostle.

A third motive for a lifestyle of poverty can be found in the New Testament. The poverty demanded in the Gospel, as the incident of the rich young man particularly shows (Mk 10: 17ff), is a prerequisite for the following of Jesus, and simultaneously a matter of giving one's wealth to the poor in order to follow him. . . . J.B. Metz remarks: "Poverty as a protest against the dictatorship of ownership and possession, of downright self-assertion . . . drives one into actual solidarity with those of the poor for whom poverty is not a virtue but their situation in life, and an unreasonable social imposition."

—Gisbert Greshake, *The Meaning of*
the Priesthood, 139–40

In what ways does my simplicity of life witness to the Gospel?

> For this we toil and struggle, because we have set our hope on the living God, who is the savior of all, especially of those who believe. (1 Tim 4:10)

Our pastoral activity demands that we should be close to people and all their problems, whether these problems be personal, family or social ones, but it also demands that we should be close to all these problems "in a priestly way." Only then, in the sphere of all those problems, do we remain ourselves. Therefore if we are really of assistance in those human problems, and they are sometimes very difficult ones, then we keep our identity and are really faithful to our vocation. With great perspicacity we must seek, together with all men, truth and justice, the true and definitive dimension of which we can only find in the Gospel, or rather in Christ Himself.

Our task is to serve *truth and justice* in the dimensions of human "temporality," but *always in a perspective that is the perspective of eternal salvation.* This salvation takes into account the temporal achievements of the human spirit in the spheres of knowledge and morality, as the Second Vatican Council wonderfully recalled; but it is not identical with them, and in fact it goes higher than them: "The things that no eye has seen and no ear has heard . . . all that God has prepared for those who love him." Our brethren in the faith, and unbelievers too, expect us always to be able to show them this perspective, to become real witnesses to it, to be dispensers of grace, to be servants of the word of God. They expect us to be men of prayer.

—Saint John Paul II, Letter to Priests for
Holy Thursday, 1979

I find so much more peace in my life when I keep my ministry in proper perspective.

July 16   Placing Our Celibacy Within Mary's Heart

[S]ome . . . have renounced marriage for the sake of the kingdom of heaven. (Matt 19:12)

The analogy between the Church and the Virgin Mother has a special eloquence for us, who link our priestly vocation to celibacy, that is, to "making ourselves eunuchs for the sake of the kingdom of heaven." We recall the conversation with the apostles, in which Christ explained to them the meaning of this choice and we seek to understand the reasons fully. We freely renounce marriage and establishing our own family, in order to be better able to serve God and neighbor. It can be said that we renounce fatherhood "according to the flesh," in order that there may grow and develop in us fatherhood "according to the Spirit," which, as has already been said, possesses at the same time maternal characteristics. Virginal fidelity to the Spouse, which finds its own particular expression in this form of life, enables us to share in the intimate life of the Church, which, following the example of the Virgin, seeks to keep "whole and pure the fidelity she has pledged to her Spouse."

By reason of this model—of the prototype which the Church finds in Mary—it is necessary that our priestly choice of celibacy for the whole of our lives should also be placed within her heart. We must have recourse to this Virgin Mother when we meet difficulties along our chosen path. With her help we must seek always a more profound understanding of this path, an ever more complete affirmation of it in our hearts. Finally, in fact, there must be developed in our life this fatherhood "according to the Spirit," which is one of the results of "making ourselves eunuchs for the sake of the kingdom of God."

—Saint John Paul II, Letter to Priests for
Holy Thursday, 1988

In the challenges of celibate life, I am called to turn to the Virgin Mother, who accompanies me along this chosen path.

A Prayer for All Priests July 17

> Since you have purified yourselves by obedience to the truth for sincere mutual love, love one another intensely from a [pure] heart. (1 Pet 1:22)

On this priestly Thursday I ask the Lord Jesus to preserve the joy sparkling in the eyes of the recently ordained who go forth to devour the world, to spend themselves fully in the midst of God's faithful people, rejoicing as they prepare their first homily, their first Mass, their first Baptism, their first confession . . . It is the joy of being able to share with wonder, and for the first time as God's anointed, the treasure of the Gospel and to feel the faithful people anointing you again and in yet another way: by their requests, by bowing their heads for your blessing, by taking your hands, by bringing you their children, by pleading for their sick . . . Preserve, Lord, in your young priests the joy of going forth, of doing everything as if for the first time, the joy of spending their lives fully for you.

On this priestly Thursday I ask the Lord Jesus to confirm the priestly joy of those who have already ministered for some years. The joy which, without leaving their eyes, is also found on the shoulders of those who bear the burden of the ministry, those priests who, having experienced the labours of the apostolate, gather their strength and rearm themselves: "get a second wind", as the athletes say. Lord, preserve the depth, wisdom and maturity of the joy felt by these older priests. May they be able to pray with Nehemiah: "the joy of the Lord is my strength" (cf. Neh 8:10).

Finally, on this priestly Thursday I ask the Lord Jesus to make better known the joy of elderly priests, whether healthy or infirm. It is the joy of the Cross, which springs from the knowledge that we possess an imperishable treasure in perishable earthen vessels. May these priests find happiness wherever they are; may they experience already, in the passage of the years, a taste of eternity (Guardini). May they know the joy of handing on the torch, the joy of seeing new generations of their spiritual children, and of hailing the promises from afar, smiling and at peace, in that hope which does not disappoint.

—Pope Francis, Homily for the Chrism Mass,
April 17, 2014

I reflect on the many priests whom I have known in my life, praying first for the deceased, that they might know Christ's lasting joy. I also pray for the living, that their lives may radiate the priestly joy so evident in the life of Pope Francis.

> Be like a father to orphans, / and take the place of a husband to widows. / Then God will call you his child, / and he will be merciful to you and deliver you from the pit. (Sir 4:10)

The priest is configured to Christ and filled with his grace to overflowing. It makes of him more than he could ever hope to be in his natural condition. He has, after all, given himself away entirely. He has given up family, home, possessions, worldly power, not out of denial but out of superabundance. There is no room for such things! In this he imitates Christ. As Josef Ratzinger puts it in another context, "[E]xcess is . . . the real foundation and form of the history of salvation, which in the last analysis is nothing other than the truly breathtaking fact that God, in an incredible outpouring of himself, expends not only a universe but his own self in order to lead man, a speck of dust, to salvation. So excess or superfluity . . . is the real definition or mark of the history of salvation" (*Introduction to Christianity*, 197).

The priest's life is one of excess, of generosity. It is generosity, not stinginess, that is the cause of celibacy. We can again see an analogy in marriage. It is not that a married man gives up other women; rather, it is that his whole being is so filled with his beloved that there is no room for other women. It is not that a priest has given up a wife and family; rather, it is that his whole being is so filled with, so configured to Christ that there is no room for anything else. And in surrendering himself to Christ he finds that he, as his Lord, has surrendered himself to everyone he encounters.

—John M. Haas, "The Sacral Character of the Priest as the
Foundation for his Moral Life and Teaching," 137

Lord Jesus, fill me with the same compassion that brimmed in your heart. May I generously serve you in each and every person I meet.

Our Marys and Marthas

> As they continued their journey he entered a village where a woman whose name was Martha welcomed him. She had a sister named Mary [who] sat beside the Lord at his feet listening to him speak. (Luke 10:38-39)

In order to live as a celibate in a mature and untroubled way it seems particularly important that the priest should develop deep within himself *the image of women as sisters*. In Christ, men and women are brothers and sisters, independently of any bonds of family relationship. This is a universal bond, thanks to which the priest can be open to every new situation, even the most foreign from an ethnic or cultural standpoint . . .

Certainly "woman as sister" represents a *specific manifestation of the spiritual beauty of women*; but it is at the same time a revelation that they are in a certain sense "set apart." If the priest, with the help of divine grace and under the special protection of Mary, Virgin and Mother, gradually develops such an attitude towards women, he will see his ministry met by *a sense of great trust* precisely on the part of women whom he regards, in the variety of their ages and life situations, as sisters and mothers.

The figure of woman as sister has considerable importance in our Christian civilization, in which countless women have become *sisters to everyone*, thanks to their exemplary attitude towards their neighbor, especially to those most in need. *A "sister" is a guarantee of selflessness:* in the school, in the hospital, in prison and in other areas of social service. . . . This selfless gift of femininity "as sister" lights up human existence, evokes the best sentiments of which human beings are capable and always leaves behind gratitude for the good freely offered.

—Saint John Paul II, Letter to Priests for
Holy Thursday, 1995

Jesus, my Brother, I pray for the grace to recognize the dignity of every woman, that I might see in each one my sister or mother or friend.

I came so that they might have life and have it more abundantly.
(John 10:10)

Like Christ Himself, His minister is wholly and solely intent on the things of God and the Church, and he imitates the great High Priest who lives ever in the presence of God in order to intercede in our favor. So he receives joy and encouragement unceasingly from the attentive and devout recitation of the Divine Office, by which he dedicates his voice to the Church who prays together with her Spouse, and he recognizes the necessity of continuing his diligence at prayer, which is the profoundly priestly occupation.

The rest of a priest's life also acquires a greater richness of meaning and sanctifying power. In fact, his individual efforts at his own sanctification find new incentives in the ministry of grace and in the ministry of the Eucharist, in which "the whole spiritual good of the Church is contained": acting in the person of Christ, the priest unites himself most intimately with the offering, and places on the altar his entire life, which bears the marks of the holocaust.

. . . Christ spoke of Himself when He said: "Unless a grain of wheat falls into the earth and dies, it remains alone; but if it dies, it bears much fruit." And the Apostle Paul did not hesitate to expose himself to a daily death in order to obtain among his faithful glory in Christ Jesus. In a similar way, by a daily dying to himself and by giving up the legitimate love of a family of his own for the love of Christ and of His kingdom, the priest will find the glory of an exceedingly rich and fruitful life in Christ, because like Him and in Him, he loves and dedicates himself to all the children of God.

—Blessed Pope Paul VI,
Sacerdotalis Caelibatus, 28–30

What has been the effect in my life of consciously placing my whole life upon the altar?

But I say to you, everyone who looks at a woman with lust has already committed adultery with her in his heart. (Matt 5:28)

The vocation to celibacy needs to be consciously protected by keeping special watch over one's feelings and over one's whole conduct. In particular, it must be protected by those priests who, following the discipline in force in the Western Church and so highly esteemed by the Eastern Church, have chosen celibacy for the sake of the Kingdom of God. If in a relationship with a woman the gift and the choice of celibacy should become endangered, the priest cannot but strive earnestly to remain faithful to his own vocation. Such a defense would not mean that marriage in itself is something bad, but that for him the path is a different one.

The Lord's prayer: "And lead us not into temptation, but deliver us from evil," takes on a specific meaning in the context *of contemporary civilization*, steeped as it is in elements of hedonism, self-centeredness and sensuality. Pornography is rampant, debasing the dignity of women and treating them exclusively as objects of sexual pleasure. *These aspects of present-day civilization certainly favor neither marital fidelity nor celibacy for the sake of the Kingdom of God.* Therefore if the priest does not foster in himself genuine dispositions of faith, hope and love of God, he can easily yield to the allurements of the world. On this Holy Thursday then, dear Brother Priests, how can I fail to *exhort you to remain faithful to the gift of celibacy* which Christ has given us? In it is contained a spiritual treasure which belongs to each of us and to the whole Church.

—Saint John Paul II, Letter to Priests for
Holy Thursday, 1995

Lord Jesus, give me the grace to see that celibacy is a most Christ-like way to show my love to others. Deliver me from the selfishness of lust.

> [We are] always carrying about in the body the dying of Jesus, so that
> the life of Jesus may also be manifested in our body. (2 Cor 4:10)

O Jesus, you want to continue Your sufferings in me for my own salvation and that of the whole world, and for the glory of your Father. By my sufferings and agony, You want to fill up what is wanting in Your sufferings for your Body, which is the Church. And so I shall receive in my life again and again a share in your agony in the Garden of Olives, a very small share, but nevertheless a real one. My "holy hours," those hours when I honor Your agony in the Garden of Olives, will be made in the truest sense not during the peaceful hours of pious devotions in church. My real "holy hours" are those hours when sufferings of body and soul come to overwhelm me. Those hours when God hands me the chalice of suffering. Those hours when I weep for my sins. Those hours when I call out to Your Father, O Jesus, and do not seem to be heard. Those hours when faith is agonizingly difficult, hope seems to be giving way to despair, and love seems to have died in my heart. They are the real "holy hours" in my life, those hours when Your grace working in my heart draws me mysteriously into Your agony in the garden. When those hours come upon me, O Lord, have mercy on me.

Give me the grace to say "yes," "yes" to even the most bitter hours, "yes" to everything, for everything that happens in those hours, even what results from my own guilt, is the will of Him Who is eternal love. May He be blessed forever.

—Karl Rahner, *Watch and Pray with Me*, 28–29

What have been the holiest hours of my priestly life?

What is man that you are mindful of him, / and a son of man that you care for him? / Yet you have made him little less than a god, / crowned him with glory and honor. (Ps 8:5-6)

A number of factors seem to be working toward making people today more deeply aware of the dignity of the human person and more open to religious values, to the Gospel and to the priestly ministry.

Despite many contradictions, society is increasingly witnessing a powerful thirst for justice and peace; a more lively sense that humanity must care for creation and respect nature; a more open search for truth; a greater effort to safeguard human dignity; a growing commitment in many sectors of the world population to a more specific international solidarity and a new ordering of the world in freedom and justice. Parallel to the continued development of the potential offered by science and technology and the exchange of information and interaction of cultures, there is a new call for ethics, that is, a quest for meaning—and therefore for an objective standard of values which will delineate the possibilities and limits of progress.

In the more specifically religious and Christian sphere, ideological prejudice and the violent rejection of the message of spiritual and religious values are crumbling and there are arising new and unexpected possibilities of evangelization and the rebirth of ecclesial life in many parts of the world. These are evident in an increased love of the sacred Scriptures; in the vitality and growing vigor of many young churches and their ever-larger role in the defense and promotion of the values of human life and the person.

—Saint John Paul II, *Pastores Dabo Vobis*, 6

Lord Jesus, bless all priests with the grace to give positive witness to the goodness and hope that are ever present in our world. May the world see us as men of courage and compassion.

Whoever wishes to come after me must deny himself, take up his cross, and follow me. (Mark 8:34)

Clerics should participate in the fulfillment of Christianity. This cannot exist without patience. Patience is a sign that the soul is intimately united to God and that it is rooted in perfection. For it must be very much in God and fully possessed by him in order to bear difficulties and torments with peace, tranquility, and even joy and beatitude in one's heart.

Priests and pastors should have a very high degree of patience because, in Jesus Christ and with Jesus Christ, they are both priests and victims for the sins of the world. Jesus Christ the priest wished to be the victim of his sacrifice. He became the host-victim for all people. Since priests are like sacraments and representations of him who lives in them to continue his priesthood and whom he clothes with his external conduct and his interior dispositions, as well as with his power and his person, he wishes furthermore that they be interiorly rooted in the spirit and dispositions of the host-victim in order to suffer, endure, do penance, in short, to immolate themselves for the glory of God and the salvation of the people.

In imitation of our Lord, priests should not only be victims for sin through persecution, penance, internal and external sufferings, but also they should be like the victims of a holocaust. This is their true vocation. For they should not merely suffer, as he did, all sorts of difficulties both for their own sins and the sins of the people entrusted to them, but even more they should be entirely consumed with him through love.

—Jean-Jacques Olier, "Introduction to
the Christian Life and Virtues"

With what spirit do I accept the crosses that are part of my priestly life?

> I pray for them. I do not pray for the world but for the ones you have given me, because they are yours . . . (John 17:9)

The Book of Genesis speaks of the divine creative act in the context of the vocation to marriage: "Therefore a man leaves his father and his mother and cleaves to his wife" (Gen 2:24). The vocation to marriage obviously assumes and requires that the environment in which one lives is made up of both men and women.

In this setting however there arise not only vocations to marriage but also *vocations to the priesthood and the consecrated life.* These do not develop in isolation. Every candidate for the priesthood, . . . has the experience of his own family and of school, where he was able to meet many young people . . . of both sexes. In order to live as a celibate in a mature and untroubled way it seems particularly important that the priest should develop deep within himself *the image of women as sisters . . .*

Our thoughts and prayers turn in a special way to *our brothers in the priesthood who meet with difficulties in this area,* and to all those who precisely because of a woman *have abandoned the priestly ministry.* Let us commend to Mary Most Holy, Mother of Priests, and to the intercession of the countless holy priests in the Church's history the difficult time which they are experiencing, and let us implore for them *the grace of a return to their first fervour* (cf. Rev 2:4-5). The experience of my own ministry confirms that such returns do occur and that even today they are not rare. God remains faithful to his covenant with man in the Sacrament of Holy Orders.

—Saint John Paul II, Letter to Priests for
Holy Thursday, 1995

Lord Jesus, bless those who have left the active priestly ministry. I pray particularly for . . .

> [God] saved us and called us to a holy life, not according to our works but according to his own design and the grace bestowed on us in Christ Jesus before time began, but now made manifest through the appearance of our savior Christ Jesus . . . (2 Tim 1:9-10)

The priest, as steward of the "mysteries of God," is at the service of the common priesthood of the faithful. By proclaiming the word and celebrating the sacraments, especially the Eucharist, he makes the whole People of God ever more aware of its share in Christ's priesthood, and at the same time encourages it to live that priesthood to the full. When, after the consecration, he says the words *Mysterium fidei*, all are invited to ponder the rich existential meaning of this proclamation, which refers to the mystery of Christ, the Eucharist, and the priesthood.

Is this not the deepest reason behind the priestly vocation? Certainly it is already fully present at the time of ordination, but it needs to be interiorized and deepened for the rest of the priest's life. Only in this way can a priest discover in depth the great treasure which has been entrusted to him. Fifty years after my ordination, I can say that in the words *Mysterium fidei* we find ever more each day the meaning of our own priesthood. Here is the measure of the gift which is the priesthood, and here is also the measure of the response which this gift demands. *The gift is constantly growing!* And this is something wonderful. It is wonderful that a man can never say that he has fully responded to the gift. It remains both a gift and a task: always! To be conscious of this is essential if we are to live our own priesthood to the full.

—Saint John Paul II, *Gift and Mystery*, 78–79

Lord Jesus, pour out your priestly spirit upon me, so that I can understand my ministry as both gift and task, always grateful yet probing its greater mystery.

Do not fear, for I have redeemed you; / I have called you by name: you are mine. (Isa 43:1)

Priestly ordination not only confers a new mission in the Church, a ministry, but a new "consecration" of a person, one linked to the character imprinted by the sacrament of Orders as a spiritual, indelible sign of a special belonging to Christ in being, and consequently, in acting. The perfection required of the presbyter is thus commensurate with his sharing in the priesthood of Christ as the author of redemption: the minister cannot be exempted from reproducing in himself the sentiments, inner tendencies and intentions, the spirit of sacrifice to the Father and of service to the brethren that is proper to Christ himself.

The priest has a sort of mastery of grace, which allows him to enjoy union with Christ and at the same time to be devoted to the pastoral service of his brothers and sisters. As the Council says, since the priest "in his own way assumes the person of Christ he is endowed with a special grace. By this grace he, through his service of the people committed to his care and all the People of God, is able the better to pursue the perfection of Christ, whose place he takes. The human weakness of his flesh is remedied by the holiness of him who became for us a high priest 'holy, innocent and undefiled, separated from sinners.'" In this condition the priest is bound to a special *imitation of Christ the Priest*, which is the result of the special grace of Orders: the grace of *union with Christ the Priest and Victim*, and, by virtue of this same union, the grace of *good pastoral service to his brothers and sisters*.

—Saint John Paul II, General Audience, May 26, 1993

In what ways do I live with a daily consciousness of being consecrated to Christ?

July 28   Practicing the Two Great Commandments

[Jesus] said to him, "You shall love the Lord, your God, with all your heart, with all your soul, and with all your mind. . . . The second is like it: You shall love your neighbor as yourself." (Matt 22:37, 39)

Because you are priests, . . . all that you do, feel and think as you move through this changing life, is going to affect all the other souls whom you touch, and condition their relation with that unchanging Real. Through you, they may be attracted to or repelled by the spiritual life. You are held tight in that double relationship; to those changing other souls, and to that changeless God. What you are like, and what your relation to God is like; this must and will affect all those whom you visit, preach to, pray with, and to whom you give the sacraments. It will make the difference between Church services which are spiritual experiences to those attending them, and Church services which consist in the formal recitation of familiar words. We, the laity, know instantly the difference between the churches which are served with love and devotion and those which are not. And we know from this, what their ministers are like. And what you are like, is going to depend on your secret life of prayer; on the steady orientation of your souls to the Reality of God. Called upon to practice in their fullness the two great commandments, you can only hope to get the second one right, if you are completely controlled by the first. And that will depend on the quality of your secret inner life.

Now by the quality of our inner lives I do not mean something characterized by ferocious intensity and strain. I mean rather such a humble and genial devotedness as we find in the most loving of the saints. I mean the quality which makes contagious Christians; makes people catch the love of God from you.

—Evelyn Underhill, *Concerning the Inner Life*, 95–96

In what ways do others see me as humble, genial, devoted, and loving?

Christis: Our Model of Priestly Poverty

> I tell you truly, this poor widow put in more than all the rest; for those others have all made offerings from their surplus wealth, but she, from her poverty, has offered her whole livelihood. (Luke 21:3-4)

It is comforting to note that over the course of time and under the influence of ancient and modern saints, the clergy has acquired an increasing awareness of a call to Gospel poverty, both as a spirit and as a practice corresponding to the demands of priestly consecration.

. . . Gospel poverty entails no distain for earthly goods, which God has put at man's disposal for his life and his cooperation in the plan of creation. According to the Second Vatican Council, the presbyter, like every other Christian, having a mission of praise and thanksgiving, must acknowledge and glorify the generosity of the heavenly Father who is revealed in created goods.

Nevertheless, the Council goes on to say that priests, although living in the midst of the world, must always keep in mind that, as the Lord said, they do not belong to the world, and therefore, they must be freed from every disordered attachment in order to obtain "that spiritual insight through which is found a right attitude to the world and to earthly goods."

The spirit of poverty modeled by Jesus Christ, the High Priest, should inspire the priest's behavior, characterize his attitude, life and very image as a pastor and man of God. It is expressed in disinterest and detachment towards money, in renunciation of all greed for possessing earthly goods, in a simple lifestyle, in the choice of a modest dwelling accessible to all, in rejecting everything that appears to be luxurious, while striving to give himself more and more freely to the service of God and the faithful.

—Saint John Paul II, General Audience, July 21, 1993

Lord Jesus, give me the grace to cultivate an interior detachment from earthly goods and a generous openness to the needs of others.

> Jesus, looking at him, loved him and said to him, "You are lacking in one thing. Go, sell what you have, and give to [the] poor and you will have treasure in heaven; then come, follow me." (Mark 10:21)

The priest must be one who himself is a follower of Christ and is like him penetrated by the love of God: how else would he be able to invite others to follow, and how could he credibly communicate God's love? He must be one who himself has a radical hope and relies on God's new world: how else could he arouse in men a hope of the kingdom of God? Consequently, the priest not only has an official mission, but he is also personally called to make God's kingdom the centre of his life and to follow the way of Jesus with special earnestness, radically and visibly.

This unreserved commitment is a continual adventure, a journey into the unknown, something which strictly speaking demands "all or nothing." In his exposition of New Testament discipleship, D. Bonhoeffer has very clearly pointed to the temptation to turn discipleship into something entirely visible, commonsensical and easy to understand: Suppose the disciple makes himself available but reserves a right to set out his own conditions. Obviously at this point following ceases to be following, for when God's call comes to man, only an unreserved consent is possible. Certainly God does not extinguish the smoking flax, as the Scripture says: yet he is a consuming fire that wishes to take hold of everything. Consequently, what Kierkegaard says is true: "To seek close union with God in any other way than by being wounded is . . . impossible. . . . One who seeks union with God without total surrender does not achieve it. In relationship with God it is impossible to seek union to a certain extent only, since he is the very opposite of everything that is limited in degree."

—Gisbert Greshake, *The Meaning of*
Christian Priesthood, 114–15

Lord Jesus, give me the courage to pray for the grace of total surrender. Grant that I may seek union with God in no other way than by being wounded in his service.

Give Me, Lord, Your Very Heartbeat July 31

I will appoint for you shepherds after my own heart, / who will shepherd you wisely and prudently. (Jer 3:15)

Lord, . . . your goodness drew the multitudes; the sick and infirm felt instinctively that you would have pity on them; you so electrified the crowds that they forgot to eat; with a knowledge of everyday life you could offer parables that everyone understood, parables both vigorous and esthetic. Your friendship was for everyone, but you manifested a special love for some, like John, and a special friendship for some, like Lazarus, Martha and Mary. . . .

You were in constant contact with your Father in prayer and your formal prayer, often lasting all night, was certainly a source of the luminous transcendence noticed by your contemporaries. Your presence instilled respect, consternation, trembling, admiration, and sometimes even profound fear from various types and classes of people.

Teach me your way of looking at people: as you glanced at Peter after his denial, as you penetrated the heart of the rich young man and the hearts of your disciples.

I would like to meet you as you really are, since your image changes those with whom you come into contact. Remember John the Baptist's first meeting with you? And the centurion's feeling of unworthiness? And the amazement of all those who saw miracles and other wonders? How you impressed your disciples, the rabble in the Garden of Olives, Pilate and his wife, and the centurion at the foot of the cross. . . .

Give me that grace, that sense of Christ, your very heartbeat, so that I may live all of my life, interiorly and exteriorly, proceeding and discerning with your spirit, exactly as you did during your mortal life.

—Pedro Arrupe, "Our Way of Proceeding,"
The Spiritual Legacy of Pedro Arrupe, S.J., 81–82

"Lord Jesus, make my heart like unto thine."

> Amen, I say to you, there is no one who has given up house or brothers or sisters or mother or father or children or lands for my sake and for the sake of the gospel who will not receive a hundred times more now in this present age . . . (Mark 10:29-30)

The call to pray with families and for families, dear Brothers, concerns each one of you in a very personal way. We owe our life to our parents and we owe them a *permanent debt of gratitude.* Whether they are still alive or have already passed into eternity, we are united with them by a close bond which time does not destroy. While we owe our vocation to God, a significant role in it is also to be attributed to our parents. The decision of a son to dedicate himself to the priestly ministry, particularly in mission lands, is no small sacrifice for his parents. This was true also in the case of our own dear ones, yet they offered their feelings to God, letting themselves be guided by a deep faith. They then followed us with their prayer, just as Mary did with Jesus when he left the home at Nazareth . . .

What an experience it was for each of us, and, at the same time, for family and friends, when we celebrated our first Holy Mass! What a great thing that celebration was for our parishes and the places where we grew up! Every new vocation makes the parish aware of the fruitfulness of its *spiritual motherhood.* . . . Every priest can say of himself: "I am indebted to God and to others." There are many people who have accompanied us with their thoughts and prayers, . . . This great *prayerful solidarity* is a source of strength for me. People really do place their trust in our vocation to serve God.

—Saint John Paul II, Letter to Priests for
Holy Thursday, 1994

Lord Jesus, I prayerfully commend my family and loved ones to your care, in gratitude for the blessing that they have been in my priestly ministry.

A Priest's Poverty of Spirit   August 2

> LORD, my allotted portion and my cup, / you have made my destiny
> secure. (Ps 16:5)

When the priest in the pulpit asks the people to contribute to a diocesan
expansion plan, does he first reach into his own pocket? When on Mission
Sunday he urges the parishioners to make a sacrifice to spread the Church
in Africa, Asia or elsewhere, does he play his primary role in sacrifice? It
is not fitting to ask others to give to a cause without setting the example.
Can the Lord look on us with more favor than He looked on Achan [who
pillaged Jericho] if we hide our bank accounts when the needs of the world
are so pressing? And what blessings does He bestow on priests who give
until it hurts, and then a little more? Fortunately, such priests are more
numerous than is sometimes recognized . . .

Poverty of spirit does not begin with an act of the will to do with less; it
begins with the Spirit of Christ in us. External poverty follows the internal.
Indifference to the accumulation of possessions follows zeal for Christ. The
greater the concern with material things, the less is the dedication to the
Spirit. Some priests may exhibit the externals of poverty, or what passes
for such. They may be careless about the way they dress and act, but these
things have no relation to poverty of spirit. They may reflect simply a lack
of dignity and culture, a lust for saving or a general carelessness about the
dignity of one's person. . . .

Three aspects of priestly poverty can be distinguished. In the priest's
personal life, poverty directs him to limit himself to the strictly necessary.
In his apostolate, poverty of spirit inspires him to use spiritual means to
attain his apostolic goals. In his use of resources, poverty obliges him to
count only on God.

—Fulton J. Sheen, *The Priest Is Not His Own*, 126–27

In what ways is my lifestyle a living sermon on the importance of poverty
of spirit?

For if by that one person's transgression the many died, how much more did the grace of God and the gracious gift of the one person Jesus Christ overflow for the many. (Rom 5:15)

The priest is the instrument for the forgiveness of sins. God's forgiveness is given to us in the Church, it is transmitted to us by means of the ministry of our brother, the priest; and he too is a man, who, like us in need of mercy, truly becomes the instrument of mercy, bestowing on us the boundless love of God the Father. Priests and bishops too have to go to confession: we are all sinners. Even the Pope confesses every 15 days, because the Pope is also a sinner. And the confessor hears what I tell him, he counsels me and forgives me, because we are all in need of this forgiveness. Sometimes you hear someone claiming to confess directly to God . . . Yes, as I said before, God is always listening, but in the Sacrament of Reconciliation he sends a brother to bestow his pardon, the certainty of forgiveness, in the name of the Church.

The service that the priest assumes a ministry, on behalf of God, to forgive sins is very delicate and requires that his heart be at peace, that the priest have peace in his heart; that he not mistreat the faithful, but that he be gentle, benevolent and merciful; that he know how to plant hope in hearts and, above all, that he be aware that the brother or sister who approaches the Sacrament of Reconciliation seeking forgiveness does so just as many people approached Jesus to be healed. The priest who is not of this disposition of mind had better not administer this sacrament until he has addressed it. The penitent faithful have the right, all faithful have the right, to find in priests servants of the forgiveness of God.

. . . Let us not forget that God never tires of forgiving us; through the ministry of priests he holds us close in a new embrace and regenerates us and allows us to rise again and resume the journey. For this is our life: to rise again continuously and to resume our journey.

—Pope Francis, General Audience,
November 20, 2013

Pope Francis asks his priests, "As members of the Church are we conscious of the beauty of this gift that God himself offers us? Do we feel the joy of this cure, of this motherly attention that the Church has for us?"

The Matchless Example of the Curé of Ars   August 4

LORD, my allotted portion and my cup, / you have made my destiny secure. (Ps 16:5)

A predecessor [in the priesthood] who remains particularly present in the memory of the Church, and he will be especially commemorated this year, on the second centenary of his birth: Saint John Mary Vianney, the Curé of Ars.

Together we wish to thank Christ, the Prince of Pastors, for this extraordinary model of priestly life and service which the saintly Curé of Ars offers to the whole Church, and above all to us priests. How many of us prepared ourselves for the Priesthood, or today exercise the difficult task of caring for souls, having before our eyes the figure of Saint John Mary Vianney! His example cannot be forgotten. More than ever we need his witness, his intercession, in order to face the situations of our times when, in spite of a certain number of hopeful signs, evangelization is being contradicted by a growing secularization, when spiritual discipline is being neglected, when many are losing sight of the Kingdom of God, when often, even in the pastoral ministry, there is a too exclusive concern for the social aspect, for temporal aims. In [his] century the Curé of Ars had to face difficulties which were perhaps of a different kind but which were no less serious. By his life and work he represented, for the society of his time, a great evangelical challenge that bore astonishing fruits of conversion. Let us not doubt that he still presents to us today the great evangelical challenge.

I therefore invite you now to meditate on our Priesthood in the presence of this matchless pastor who illustrates both the fullest realization of the priestly ministry and the holiness of the minister.

—Saint John Paul II, Letter to Priests for
Holy Thursday, 1986

Lord Jesus, guide my steps along the path of holiness marked out by the humble priest John Vianney.

I urge you therefore, brothers, by the mercies of God, to offer your bodies as a living sacrifice, holy and pleasing to God, your spiritual worship. (Rom 12:1)

Dear Brothers in the Priesthood! This ministry forms a new life in us and around us. *The Eucharist evangelizes* our surroundings and confirms us in the hope that Christ's words will not pass away (cf. Lk 21:33). His words will remain, for they are rooted in the Sacrifice of the Cross: we are special witnesses and privileged ministers of the permanence of this truth and of God's love. We can therefore rejoice together when people feel the need for the new Catechism, or are prompted to read the Encyclical *Veritatis Splendor.* All of this strengthens us in the conviction that our *ministry of the Gospel becomes fruitful through the power of the Eucharist.*

. . . What unfathomable riches the Church offers us during the *Sacred Triduum* . . . My words are but a partial reflection of the feelings which each of you undoubtedly experiences in his heart. Perhaps this Letter for Holy Thursday will help to ensure that the many different manifestations of Christ's gift implanted in so many hearts will come together before the majesty of the great "mystery of faith" in a meaningful sharing of what the Priesthood is and will always be within the Church. May our union around the altar embrace all those who are marked by *the indelible sign of this Sacrament*, including those brothers of ours who in some way or other have distanced themselves from the sacred ministry. I trust that this remembrance will lead each of us to live ever more deeply the excellence of the gift which is the Priesthood of Christ.

—Saint John Paul II, Letter to Priests for
Holy Thursday, 1994

Lord Jesus, I pray with the Holy Father for all priests who have distanced themselves from the sacred ministry. I remember especially . . .

Dying with Christ on the Cross August 6

> Whoever wishes to come after me must deny himself, take up his cross, and follow me. (Mark 8:34)

[Consider] at once the beauty and the terror of the priestly vocation. A man, weak as other men, imperfect as they are, perhaps less well endowed than many of those to whom he is sent, perhaps even less inclined to be virtuous than some of them, finds himself caught, without possibility of escape, between the infinite mercy of Christ and the almost infinite dreadfulness of man's sin. He cannot help but feel in the depths of his heart something of Christ's compassion for sinners, something of the eternal Father's hatred of sin, something of the inexpressible love that drives the Spirit of God to consume sin in the fires of sacrifice. At the same time he may feel in himself all the conflicts of human weakness and irresolution and dread, the anguish of uncertainty and helplessness and fear, the inescapable lure of passion. All that he hates in himself becomes more hateful to him, by reason of his close union with Christ. But also by reason of his very vocation he is forced to face resolutely the reality of sin in himself and in others. He is bound by his vocation to fight this enemy. He cannot avoid the battle. And it is a battle that he alone can never win. He is forced to let Christ Himself fight the enemy in him. He must do battle on the ground chosen not by himself but by Christ. That ground is the hill of Calvary and the Cross. For, to speak plainly, the priest makes no sense at all in the world except to perpetuate in it the sacrifice of the Cross, and to die with Christ on the Cross for the love of those whom God would have him save.

—Thomas Merton, *No Man Is an Island*, 115

I ponder the times when the shadow of the cross has been cast over my priestly life.

> Owe nothing to anyone, except to love one another; for the one who loves another has fulfilled the law. (Rom 13:8)

Let us recall how Jesus named twelve as his companions. The call to priestly service includes an invitation to special intimacy with Christ. The lived experience of priests in every generation has led them to discover in their own lives and ministry the absolute centrality of their personal union with Jesus, of being his companions. No one can effectively bring the good news of Jesus to others unless he himself has first been his constant companion through personal prayer, unless he has learned from Jesus the mystery to be proclaimed.

This union with Jesus, modeled on his oneness with his Father, has a further intrinsic dimension, as his own prayer at the Last Supper reveals: "that they may be one, Father, even as we are one" (Jn 17:11). His priesthood is one, and this unity must be actual and effective among his chosen companions. Hence unity among priests, lived out in fraternity and friendship, becomes a demand and an integral part of the life of a priest.

Unity among priests is not a unity or fraternity that is directed towards itself. It is for the sake of the Gospel, to symbolize, in the living out of the priesthood, the essential direction to which the Gospel calls all people: to the union of love with him and one another . . .

Indeed, how will the world come to believe that the Father has sent Jesus unless people can see in visible ways that those who believe in Jesus have heard his commandment to "love one another"? And how will believers receive a witness that such love is a concrete possibility unless they find it in the example of the unity of their priestly ministers, of those whom Jesus himself forms into one priesthood as his own companions?

> —Saint John Paul II, Homily for a Holy Mass for
> the American Priests, October 4, 1979

How regularly do I seek the companionship of priests, not only for my own good, but for theirs?

> At that very moment [Jesus] rejoiced [in] the holy Spirit and said, "I give you praise, Father, Lord of heaven and earth, for although you have hidden these things from the wise and the learned you have revealed them to the childlike." (Luke 10:21)

The more mature I grow in years and experience the more I recognize that the surest way to make myself holy and to succeed in the service of the Holy See lies in the constant effort to reduce everything, principles, aims, position business, to the utmost simplicity and tranquility; I must always take care to strip my vines of all useless foliage and spreading tendrils, and concentrate on what is truth, justice and charity, above all charity. Any other way of behaving is nothing but affectation and self-assertion; it soon shows itself in its true colours and becomes a hindrance and a mockery.

Oh, the simplicity of the Gospel, of *The Imitation of Christ*, of *The Little Flowers of St. Francis* and of the most exquisite passages in St. Gregory, in his *Moralia* . . . I enjoy these pages more and more and return to them with joy. All the wiseacres of this world, and all the cunning minds, including those in Vatican diplomacy, cut such a poor figure in the light of the simplicity and grace shed by this great and fundamental doctrine of Jesus and his saints! This is the surest wisdom, that confounds the learning of this world and, with courtesy and true nobility, is consistent, equally well and even better, with the loftiest achievements in the sphere of science, even of secular and social science, in accordance with the requirements of time, place and circumstance. "This is the height of philosophy, to be simple with prudence," as was said by St. John Chrysostom great patron saint of the East.

Jesus, preserve in me the love and practice of this simplicity which, by keeping me humble, makes me more like you and draws and saves the souls of men.

—Saint John XXIII, *Journal of a Soul*, 326–27

Can I pray daily for this simplicity of heart, this simplicity of life?

> But we hold this treasure in earthen vessels, that the surpassing power
> may be of God and not from us. (2 Cor 4:7)

Our witness to Christ is often very imperfect and deficient. How consoling it is for us to have the assurance that it is primarily He, the Spirit of
Truth, who bears witness to Christ. May our human witness be open above
all to His witness! For it is the Spirit Himself who "searches . . . the depths
of God" and alone can bring these "depths," these "mighty works of God" to
the minds and hearts of those to whom we are sent as servants of the Gospel
of salvation. The more overwhelmed we feel by our mission, the more open
we must be to the action of the Holy Spirit, especially when the resistance
of minds and hearts, the resistance of a culture begotten under the influence
of "the spirit of the world," becomes particularly obvious and powerful.

"The Spirit helps us in our weakness . . . and intercedes for us with
sighs too deep for words." Despite the resistance of minds and hearts and
of a culture steeped in "the spirit of the world," there nevertheless persists
in all of creation the "longing" spoken of by St. Paul in the Letter to the
Romans: "The whole creation has been groaning in travail together until
now," that it may "obtain the glorious liberty of the children of God." May
this vision of St. Paul not fade from our priestly consciousness, and may
it support us in our life and service! Then we shall better understand why
the priest is necessary for the world and for mankind.

—Saint John Paul II, Letter to Priests for
Holy Thursday, 1991

Jesus, my Brother and Friend, I am overwhelmed at times by my weakness
and unworthiness. I commend my ministry completely into your loving
hands!

A Call to Unpossessive Generosity

> [Love] bears all things, believes all things, hopes all things, endures all things. (1 Cor 13:7)

[Chastity] is that utterly generous and unpossessive love by which the Father gives all that he is to the Son, including his divinity. It is not a sentiment or a feeling, but the love that grants the Son being. All human love, of married people or religious, should seek to live and share in this mystery, in its unpossessive generosity.

We must be completely unambiguous as to what this loving demands of us who are vowed to chastity. It means not just that we do not marry but that we abstain from sexual activity. It asks of us a real and clear renunciation, an asceticism. If we pretend otherwise and willingly accept compromises, then we enter upon a path that may be ultimately impossible to sustain and cause us and others terrible unhappiness.

The first thing that we are asked to do is to believe that the vow of chastity really can be a way of loving, that though we may pass through moments of frustration and desolation, it is a path that can lead to our flourishing as affectionate, whole human beings. The older members of our community are often signs of hope for us. We meet men and women who have passed through the trials of chastity, and emerged into the liberty of those who can love freely. They can be for us signs that with God nothing is impossible. . . .

Our communities should be places in which brothers or sisters must give each other courage when one person's heart hesitates, forgiveness when another fails and truthfulness when anyone is tempted by self-deceit. We must believe in the goodness of our brothers or sisters when they cease to believe it of themselves.

—Timothy Radcliffe, OP, *Sing a New Song:*
The Christian Vocation, 48–50

I am called to pray daily that my loving may be ever more generous and unpossessive, that in the hard times, love has the power to endure.

August 11   In the Upper Room and at Gethsemane

Probe me, God, know my heart; / try me, know my thoughts. (Ps 139:23)

In our priestly life prayer has a variety of forms and meanings: personal, communal and liturgical (public and official). However, at the basis of these many forms of prayer there must always be that most profound foundation which corresponds to our priestly existence in Christ, insofar as it is a specific realization of Christian existence itself and even with a wider radius of human existence. For prayer is a connatural expression of the awareness that we have been created by God and still more as we clearly see from the Bible that the Creator has manifested himself to man as the God of the Covenant.

The prayer which corresponds to our priestly existence naturally includes everything that derives from our being Christians, or even simply from our being men made "in the image and likeness" of God. It also includes our awareness of our being men and Christians as priests. And it seems we can more fully discover this on Holy Thursday, as we go with Christ, after the Last Supper, to Gethsemane. For here we are witnesses of the prayer of Jesus himself, the prayer which immediately precedes the supreme fulfillment of his Priesthood through the sacrifice of himself on the Cross. "As a high priest of the good things to come . . . he entered once for all into the Holy Place . . . by his own blood." In fact, if he was a priest from the beginning of his existence, nevertheless he "became" in a full way the unique priest of the new and eternal Covenant through the redemptive sacrifice which had its beginning in Gethsemane. This beginning took place in a context of prayer.

—Saint John Paul II, Letter to Priests for
Holy Thursday, 1987

In what ways does my prayer reflect the depth of my common humanity with all people, my fellowship with Christians, my identity as priest?

Priests: Contagious Christians

I have told you this so that my joy may be in you and your joy may be complete. (John 15:11)

The quality which makes contagious Christians enables people catch the love of God from you. . . . If you yourselves feel the love, joy and peace, the utter delightfulness of the consecrated life and this to such an extent, then every formal act of worship in church is filled with the free spontaneous worship of your soul. That is what wins people above all. It raises the simplest vocal prayer, the most commonplace of hymns, the most elaborate ceremonial action, to the same level of supernatural truth. People want to see and feel this in those who come to them with the credentials of religion: the joy, the delightfulness, the transfiguration of hard dull work and of suffering, which irradiate the real Christian life. You can't do more for anybody than give them that, can you? for that means real redemption here and now; the healing of all our psychic conflicts, all our worries and resistances and sense of injustice.

You are sent to a world full of tortured, twisted, overdriven souls: and sometimes nowadays you are told that in order to help them better, you ought to study psychology . . . I do not deny that this may be very useful knowledge for the clergy, and save them from many disastrous mistakes. But all the same, I think it would be much more practical, more use to your people in the end, to spend that time and strength in deepening and increasing your own love of God: for it is only through adoration and attention that we make our personal discoveries about Him. How are you going to show these souls who need it so dreadfully, the joy and delightfulness of God and surrender to God, unless you have it yourselves?

—Evelyn Underhill, *Concerning the Inner Life*, 96–97

Do I understand what it is that God's people are looking for in my ministry?

> Come to him, a living stone, rejected by human beings but chosen and precious in the sight of God, and, like living stones, let yourselves be built into a spiritual house to be a holy priesthood to offer spiritual sacrifices acceptable to God through Jesus Christ. (1 Pet 2:4-5)

Together with John, the Apostle and Evangelist, we turn the gaze of our soul towards that "woman clothed with the sun," who appears on the eschatological horizon of the Church and the world in the Book of Revelation. It is not difficult to recognize in her the same figure who, at the beginning of human history, after original sin, was foretold as the Mother of the Redeemer. In the Book of Revelation we see her, on the one hand, as the exalted woman in the midst of visible creation, and on the other, as the one who continues to take part in the spiritual battle for the victory of good over evil. This is the combat waged by the Church in union with the Mother of God, her "model," "against the world rulers of this present darkness, against the spiritual hosts of wickedness," as we read in the Letter of the Ephesians.

The beginning of this spiritual battle goes back to the moment when man "abused his liberty at the urging of personified Evil and set himself against God and sought to find fulfillment apart from God." One can say that man, blinded by the prospect of being raised beyond the measure of the creature which he was—in the words of the tempter: "you will become as God"—has ceased to seek the truth of his own existence and progress in Him who is "the first-born of all creation"; and has ceased to give this creation and himself in Christ to God, from whom everything takes its origin. Man has lost the awareness of being the priest of the whole visible world, turning the latter exclusively towards himself.

—Saint John Paul II, Letter to Priests for
Holy Thursday, 1988

Jesus, Eternal High Priest, may I be ever conscious of the priestly dignity given to me in baptism. May I readily nurture this priestly dignity in my fellow Christians.

Being Icons of the Gospel August 14

Be imitators of me, as I am of Christ. (1 Cor 11:1)

One who has the office of passing on the salvation of God's kingdom must be possessed and affected by it in his own person. This is particularly obvious in Paul, the model and type of church office, the model "official" or office-bearer of the official Church. For him, it is simply a matter of fact that the Cross and Resurrection (that dual event which is the dawning of God's kingdom) must be put in practice in his own life prior to being proclaimed to others and proposed to the community: "always carrying about in the body the death of Jesus, that the life of Jesus also may be manifested in our body. For we who live are constantly being delivered over to death for the sake of Jesus, that the life of Jesus also may be manifested in our mortal flesh" (2 Cor 4:10 ff). That means: Cross and Resurrection, the centre of Paul's apostolic activity, must become the fundamental principle of his own life, and must become visible in him. For this reason Paul does not merely proclaim the Gospel: he exemplifies it in his whole life. For this reason also he can say to the communities: "Be followers of me, as I am of Christ" (1 Cor 11:1).

In the Apostle's lifestyle the community has before its eyes a concrete model of its Christian life, which results from imitation of Christ and expectation of the coming kingdom. Christ is, so to speak, shown and held up before it in the personal life of the Apostle. This does not mean merely moral exemplarity; Paul points candidly to the weakness, suffering and contradiction experienced in his apostolic life, since in the endurance of adversity both the form of Christ crucified and the reality of his hidden risen life become visible.

—Gisbert Greshake, *The Meaning of
Christian Priesthood*, 112–13

In what ways is Christ my breath, my life, my all?

He went down with them and came to Nazareth, and was obedient to them; and his mother kept all these things in her heart. (Luke 2:51)

In the midst of the People of God that looks to Mary with immense love and hope, you must look to her with exceptional hope and love. Indeed, you must proclaim Christ who is her Son; and who will better communicate to you the truth about Him than His Mother? You must nourish human hearts with Christ: and who can make you more aware of what you are doing than she who nourished Him? "Hail, true Body, born of the Virgin Mary." In our "ministerial" Priesthood there is the *wonderful and penetrating dimension of nearness to the Mother of Christ.* So let us try to live in that dimension. If I may be permitted to speak here of my own experience, I will say to you that in writing to you I am referring especially to my own personal experience.

As I communicate all this to you, at the beginning of my service to the universal Church, I do not cease to ask God to fill you, priests of Jesus Christ, with every blessing and grace, and as a token of this communion in prayer I bless you with all my heart, in the name of the Father and of the Son and of the Holy Spirit.

Accept this blessing. Accept the words of the new Successor of Peter, that Peter whom the Lord commanded: "And once you have recovered, you in your turn must strengthen your brothers." Do not cease to pray for me together with the whole Church, so that I may respond to that exigency of a primacy of love that the Lord made the foundation of the mission of Peter, when He said to him: "Feed my lambs." Amen.

—Saint John Paul II, Letter to Priests for
Holy Thursday, 1979

Mary, Mother of the Redeemer, bless me with the grace to always remain faithful to your Son, even to the foot of the cross.

"Come," says my heart, "seek [God's] face"; / your face, LORD, do I seek! (Ps 27:8)

Whenever we pick up the breviary, we pick up Japan and Africa, two billion unbelievers, fallen-away Catholics, the burden of the Churches throughout the world. If millions are reluctant to pray, do we not feel their reluctance? If the unconverted drag their feet, how can we take wings and fly? Three times during His Agony, Our Lord came back to His three Apostles, seeking consolation. The breviary is not a personal prayer; it is an official prayer and therefore is weighted down "with the burden of the Churches". And until we realize that we are vocalizing the prayer of the Church, will we understand both its beauty and its burden?

Our Lord poured forth His personal prayers to His Father on the mountaintop, but when He prayed for His enemies, He was bleeding on a gibbet (Lk 23:34). The more His prayer was related to Redemption, the more He suffered . . .

If God will be with me, Jacob said, and watch over me on this journey of mine, and give me bread to eat and clothes to cover my back, till at last I return safe to my father's house, then the Lord shall be my God (Genesis 28:20-21).

Jacob loved God while loving himself. But in the breviary we are making an act of love, not only for the Church, but also for her enemies. The breviary, like the angel, is the test of our strength; as the angel shook Jacob and made him reel and roll, so the breviary tests our endurance. If the breviary be approached as a work, as a wrestling with God, as an intercession on the cross, as something intended to bring us not consolation but struggle, we shall eventually learn to enjoy the battle and turn it to the glory of God.

—Fulton J. Sheen, *The Priest Is Not His Own*, 144–45

I give serious consideration to the place that the Breviary plays in my daily life.

I no longer call you slaves, because a slave does not know what his master is doing. I have called you friends, because I have told you everything I have heard from my Father. (John 15:15)

It was precisely in the Upper Room that these words were spoken, in the immediate context of the institution of the Eucharist and of the ministerial Priesthood. Christ made known to the Apostles, and to all those who inherit from them the ordained Priesthood, that in this vocation and for this ministry they must become His friends—they must become the friends of that mystery which He came to accomplish. To be a priest means to enjoy special friendship with the mystery of Christ, with the mystery of the Redemption, in which He gives His flesh "for the life of the world." We who celebrate the Eucharist each day, the saving sacrament of the body and blood, must have a particular intimacy with the mystery from which this sacrament takes its beginning. The ministerial Priesthood is explainable only and exclusively in the framework of this divine mystery—and only within this framework is it accomplished.

In the depths of our priestly being, thanks to what each one of us became at the moment of our ordination, we are "friends": we are witnesses who are particularly close to this Love, which manifests itself in the Redemption. "For God so loved the world that he gave his only Son, that whoever believes in him should not perish but have eternal life." This is the definition of love in its redemptive meaning. This is the mystery of the Redemption, defined by love. It is the only begotten Son who takes this love from the Father and who gives it to the Father by bringing it to the world.

—Saint John Paul II, Letter to Priests for
Holy Thursday, 1983

In what ways have I nurtured this friendship with Christ, and how have I shown it to others?

I Will Make the Whole Earth My Altar   August 18

> Give thanks to the LORD, who is good, / whose mercy endures forever. / Who can recount the mighty deeds of the LORD, / proclaim in full God's praise? (Ps 106:1-2)

Since once again, Lord—though this time not in the forests of the Aisne but in the steppes of Asia—I have neither bread, nor wine, nor altar, I will raise myself beyond these symbols, up to the pure majesty of the real itself; I, your priest, will make the whole earth my altar and on it will offer you all the labours and sufferings of the world.

Over there, on the horizon, the sun has just touched with light the outermost fringe of the eastern sky. Once again, beneath this moving sheet of fire, the living surface of the earth wakes and trembles, and once again begins its fearful travail. I will place on my paten, O God, the harvest to be won by this renewal of labour. Into my chalice I shall pour all the sap which is to be pressed out this day from the earth's fruits.

My paten and my chalice are the depths of a soul laid widely open to all the forces which in a moment will rise up from every corner of the earth and converge upon the Spirit. Grant me the remembrance and the mystic presence of all those whom the light is now awakening to the new day.

One by one, Lord, I see and I love all those whom you have given me to sustain and charm my life. One by one also I number all those who make up that other beloved family which has gradually surrounded me, its unity fashioned out of the most disparate elements, with affinities of the heart, of scientific research and of thought. And again one by one—more vaguely it is true, yet all inclusively—I call before me the whole vast anonymous army of living humanity; those who surround me and support me though I do not know them; those who come and those who go; . . . those who today will take up again their impassioned pursuit of the light.

> —Pierre Teilhard de Chardin,
> "The Mass on the World," 145–46

I am invited today to contemplate the cosmic dimensions of the priesthood.

> I am the good shepherd, and I know mine and mine know me, just as the Father knows me and I know the Father; and I will lay down my life for the sheep. (John 10:14-15)

Jesus Christ is in our midst and He says to us: "I am the Good Shepherd." It is precisely He who has "made" shepherds of us too. And it is He who "goes about all the cities and villages," wherever we are sent in order to perform our priestly and pastoral service.

It is He, Jesus Christ, who teaches, who preaches the Gospel of the Kingdom and heals every human disease and infirmity wherever we are sent for the service of the Gospel and the administration of the Sacraments.

It is precisely He, Jesus Christ, who continually feels compassion for the crowds and for every tired and exhausted person, like a "sheep without a shepherd." Dear brothers! In this liturgical assembly of ours let us ask Christ for just one thing: that each of us may learn to serve better, more clearly and more effectively, His presence as Shepherd in the midst of the people of today's world!

This is also most important for ourselves, so that we may not be ensnared by the temptation of "uselessness," that is to say, the temptation to feel that we are not needed. Because it is not true. We are more necessary than ever, because Christ is more necessary than ever! The Good Shepherd is more than ever necessary! We have in our hands—precisely in our "empty hands"—the power of the means of action that the Lord has given to us. . . .

There is no doubt about it, dear brothers: with the good use of these "poor means" (but divinely powerful ones!) you will see blossoming along your path the wonders of the infinite Mercy of God.

—Saint John Paul II, Homily for Priests at
the Jubilee of Redemption, April 24, 1984

Lord Jesus, renew my priestly heart with the tenderness of a shepherd's love, with the abiding mercy that fills your own Sacred Heart.

God Knows Those Whom He Has Called   August 20

You formed my inmost being; / you knit me in my mother's womb. / I praise you, because I am wonderfully made; / wonderful are your works! / My very self you know. / My bones are not hidden from you, / When I was being made in secret, / fashioned in the depths of the earth. / Your eyes saw me unformed; / in your book all are written down; / my days were shaped, before one came to be. (Ps 139:13-16)

God beholds thee individually, whoever thou art. He "calls thee by thy name." He sees thee, and understands thee, as He made thee. He knows what is in thee, all thy own peculiar feelings and thoughts, thy dispositions and likings, thy strength and thy weakness. He views thee in thy day of rejoicing and thy day of sorrow. He sympathizes in thy hopes and thy temptations. He interests Himself in all thy anxieties and remembrances, all the risings and failings of thy spirit. He has numbered the very hairs of thy head and the cubits of thy stature. He compasses thee round and bears thee in His arms; He takes thee up and sets thee down. He notes thy very countenance, whether smiling or in tears, whether healthful or sickly. He looks tenderly upon thy hands and thy feet; He hears thy voice, the beating of thy heart, and thy very breathing. Thou dost not love thyself better than He loves thee. Thou canst not shrink from pain more than He dislikes thy bearing it; and if He puts it on thee, it is as thou wilt put it on thyself, if thou art wise, for a greater good afterwards.

—Blessed John Henry Newman,
Parochial and Plain Sermons, 5:124–25

I open the book of my life to the living God. I rejoice in his loving acceptance of all that I've been and all that I am and all that I shall yet become.

> For if we live, we live for the Lord, and if we die, we die for the Lord; so then, whether we live or die, we are the Lord's. (Rom 14:8)

We would likewise admonish the priest that in the last analysis, it is not for himself alone that he has to sanctify himself, for he is the workman whom Christ went out . . . to hire into his vineyard (Mt 16:24). Therefore, it is his duty to uproot unfruitful plants and to sow useful ones, to water the crop and to guard lest the enemy sow cockle among it. Consequently, the priest must be careful not to allow an unbalanced concern for personal perfection to lead him to overlook any part of the duties of his office which are conducive to the welfare of others. . . .

In the midst of all these duties, the priest shall have ever present to his mind the striking admonition given by St. Paul: Neither he who plants is anything, nor he who waters, but God who gives the increase (1 Cor 3:7). It may be that we go and sow the seed with tears; it may be that we tend its growth at the cost of heavy labor; but to make it germinate and yield the hoped for fruit, that depends on God alone and his powerful assistance. This further point also is worthy of profound consideration, namely that men are but the instruments whom God employs for the salvation of souls; they must, therefore, be instruments fit to be employed by God.

. . . There is, indeed, only one thing that unites man to God, one thing that makes him pleasing to God and a not unworthy dispenser of his mercy; and that one thing is holiness of life and conduct. If this holiness, which is the true super-eminent knowledge of Jesus Christ, is wanting in the priest, then everything is wanting.

—Saint Pius X, *Haerent Animo*

Many times a day I need to bring to clarity my singular purpose: to live for God.

Mary and the Eucharist

> When Jesus saw his mother and the disciple there whom he loved, he said to his mother, "Woman, behold, your son." Then he said to the disciple, "Behold, your mother." (John 19:26)

The Last Supper, at which Christ instituted the sacraments of the Sacrifice and the Priesthood of the New Covenant, is the beginning of the *Triduum Paschale*. At its centre is the Body of Christ. It is precisely this Body which, before being subjected to suffering and death, is offered at the Last Supper as food in the institution of the Eucharist. Christ takes bread in his hands, breaks it and gives it to his Apostles with the words: "Take; eat: this is my Body" (Mt 26:26). In this way he institutes the sacrament of his Body, that Body which, as the Son of God, he had taken from his Mother, the Immaculate Virgin. Then, taking the cup, he offers to the Apostles his own Blood under the species of wine, saying: "Drink of it, all of you; for this is my Blood of the covenant, which is poured out for many for the forgiveness of sins" (Mt 26:27-28). Here too it is the Blood which gave life to the Body received from the Virgin Mother: Blood which had to be shed, in fulfilment of the mystery of the Redemption, in order that the Body received from his Mother could—as Corpus *immolatum in cruce pro homine*—become for us and for all mankind the sacrament of eternal life, the viaticum for eternity . . .

Even though the Holy Thursday liturgy does not speak of Mary—rather we find her on Good Friday at the foot of the Cross with the Apostle John—it is difficult not to sense her presence at the institution of the Eucharist, the anticipation of the Passion and Death of the Body of Christ, that Body which the Son of God had received from the Virgin Mother at the moment of the Annunciation.

—Saint John Paul II, Letter to Priests for
Holy Thursday, 1995

My Eucharistic Lord, as you are truly present in the sacred liturgy, grant me the grace to know in that mystery the loving presence of Mary, your Mother.

August 23   The Priest Seeks Another Fatherhood

[S]ome . . . have renounced marriage for the sake of the kingdom of heaven. (Matt 19:12)

The Latin Church has wished . . . that *all those who receive the sacrament of Orders should embrace this renunciation "for the sake of the kingdom of heaven."* . . . We are all aware that "we have this treasure in earthen vessels" yet we know very well that it is precisely a treasure.

. . . Through his celibacy, the priest becomes the "man for others," in a different way from the man who, by binding himself in conjugal union with a woman, also becomes, as husband and father, a man "for others," especially in the radius of his own family: for his wife, and, together with her, for the children, to whom he gives life. The priest, by renouncing this fatherhood proper to married men, seeks another fatherhood and, as it were, even another motherhood, recalling the words of the Apostle about the children whom he begets in suffering. These are children of his spirit, people entrusted to his solicitude by the Good Shepherd. These people are many, more numerous than an ordinary human family can embrace. The pastoral vocation of priests is great, and the Council teaches that it is universal: it is directed towards the whole Church, and therefore it is of a missionary character. Normally, it is linked to the service of a particular community of the People of God, in which each individual expects attention, care and love. The heart of the priest, in order that it may be available for this service, must be free. Celibacy is a sign of a freedom that exists for the sake of service.

—Saint John Paul II, Letter to Priests for
Holy Thursday, 1979

Lord Jesus, as I seek daily to imitate you, help me to see that the call to celibacy is a call to free and generous service to all of God's people.

> Amen, amen, I say to you, whoever believes in me will do the works that I do, and will do greater ones than these, because I am going to the Father. (John 14:12)

Our Lord Jesus Christ did not hesitate to confide the formidable task of evangelizing the then-known world to a handful of men to all appearances lacking in number and quality. He bade this little flock not to lose heart, for, thanks to His constant assistance, through Him and with Him, they would overcome the world. Jesus has also taught us that the kingdom of God has an intrinsic and unobservable dynamism which enables it to grow "without [man's] knowing it." The harvest of God's kingdom is great, but the laborers, as in the beginning, are few. Actually, they have never been as numerous as human standards would have judged sufficient. But the heavenly King demands that we pray "the Lord of the harvest to send out laborers into His harvest." The counsels and prudence of man cannot supersede the hidden wisdom of Him who, in the history of salvation, has challenged man's wisdom and power by His own foolishness and weakness.

Supported by the power of faith, We express the Church's conviction on this matter. Of this she is certain: if she is prompter and more persevering in her response to grace, if she relies more openly and more fully on its secret but invincible power, if, in short, she bears more exemplary witness to the mystery of Christ, then she will never fall short in the performance of her salvific mission to the world—no matter how much opposition she faces from human ways of thinking or misrepresentations. We must all realize that we can do all things in Him who alone gives strength to souls and increase to His Church.

—Blessed Pope Paul VI,
Sacerdotalis Caelibatus, 28–30

Lord Jesus, help me never to forget that it is you who is living your life again in me, it is you who is living your priesthood in me.

> We are afflicted in every way, but not constrained; perplexed, but not driven to despair; persecuted, but not abandoned; struck down, but not destroyed; always carrying about in the body the dying of Jesus, so that the life of Jesus may also be manifested in our body. (2 Cor 4:8-10)

The followers of Christ, all who wish to walk in His footsteps and press towards the goal of sanctity, must cultivate the same attitude towards life that He had. They must be prepared to face the tasks that Providence assigns to them regardless of success or failure. If they shrink from the work God imposes on them, and take up only that in which they foresee success, in order to enjoy the satisfaction of feeling themselves efficient, and being thought so by others, they miss the whole meaning and purpose of life, and arrive at old age with empty hands. Our existence on earth, with its enterprises and its toils, is given us to be used for the transformation of our souls, and not for the flattering of our inordinate desires of excellence. The true disciple of the Divine Master does not desist from his efforts to create in himself and around himself the reign of justice, because he is thwarted and cannot have his own way in dealing with circumstances. He realizes that things are all wrong not when *he* cannot have his way with things, but when God cannot have is His way with *him*. We are not meant to mold persons and events to our will, but rather to be molded by life's contacts to the form preordained for us by God. If we achieve great things outside of ourselves, and the achieving of them does not affect any change or development in ourselves, we have done nothing. *Life's purpose is to purify us, not gratify us.* It is not a theatre where we are called upon to play a brilliant part with the view of gaining the applause of the audience, nor an arena in which to achieve a success to be greeted by the acclamations of the onlookers, *but a process, by which our souls are to be made strong with the strength of supernatural life . . . .* Existence for the Christian is not a cozy fireside by which to sit and warm himself, but a furnace in which he is to be plunged in order to be refined as silver or annealed as steel.

—Edward Leen, *In the Likeness of Christ*, 237–39

Purify my desires, O Lord, so that I am always and in all ways ready to do your will.

Ministry Under the Cross August 26

> [We are] always carrying about in the body the dying of Jesus, so that the life of Jesus may also be manifested in our body. (2 Cor 4:10)

A review of the place of a theology of the Cross in the whole development of Christian tradition reveals its potential, not only to inspire deeply affective and spiritual bonds of identity with the Crucified One of Christian faith, liturgy and proclamation, but also to become the stimulus and ground for the most profound involvement with the crucified ones of the world . . . Ministry under the Cross is truly a ministry at the heart of the world.

Like Jesus the Redeemer on the Cross, the Church and her ministry is called to assume a Form that is appropriate to a broken world. The call of the priesthood as an objective ministry in the Church is a call to live the Cross both ecclesially and personally. Election to the priesthood, Balthasar states, is equivalent to being made "a libation for the sacrifice and the service of faith," and is a participation in the responsibilities of the Good Shepherd who lays down his life for his sheep (Jn 10:15). Having been entrusted with pastoral office, priests, therefore, are required to give their lives away in configuration to the Priesthood and Person of Christ himself.

The absolute demands of this office weigh heavily on the person who is called: pastoral love takes on the Form of the Cross. Acquiring this Form of life requires a wholehearted surrender . . . The mysteries of the Lord's Eucharistic self-giving love unfold in the life of his ministers: like him, they are to be taken and blessed, broken and given, not only in terms of liturgical gesture, but in the praxis of loving the community following the example of Jesus when he washes the disciples' feet on Holy Thursday (Jn 13:1).

—Dermot Power, *A Spiritual Theology of the Priesthood*, 47–48

Lord Jesus crucified, give me the grace to see in the crosses in my ministry a privileged share in your own passion.

I give thanks to my God always, remembering you in my prayers, as I hear of the love and the faith you have in the Lord Jesus and for all the holy ones, so that your partnership in the faith may become effective in recognizing every good there is in us that leads to Christ. (Phlm 4-6)

"The priest's identity, like every Christian identity, has its source in the Blessed Trinity," which is revealed and is communicated to people in Christ, establishing, in him and through the Spirit, the Church as "the seed and the beginning of the kingdom." The apostolic exhortation *Christifideles Laici*, . . . presents the Church as *mystery, communion and mission*: "She is *mystery* because the very life and love of the Father, Son and Holy Spirit are the gift gratuitously offered to all those who are born of water and the Spirit (cf. Jn. 3:5) and called to relive the very *communion* of God and to manifest it and communicate it in history [mission]."

It is within the Church's *mystery*, as a mystery of Trinitarian communion in missionary tension, that every Christian identity is revealed, and likewise the specific identity of the priest and his ministry. Indeed, the priest, by virtue of the consecration which he receives in the sacrament of orders, is sent forth by the Father through the mediatorship of Jesus Christ, to whom he is configured in a special way as head and shepherd of his people, in order to live and work by the power of the Holy Spirit in service of the Church and for the salvation of the world.

In this way the fundamentally "relational" dimension of priestly identity can be understood. Through the priesthood which arises from the depths of the ineffable mystery of God, that is, from the love of the Father, the grace of Jesus Christ and the Holy Spirit's gift of unity, the priest sacramentally enters into communion with the bishop and with other priests in order to serve the People of God who are the Church and to draw all mankind to Christ.

—Saint John Paul II, *Pastores Dabo Vobis*, 12

Heavenly Father, you have called us to be configured to Christ, the eternal high priest. Help me each day to prayerfully recommit myself to your service.

> I urge you, [brothers,] by our Lord Jesus Christ and by the love of the
> Spirit, to join me in the struggle by your prayers to God on my behalf
> . . . (Rom 15:30)

A form of spiritual motherhood . . . has always silently accompanied the chosen ranks of priests in the course of the Church's history. It is the concrete entrustment of our ministry to a specific face, to a consecrated soul who has been called by Christ and therefore chooses to offer herself, with the necessary suffering and the inevitable struggles of life, to intercede for our priestly existence, thereby dwelling in Christ's sweet presence.

This motherhood, which embodies Mary's loving face, should be prayed for because God alone can bring it into being and sustain it. In this regard there are plenty of wonderful examples; only think of St. Monica's beneficial tears for her son Augustine, for whom she wept "more than mothers weep when lamenting their dead children" (St. Augustine, *Confessions III*, 11). . . .

Since it is impossible to be true mendicants before Christ, marvelously concealed in the Eucharistic Mystery, without being able in practice to ask for the effective help and prayers of those whom he sets beside us, let us not be afraid to entrust ourselves to the motherhoods that the Spirit will certainly bring into being for us.

. . . Let us remember the words of the Holy Curé of Ars, Patron of Parish Priests: "If I already had one foot in Heaven and I was told to return to the earth to work to convert sinners, I would gladly return. And if, to do this, it were necessary that I remain on earth until the end of the world, always rising at midnight and suffering as I suffer, I would consent with all my heart" (Bro. Athanase, *Procès de l'Ordinaire*, p. 883).

> —Pope Benedict XVI, Letter on the Occasion of the
> World Day of Prayer for the Sanctification of Priests

As I am in need of the prayers of others to sustain me in ministry, so I recommit myself to praying for my brother priests.

August 29 Mary, Model of the Ministerial Priesthood

When Jesus saw his mother and the disciple there whom he loved, he said to his mother, "Woman, behold your son." Then he said to the disciple, "Behold, your mother." And from that hour the disciple took her into his home. (John 19:26-27)

Dear Brothers, the priesthood which today we recall with such veneration as our special inheritance *is a ministerial priesthood! We are at the service of the People of God! We are at the service of its mission! This priesthood of ours must guarantee the participation of everyone*—men and women alike—in the threefold prophetic, priestly and royal mission of Christ. And not only is the Sacrament of Holy Orders ministerial: *above all else the Eucharist itself is ministerial.* When Christ affirms that: "This is my Body which is given for you . . . This cup which is poured out for you is the new covenant in my Blood" (Lk 22:19, 20), he reveals his greatest service: *the service of the Redemption,* in which the Only-Begotten and Eternal Son of God becomes the *Servant of man* in the fullest and most profound sense.

Beside *Christ the Servant,* we cannot forget the one who is "the Handmaid," Mary. St. Luke tells us that, at the decisive moment of the Annunciation, the Virgin expressed her "fiat" in these words: "Behold, I am the handmaid of the Lord" (Lk 1:38). The relationship of priests to women as mothers and sisters is enriched, thanks to the *Marian tradition,* by another aspect: that of service *in imitation of Mary the Handmaid.* If the priesthood is by its nature ministerial, we must live it in union with the Mother *who is the Handmaid of the Lord.* Then our priesthood will be kept safe in her hands, indeed in her heart, and we shall be able to open it to everyone. In this way our priesthood, in all its dimensions, will be fruitful and salvific.

—Saint John Paul II, Letter to Priests for
Holy Thursday, 1995

Mary, Mother of Priests, bless me and all those in priestly ministry with your true spirit of servanthood in our ministry to God's people.

No Counterfeiters Need Apply

Whoever belongs to God hears the words of God . . . (John 8:47)

It is not only because the official Church must be guided by the basic attitudes of Jesus that priesthood involves obedience. The most important reason of all is that the bearer of church office has the obligation to pass on something which he does not possess of himself but which he himself obeys and must pass on to others. Consequently, a priest who does not first listen before he delivers the message is fundamentally a counterfeiter who is not circulating genuine currency and real values but instead is carrying out a deception with sham metal of his own making. Priestly office, therefore, is either founded on personal listening to the word of God or else degenerates into a "popedom" which merely discharges functions. How can a person prepare a community for the kingdom of God, and proclaim the word of God to it, if he has not first listened to it himself? If someone seeks his advice, how can one say with authority "Do this, or that!" if he has not first listened to God in prayer and asked him what is his will for this person.

Besides this readiness to listen, the candidate for ordination, at the ordination itself, makes a public and binding surrender of his freedom in carrying out the pastoral work of the Church, a work for which the bishop (and the major superior in a religious order) bears the ultimate responsibility. This promise of obedience is the concrete answer of those whom God and the Church have called to the official mission. Strictly speaking the promise of obedience is made, not to the bishop, but to God, who draws and encourages the candidate to this offering of his freedom, and to the community, which needs the availability of the priest.

—Gisbert Greshake, *The Meaning of Christian Priesthood*, 134

In what way is my personal prayer marked by a readiness to listen?

"This is the time of fulfillment. The kingdom of God is at hand. Repent, and believe in the gospel." (Mark 1:15)

His sharing in Christ's priesthood cannot fail to arouse in the presbyter a sacrificial spirit too, a type of *pondus crucis*, the burden of the cross, which is expressed especially in mortification. As the Council says, "Christ, whom the Father sanctified or consecrated and sent into the world, 'gave himself for us to redeem us from all iniquity and to purify for himself a people of his own who are zealous for good deeds'. . . . In a similar way, priests, who are consecrated by the anointing of the Holy Spirit and sent by Christ, mortify the works of the flesh in themselves and dedicate themselves completely to the service of the people, and so are able, in the holiness with which they have been enriched in Christ, to make progress towards the perfect man."

This is the ascetical aspect of the way of perfection, which for the priest cannot be lacking in renunciation and struggle against every sort of desire and yearning that would induce him to seek the good things of this world, thus compromising his interior progress. This is the "spiritual combat" of which the ascetical masters speak and which is required of every follower of Christ, but especially of every minister in the work of the cross, called to reproduce in himself the image of Him who is *Sacerdos et Hostia*.

Obviously, one always needs to be open and responsive to the grace which itself comes from him who begets "any measure of desire or achievement," but who also demands that one use the means of mortification and self-discipline without which one remains impervious soil.

—Saint John Paul II, General Audience, May 26, 1993

Is my priestly life marked by a spirit of daily self-denial? Has the soil of my life become impervious to God's grace?

Companions in His Service

> He said to them, "Come after me, and I will make you fishers of men."
> (Matt 4:19)

Our priestly vocation is given by the Lord Jesus himself. It is a call which is personal and individual: we are called by name as was Jeremiah. It is a call to service: we are sent out to preach the Good News, to "give God's flock a shepherd's care" . . .

Priesthood is not merely a task which has been assigned; it is a vocation, a call to be heard again and again. To hear this call and to respond generously to what this call entails is a task for each priest, but it is also a responsibility for the Senates of Priests. This responsibility means deepening our understanding of the priesthood as Christ instituted it, as he wanted it to be and to remain, and as the Church faithfully explains it and transmits it. Fidelity to the call to the priesthood means building up this priesthood with God's people by a life of service according to apostolic priorities: concentration "on prayer and the ministry of the word" (Acts 6:4).

In the Gospel of Saint Mark the priestly call of the Twelve Apostles is like a bud whose flowering displays a whole theology of priesthood. In the midst of Jesus' ministry, we read that "he went up the mountain and summoned the men he himself had decided on, who came and joined him. He named twelve as his companions whom he would send to preach the good news . . . " The passage then lists the names of the Twelve (Mk 3, 13-14). Here we see three significant aspects of the call given by Jesus: he called his first priests individually and by *name*; he called them for the service of his word, to *preach the Gospel*; and he made them his own *companions*, drawing them into that unity of life and action which he shares with his Father in the very life of the Trinity.

> —Saint John Paul II, Homily for a Holy Mass for
> the American Priests, October 4, 1979

I can really never spend enough time reflecting on the personal call that I have received from Christ. With all my weaknesses, he has chosen me as his priest and friend.

September 2   In Communion with a Fractured World

> For all of you who were baptized into Christ have clothed yourselves
> with Christ. There is neither Jew nor Greek, there is neither slave nor
> free person, there is not male and female; for you are all one in Christ
> Jesus. (Gal 3:27-28)

I recently came across a marvelous description of the Church. The Church
is the place of "the dynamic movement of gathering" first begun in Christ.

The reality of gathering expresses for me something very powerful
about the Eucharist. While presiding one Sunday morning at St. Mary's
Cathedral, this was brought home to me in a concrete way. Standing before
me was an amazing mixture of people. Ethnically, politically, economically,
theologically, people of many types and on every place of the spectrum,
responded to my "The Lord be with you," as one, "And also with you."
As the one bread and the one cup are transformed into the living presence
of Christ, all these different people enter into that one life of Christ. From
such difference, unity is made possible.

The daily Eucharist reminds me of this when I pray, "Grant that we,
who are nourished by his body and blood, may be filled with his Holy Spirit,
and become one body, one spirit in Christ" (Eucharistic Prayer III). The
Eucharist is that place where the Spirit is powerfully acting to continue the
dynamic movement of gathering people into Christ.

Our world is marked by much division, enormous economic gaps, and
by separations of fear and misunderstanding. In the Eucharist, I experience
God not simply breaking down the barriers and closing the gaps, but gathering us with all our differences into a unity that only God is big enough to
sustain and somehow transform.

In my priesthood, too, where I often feel pulled in so many directions,
I am called to be many different things to different people. The daily celebration of the Eucharist is where I find Christ gathering me back together
and showing me that he is big enough for all the diverse needs of the people.
For me, the Eucharist is the encounter with the possibility of communion
in a complicated, often fractured world.

> —Anthony Oelrich, "Communion in
> a Fractured World," 65–66

The expansive love of Christ in the Eucharist is a daily invitation for me to
open wide the doors of my priestly life to all who long for communion.

A Looking Away from Oneself   September 3

No one takes this honor upon himself but only when called by God, just as Aaron was. (Heb 5:4)

Whoever knows himself to be called by God may no longer quarrel with God concerning the call. He should manage to remain simple and childlike in his consent. Childlike, because God is the Father of those he calls, and the Father/child relationship is continually exemplified both in the orders and in the priesthood through obedience. Childlikeness can assume different forms according to the order chosen, just as obedience adapts itself to the particular rule of an order. But childlikeness it must nevertheless be, and therefore also simplicity, a looking away from one's self in order to have one's glance free for God. . . . The important thing now is to listen to God's Word, to the dialogue between Father and Son, so as to be receptive for the sonship destined for those called to the discipleship of the Lord.

Prayer should leave its stamp on a person's total attitude toward life, and it should make the one called into a kind person, a loving person who infects others with his love. They ought not only to feel loved; the question itself of love should awaken in them: "What is the nature of a love that can transform that person in such a way? How could I myself acquire such a love? How did he ever come upon it?" Such questions concerning love could be roads to God. Everything about the one called should point to God and not to himself. His apostolate will be much less one of word than one of deed, but more in the sense of "letting happen" than of actively intervening. . . . Each word of Scripture now appears new to the one called, and it exhibits a sense he had never discovered until now.

—Adrienne von Speyr, *They Followed His Call*, 36–39

My call, my prayer, my ministry. I reflect on the way that each is a gift for which I give a generous response.

September 4   Priestly Life as Eloquent Catechesis

According to the grace of God given to me, like a wise master builder I laid a foundation, and another is building upon it. But each one must be careful how he builds upon it, for no one can lay a foundation other than the one that is there, namely, Jesus Christ. (1 Cor 3:10-11)

The Catechism sets forth once more the fundamental and essential contents of Catholic faith and morality as they are believed, celebrated, lived and prayed by the Church today. It is thus a special means for deepening knowledge of the inexhaustible Christian mystery, for encouraging fresh enthusiasm for prayer intimately united with the prayer of Christ and for strengthening the commitment of a consistent witness of life.

At the same time, this Catechism is given to us as a sure point of reference for fulfilling the mission, entrusted to us in the Sacrament of Orders, of proclaiming the "Good News" to all people in the name of Christ and of the Church. Thanks to it, we can put into practice in a constantly renewed way Christ's perennial command: "Go therefore and make disciples of all nations . . . teaching them to observe all that I have commanded you" (Mt 28:19-20).

Indeed, in this summary of the deposit of faith, we can find an authentic and sure norm for teaching Catholic doctrine, for catechetical activity among the Christian people, for that "new evangelization" of which today's world has such immense need.

Dear priests, our life and ministry will themselves become an eloquent catechesis for the entire community entrusted to us, provided that they are rooted in the Truth which is Christ. Then ours will not be an isolated witness, but a harmonious one, offered by people united in the same faith and sharing in the same cup. It is this sort of vital "infectiousness" that we must together aim at, in effective and affective communion, in order to carry out the ever more urgent "new evangelization."

—Saint John Paul II, Letter to Priests for
Holy Thursday, 1993

In what ways is my life a more eloquent catechesis than the words that I speak?

To Live Rightly, Pray Rightly

> Rising very early before dawn, he left and went off to a deserted place, where he prayed. (Mark 1:35)

There is, in fact, such a necessary link between holiness and prayer that the one cannot exist without the other. The words of Chrysostom on this matter are an exact expression of the truth: "I consider that it is obvious to everyone that it is impossible to live virtuously without the aid of prayer"; and Augustine sums up shrewdly: "He truly knows how to live rightly, who rightly knows how to pray."

Christ himself, by his constant exhortations and especially by his example, has even more firmly inculcated these truths. To pray he withdrew into desert places or climbed the mountain alone; he spent whole nights absorbed in prayer; he paid many visits to the temple; even when the crowds thronged around him, he raised his eyes to heaven and prayed openly before them; when nailed to the Cross, in the agony of death, he supplicated the Father with a strong cry and tears.

Let us be convinced, therefore, that a priest must be especially devoted to the practice of prayer if he is to maintain worthily his dignity and to fulfill his duty. All too frequently one must deplore the fact that prayer is a matter of routine rather than of genuine fervor; the Psalms are recited at the appointed times in a negligent manner, a few short prayers are said in between; there is no further thought of consecrating part of the day to speaking with God, with pious aspirations to him. And it is the priest, more than any other, who is bound to obey scrupulously the command of Christ: We ought always pray (Lk 18,1), a command which Paul so insistently inculcated: Be constant in prayer, watching in it with thanksgiving (Col 4,2), pray without ceasing (1 Thes 5,17).

—Saint Pius X, *Haerent Animo*

How easily I allow prayer to slip from my daily routine; or worse, that I allow prayer to become rote, and lifeless.

September 6   In the Priest, Christ Relives His Passion

[But] whatever gains I had, these I have come to consider a loss because of Christ. More than that, I even consider everything as a loss because of the supreme good of knowing Christ Jesus my Lord. (Phil 3:7-8)

Dear brother priests, let us not be afraid of this very personal commitment—marked by asceticism and inspired by love—which God asks of us for the proper exercise of our Priesthood. Let us remember the recent reflections of the Synodal Fathers: "It seems to us that in the difficulties of today God wishes to teach us more deeply the value, importance and central place of the Cross of Jesus Christ." In the priest, Christ relives his Passion, for the sake of souls. Let us give thanks to God who thus permits us to share in the Redemption, in our hearts and in our flesh!

For all these reasons, Saint John Mary Vianney never ceases to be a witness, ever living, ever relevant, to the truth about the priestly vocation and service. We recall the convincing way in which he spoke of the greatness of the priest and of the absolute need for him. Those who are already priests, those who are preparing for the Priesthood and those who will be called to it must fix their eyes on his example and follow it. The faithful too will more clearly grasp, thanks to him, the mystery of the Priesthood of their priests. No, the figure of the Curé of Ars does not fade.

Dear brothers, may these reflections renew your joy at being priests, your desire to be priests more profoundly! The witness of the Curé of Ars contains still other treasures to be discovered . . .

We hear Christ saying to us as he said to the Apostles: "Greater love has no man than this, that a man lay down his life for his friends. . . . No longer do I call you servants . . . , I have called you friends." Before him who manifests love in its fullness, we, priests and Bishops, renew our priestly commitments.

—Saint John Paul II, Letter to Priests for
Holy Thursday, 1986

Our Holy Father exhorts us: "We pray for one another, each for his brother, and all for all."

Never Doubt Your Priesthood

> To the thirsty I will give a gift from the spring of life-giving water. The victor will inherit these gifts, and I shall be his God, and he will be my son. (Rev 21:6-7)

What we wish to say to you today is this: never doubt your priesthood. This we say for several reasons. By your ordination you have been endowed with the sacramental mystery which has conferred upon you powers that liken you to Christ: the power to celebrate the Holy Eucharist, to administer the sacrament of Penance, and so on. Through the priestly ministry that is now yours you are likened to the Apostles, you have been made ministers of the Gospel. To you are now applied in a special way the words that Christ spoke to his disciples: "As the Father has sent me, even so I send you" (Jn. 20, 21). Those words are addressed personally to each one of you.

Never doubt your priesthood. Your task is now to serve the Church and the world with all your strength. What a noble task, and how varied are the forms that it will take! How lofty too are the obligations that you have undertaken, that of holiness, of charity to all men, of sacrifice. It is the Cross that you have willingly accepted, the Cross which will give your lives a serious character, but which will make them strong.

Whatever difficulties and trials you may encounter, you are assured of never-failing help and support: the assistance of God's grace, the communion of the Church, the esteem—and the good example—of the People of God.

Therefore we repeat: never doubt your priesthood. Go forward with confidence. The Lord be with you, and may the Mother of God ever assist you.

We wish also to extend a special greeting to the parents, relatives and friends of the new priests. We pray that God will reward you for the sacrifices you have made on their behalf, and for the support and encouragement you have given them during their years of training. . . . Be sure that we shall remember you in our prayers.

—Blessed Pope Paul VI, Address to the Newly
Ordained Priests, March 20, 1972

I reflect upon the times I have doubted my priesthood, recalling with confidence the many graces of my priestly life.

> When Jesus saw his mother and the disciple there whom he loved, he said to his mother, "Woman, behold, your son." Then he said to the disciple, "Behold, your mother." (John 19:26-27)

Dear brothers, at the beginning of my ministry I entrust all of you to the Mother of Christ, who in a special way is our Mother: the Mother of priests. In fact, the beloved disciple, who, as one of the Twelve, had heard in the Upper Room the words "Do this in memory of me," was given by Christ on the Cross to His Mother, with the words: "Behold your son." The man who on Holy Thursday received the power to celebrate the Eucharist was, by these words of the dying Redeemer, given to His Mother as her "son." All of us, therefore, who receive the same power through priestly Ordination, have in a certain sense a prior right to see her as our Mother. And so I desire that all of you, together with me, should find in Mary the Mother of the Priesthood which we have received from Christ. I also desire that you should entrust your Priesthood to her in a special way. Allow me to do it myself, *entrusting to the Mother of Christ* each one of you—without any exception—in a solemn and at the same time simple and humble way. And I ask each of you, dear brothers, to do it yourselves, in the way dictated to you by your own heart, especially by your love for Christ the Priest, and also by your own weakness, which goes hand in hand with your desire for service and holiness. I ask you to do this.

—Saint John Paul II, Letter to Priests for
Holy Thursday, 1979

Mary, Mother of Priests, bless me with the humility to entrust my daily ministry to your love and protection, as I seek to serve your Son with obedient and trusting faith.

Martha, Martha, you are anxious and worried about many things. There is need of only one thing. (Luke 10:41-42)

In *The Edge of Sadness* [author Edwin O'Connor], a novel about a priest in a busy parish who through depression ends up an alcoholic, the central character, Father Kennedy, did not bother spending too much time with the Lord. Prayer and preparation for liturgical functions were activities he fitted in if there happened to be any time left over from other more pressing involvements. He gradually convinced himself that work was his prayer and that priestly work was all that was necessary. But he eventually described his own alarming situation in these words:

> What he (i.e., a priest) may not see is that he stands in some danger of losing himself in the strangely engrossing business of simply "being busy." And gradually, too, he may find that he is rather uncomfortable whenever he is not busy. He may find fewer and fewer moments in which he can absent himself from activity, in which he can be alone, can be silent, can be still, in which he can reflect and pray. . . . The loss of such moments is grave and perilous. . . . Something within him will have atrophied from disuse, something precious, something vital. It will have gone almost without his knowing it, but one day, in a great crisis, say, he will reach for it and it will not be there.

A priest in a parish must take care to find some time to be alone, to be still, to be silent, to let himself pray and reflect on his life. It is strange that the busy priest, no matter how busy he is, always seems to be able to squeeze more people into his time, but unfortunately the last person to get squeezed in is often the Lord himself. If you do not offer Christ prime time, it is not top of your list of appointments every day, you are heading for trouble. The Lord always seems to be at the end of the line waiting to be seen, waiting to be heard by the feverish character who is so busy taking care of the Lord's people.

—Gerard McGinnity, *Christmen: Experience of Priesthood Today*, 48–49

Lord, I wholeheartedly confess that I have often been too busy for prayer, too busy to nurture my friendship with you. Help me realize that "without you, I am nothing."

[H]e said to me, "My grace is sufficient for you, for power is made perfect in weakness." (2 Cor 12:9)

In today's world, as in the troubled times of the Curé of Ars, the lives and activity of priests need to be distinguished by a forceful witness to the Gospel. As Pope Paul VI rightly noted, "modern man listens more willingly to witnesses than to teachers, and if he does listen to teachers, it is because they are witnesses." Lest we experience existential emptiness and the effectiveness of our ministry be compromised, we need to ask ourselves ever anew: "Are we truly pervaded by the Word of God? Is that Word truly the nourishment we live by, even more than bread and the things of this world? Do we really know that Word? Do we love it? Are we deeply engaged with this Word to the point that it really leaves a mark on our lives and shapes our thinking?" Just as Jesus called the Twelve to be with Him, and only later sent them forth to preach, so too in our days priests are called to assimilate that "new style of life" which was inaugurated by the Lord Jesus and taken up by the Apostles.

It was complete commitment to this "new style of life" which marked the priestly ministry of the Curé of Ars. Pope John XXIII, in his Encyclical Letter "*Sacerdotii nostri primordia*," published in 1959 on the first centenary of the death of St. John Mary Vianney, presented his asceticism with special reference to the "three evangelical counsels" which the Pope considered necessary also for priests: "even though priests are not bound to embrace these evangelical counsels by virtue of the clerical state, these counsels nonetheless offer them, as they do all the faithful, the surest road to the desired goal of Christian perfection."

—Pope Benedict XVI, Letter Proclaiming
a Year for Priests, June 16, 2009

Lord Jesus, help me appreciate daily that it is knowledge and love of your Word that sustains the "new style of life" to which you summon me.

Gathering the Community September 11

Now you are Christ's body, and individually parts of it. (1 Cor 12:27)

Cultivating such an attitude [of service] toward all the lay faithful . . . who themselves have been marked by the gift of a vocation received from Christ, the priest can carry out this social task which is linked with his vocation as a pastor, that is to say, he can "gather together" the Christian communities to which he is sent. The council on several occasions emphasizes this task. For example, it says that priests "exercising . . . the function of Christ . . . gather together God's family as a brotherhood all of one mind and lead them in the Spirit, through Christ, to God the Father."

This "gathering together" is service. Each of us must be aware of gathering the community together not around ourselves but around Christ, and not for ourselves but for Christ, so that he can act in this community and at the same time in each person. He acts by the power of his Spirit, the Paraclete, in the measure of the "gift" which each person receives in this Spirit "for the common benefit."

Consequently, this "gathering together" is service, and all the more service, to the extent that the priest "presides" over the community. In this regard the council emphasizes that "priests should preside in such a way that they seek the things of Jesus, not the things which are their own. They must work together with the lay faithful."

This "gathering together" is not to be understood as something occasional but as a continuous and coherent "building up" of the community. . . . Priests must "discover with the instinct of faith, acknowledge with joy and foster with diligence the various humble and exalted charisms of the laity," as we read in the council's decree.

—Saint John Paul II, Letter to Priests for
Holy Thursday, 1989

I meditate on the many ways that I build up the community of faith by my ministry. What are the recognizable signs that the community is strengthened by my service?

> Before I formed you in the womb I knew you, / before you were born I
> dedicated you, / a prophet to the nations I appointed you. (Jer 1:5)

Who am I? Where do I come from? Where am I going? I am nothing.
Everything I possess, my being, life, understanding, will and memory—all
were given me by God, all belong to him. Twenty short years ago all that
I see around me was already here; the same sun, moon and stars, the same
mountains, seas, deserts, beasts, plants and everything was proceeding in
its appointed way under the watchful eyes of Divine Providence. And I? I
was not here. Everything was being done without me, nobody was thinking
of me, nobody could imagine me, even in dreams, because I did not exist.

And you, O God, with a wonderful gesture of love, you who are from
the beginning and before all time, you drew me forth from my nothingness,
you gave me being, life, a soul, in fact all the faculties of my body and
spirit; you opened my eyes to this light which sheds its radiance around
me, you created me. So you are my Master and I am your creature. I am
nothing without you, and through you I am all that I am. . . .

What am I set in this world to do? To serve God. He is my supreme
Master because he has created me, because he preserves my life, and so
I am his servant. Therefore my whole life must be consecrated to him, to
carry out his wishes, in all things and at all times. So, when I do not think
of God, . . . I neglect my most compelling duty, I become a disobedient
servant. And what will God do with me then? O Lord, . . . do not dismiss
me from your service, as I would only too well deserve.

Servant of God! What a proud title and what a wonderful service this is!

—Saint John XXIII, *Journal of a Soul*, 126–27

I reflect on the depth of the call that I have received from God, the God
of my vocation.

Our Sins: A Common Injury to All   September 13

> Whoever causes one of these little ones who believe in me to sin, it would be better for him to have a great millstone hung around his neck and to be drowned in the depths of the sea. (Matt 18:6)

The priest's shortcomings simply cannot be concealed. On the contrary, even the most trivial soon get known. The weakest athlete can keep his weakness secret as long as he remains at home and pits himself against nobody; but when he strips for the contest, he is soon shown up. So with other men: those who lead a retired and inactive life have their solitude as a cloak for their private faults; but when they are brought into public life, they are compelled to strip off their retirement like a garment and to show everyone their naked souls by their outward movements . . . The beauty of his soul must shine out brightly all around, to be able to gladden and enlighten the souls of all who see.

The sins of ordinary men are committed in the dark, so to speak, and ruin only those who commit them. But when a man becomes famous and is known to many, his misdeeds inflict a common injury on all. They make backsliders even more supine in their efforts for what is good, and drive to despair those who want to improve. Apart from this, the offense of the insignificant, even if made public, harms no one seriously. But those who are set upon the pinnacle of this honor not only catch every eye; more than that, however trifling their offences, these little things seem great to others, since everyone measures sin, not by the size of the offense, but by the standing of the sinner.

A priest must be sober and clear-sighted and possess a thousand eyes looking in every direction, for he lives, not for himself alone, but for a great multitude.

—Saint John Chrysostom, *On the Priesthood* III

How conscious am I of giving scandal to the weakest members of the community?

September 14 The Shepherd at the Service of Unity

> I have other sheep that do not belong to this fold. These also I must lead, and they will hear my voice, and there will be one flock, one shepherd. (John 10:16)

The relationship between the Cross and unity is revealed: the Cross is the price of unity. Above all, however, it is the universal horizon of Jesus' action that emerges.

If, in his prophecy about the shepherd, Ezekiel was aiming to restore unity among the dispersed tribes of Israel (cf. Ez 34:22-24), here it is a question not only of the unification of a dispersed Israel but of the unification of all the children of God. . . .

Jesus' mission concerns all humanity. . . . The Church must never be satisfied with the ranks of those whom she has reached at a certain point or say that others are fine as they are: Muslims, Hindus and so forth. The Church can never retreat comfortably to within the limits of her own environment. She is charged with universal solicitude; she must be concerned with and for one and all.

. . . Obviously, a priest, a pastor of souls, must first and foremost be concerned with those who believe and live with the Church, who seek in her their way of life and on their part, like living stones, build the Church, hence, also build and support the priest.

However, we must also—as the Lord says—go out ever anew "to the highways and hedges" (Lk 14:23), to deliver God's invitation to his banquet also to those who have so far heard nothing or have not been stirred within. This universal service has many forms. One of them is also the commitment to the inner unity of the Church, so that over and above differences and limitations she may be a sign of God's presence in the world, which alone can create this unity.

—Pope Benedict XVI, Homily for the Ordination to
the Priesthood, May 7, 2006

In what ways do I extend a welcoming hand to those of other faiths? How am I an agent of unity in my own ministry?

With Mary at the Altar

When Jesus saw his mother and the disciple there whom he loved, he said to his mother, "Woman, behold, your son." Then he said to the disciple, "Behold, your mother." (John 19:26-27)

There is no indication that the Mother of Christ was present in the Upper Room at the Last Supper. But she was present on Calvary, at the foot of the cross, where as the Second Vatican Council teaches, "she stood, in accordance with the divine plan, suffering grievously with her only-begotten Son, uniting herself with a maternal heart to his sacrifice, and lovingly consenting to the immolation of this victim which she herself had brought forth." How far the fiat uttered by Mary at the annunciation had taken her!

When, acting in persona Christi, we celebrate the sacrament of the one same sacrifice of which Christ is and remains the only priest and victim, we must not forget this suffering of his Mother, in whom were fulfilled Simeon's words in the Temple at Jerusalem: "A sword will pierce through your own soul also." They were spoken directly to Mary forty days after Jesus' birth. On Golgotha, beneath the cross, these words were completely fulfilled. When on the cross Mary's Son revealed himself fully as the "sign of contradiction," it was then that this immolation and mortal agony also reached her maternal heart.

Behold the agony of the heart of the Mother who suffered together with him, "consenting to the immolation of this victim which she herself had brought forth." Here we reach the high point of Mary's presence in the mystery of Christ and of the Church on earth. . . .

Dear brothers: . . . when we celebrate the Eucharist and stand each day on Golgotha, we need to have near us the one who through heroic faith carried to its zenith her union with her Son, precisely then on Golgotha.

—Saint John Paul II, Letter to Priests for
Holy Thursday, 1988

Lord Jesus, give me the heart of your mother when I am standing at the altar, so that I might fully unite my life to yours.

Rejoice in the Lord always. I shall say it again: rejoice! (Phil 4:4)

How are you going to show those souls who need it so dreadfully, the joy and delightfulness of God and surrender to God, unless you have it yourselves? But that means giving time, patience, effort to such a special discipline and cultivation of your attention as artists must give, if they are to enter deeply into the reality and joy of natural loveliness and impart it in their work. Do you see the great facts and splendors of religion with the eye of an artist and a lover, or with the eye of a man of business, or the eye of the man in the street? Is your sense of wonder and mystery keen and deep? Such a sense of wonder and mystery, such a living delight in God, is of course in technical language a grace. It is something added, given, to the natural man. But, like all other graces, its reception by us depends very largely on the exercise of our will and our desire, on our mental and emotional openness and plasticity. It will not be forced upon us. And we show our will and desire, keep ourselves plastic, in and through the character of our prayer. You remember Jeremy Taylor's saying: "Prayer is only the body of the bird—desires are its wings."

All this means that the secret prayer of the priest must have a certain contemplative color about it: that one of its main functions must be to feed and expand his sense and desire of God. Let us get this supernatural orientation firmly fixed in our minds, as the central character of a fruitful inner life.

—Evelyn Underhill, *Concerning the Inner Life*, 97–98

Lord Jesus, renew my prayer with a sense of wonder and mystery.

A Priest and His Bishop

> This is how all will know that you are my disciples, if you have love for one another. (Jn 13:35)

Priests are the visible sign of unity in the parish community, and through their loyalty to the bishop, they exercise a ministry of unity in the diocese. The council goes on to say: "presbyters for their part should keep in mind the fullness of the sacrament of order which the bishops enjoy and should reverence in their persons the authority of Christ the Supreme Pastor (PO, 7). The sacred powers of priests extend the ministry of the bishop in scope and variety.

Their common relationship with the bishop in obedience and filial affection, loyalty and willing cooperation, should establish a bond of unity among priests. The council describes them as "an intimate sacramental brotherhood" (PO, 8). Their readiness to help one another, whether diocesan or regular, flows from the nature of the presbyteral order. The brotherly bond that exists among them means that they have an obligation to care for one another and a responsibility toward those in difficulty. It also means taking time to help one another, "even discreetly warning them when necessary" (ibid.).

The role of priests as the bishop's vicar implies both courage and humility. They courageously represent the Church's authority and compassion as the voice of the bishop who is the chief representative of Christ in the local church. For his part, the bishop is encouraged to know his priests deeply and well, to listen carefully to their analysis of the needs and possibilities of the diocesan church, and to be accessible and genuine with them—truly a father figure. This implies humility on the part of priests and deference in their obedience to the pastoral judgment and ecclesial discipline of the bishop as leader of the local church. These days, initiatives are appropriate and required in both directions between bishops and priests, if real fraternal solidarity in the one priesthood they share is to be authentic.

The spirituality of both bishops and priests will be nurtured by the development of mutual trust and common concerns. At the very least, both bishop and priests need to remember and reverence the fact that it is God who has called them to their offices of pastoral service.

—Paul J. Philibert, *Stewards of God's Mysteries*, 33–34

Lord Jesus, strengthen the bonds of love and trust between priests and bishops, so that we might manifest our unity in Christ.

And now I will no longer be in the world, but they are in the world, while I am coming to you. (John 17:11)

Scripture shows in many ways that whenever God takes men into his service and entrusts tasks to them, whenever his word seeks to appear to mankind, it is not only the individual acceptance of the person called that is required; that person is also asked to adopt a lifestyle in which his recruitment into God's service becomes sacramentally visible and is thus seen to be credible. A few pointers to this: since Abraham was to be a "blessing for all generations" (Gen 12:2), and since he and his descendants were promised "a city with strong walls, planned and built by God himself" (Heb 11:10), he had to leave his home in faith, and set out into darkness. He became a stranger without a home. It is in this way that the call he received took visible form. Moses and the prophets further develop this unity of vocation and witness of lifestyle: . . . Their vocation puts its stamp on their life, even in the most personal and intimate way (the marriage of Hosea; Jeremiah's fate and his renunciation of marriage, joy in life, success; the suffering of the Servant of God; the ascetic life of the Baptist). How could it be otherwise with Jesus! In him we find the most perfect unity of mission and life. The supremacy of God—the centre of Jesus' mission and activity—is as it were reality in himself "before" he brings it to mankind. Origen calls Jesus Christ simply the "*autobasileia*": the kingdom of God in person. He is what he does and he does what he is. In his life he is the union of sign and reality, of witness and testimony.

—Gisbert Greshake, *The Meaning of
Christian Priesthood*, 111

How does my personal and ministerial life reflect the liberating presence of the kingdom of God?

> For as often as you eat this bread and drink the cup, you proclaim the death of the Lord until he comes. (1 Cor 11:26)

Once we have begun to speak of the priest's work in the world, we must consider more expressly than we have yet done the mystery that is comparable to the heart in the body of the Church, inasmuch as it conducts with even pulse beats the nourishing strength of the blood to the individual members. The priest is the man to whom the sacrifice of the Church, the liturgical repetition of Christ's Last Supper, is committed, and because this is after all the inmost and ultimate thing in the priestly existence, we celebrate the beginning of that kind of life, not with his first baptism or with the first time he says the words of forgiveness of sin, but with the first time he celebrates the sacrifice of the altar, and we celebrate it with him.

Here at such a moment we find everything brought together: men, the Church, God, Christ, the sacrifice of the cross, the living and the dead, the poverty of earth and the blessings of heaven. For here is the glorified Lord in the midst of His community, the community of the sanctified and redeemed, whom the priest, commissioned by Christ Himself and possessing an authority that comes from above and not from below, leads in before the throne of grace, so that this community offers the eternal Father as the sacrifice of this entire Church the Lord made present by the priest's word, to the praise of His name and the salvation of all who celebrate this sacrifice and whom we remember in love and fidelity. Authorized by Christ himself, who loves His Church and has given her His own sacrifice the priest has the power to celebrate the sacrifice of eternal reconciliation in the name of all, with all, and for all.

—Karl Rahner, *Meditations on the Sacraments*, 66–67

Can I take more time in prayerful preparation for the celebration of the Eucharist, so that I am less distracted and more present to the sacred mysteries?

September 20   In Union with Christ and the Church

> I revealed your name to those whom you gave me out of the world. They belonged to you, and you gave them to me, and they have kept your word. (John 17:6)

By its very nature, the ordained ministry can be carried out only to the extent that the priest is united to Christ through sacramental participation in the priestly order, and thus to the extent that he is in hierarchical communion with his own bishop. The ordained ministry has a radical "communitarian form" and can only be carried out as "a collective work." The Council dealt extensively with this communal aspect of the nature of the priesthood, examining in succession the relationship of the priest with his own bishop, with other priests and with the lay faithful.

The ministry of priests is above all communion and a responsible and necessary cooperation with the bishop's ministry, in concern for the universal Church and for the individual particular churches, for whose service they form with the bishop a single presbyterate.

Each priest, whether diocesan or religious, is united to the other members of this presbyterate on the basis of the sacrament of holy orders and by particular bonds of apostolic charity, ministry and fraternity. All priests in fact, whether diocesan or religious, share in the one priesthood of Christ the head and shepherd; "they work for the same cause, namely, the building up of the body of Christ, which demands a variety of functions and new adaptations, especially at the present time," and is enriched down the centuries by ever new charisms.

—Saint John Paul II, *Pastores Dabo Vobis*, 17

Lord Jesus, my share in your priesthood unites me with all members of the church, but especially with my bishop and brother priests. May this unity be a source of strength and encouragement in my ministry.

What Is a Priest?

> As a shepherd examines his flock while he himself is among his scattered sheep, so will I examine my sheep. I will deliver them from every place where they were scattered on the day of dark clouds. (Ezek 34:12)

A priest is a lover of God, a priest is a lover of men,
a priest is a holy man because he walks before the face of the All-Holy.
A priest understands all things, a priest forgives all things, a priest encompasses all things.
The heart of a priest is pierced, like Christ's, with the lance of love.
The heart of a priest is open, like Christ's, for the whole world to
 walk through.

The heart of a priest is a vessel of compassion,
the heart of a priest is a chalice of love,
the heart of a priest is the trysting place of human and divine love.

A priest is a man whose goal is to be another Christ;
A priest is a man who lives to serve.

A priest is a man who has crucified himself so that he too may be lifted up
and draw all things to Christ.

A priest is a man in love with God.
A priest is a gift of God to man and of man to God.
A priest is the symbol of the Word made flesh,
a priest is the naked sword of God's justice,
A priest is the hand of God's mercy, a priest is the reflection of God's love.

Nothing can be greater in this world than a priest,
nothing but God himself.

—Catherine de Hueck Doherty, *Dear Father*, 1–2

Which image from this reading resonates with my own understanding of priestly life?

> Now if [I] do what I do not want, it is no longer I who do it, but sin
> that dwells in me. So, then, I discover the principle that when I want
> to do right, evil is at hand. For I take delight in the law of God, in my
> inner self, but I see in my members another principle at war with the
> law of my mind, taking me captive to the law of sin that dwells in my
> members. (Rom 7:20-23)

Despite the call to sanctity, despite his sacral character, the priest will
fall. There is but one perfect man, and that is Jesus Christ. "All have sinned
and fallen short of the glory of God" (Rm 3:23). "If we say, 'We are without
sin,' we deceive ourselves, and the truth is not in us" (1 Jn 1:8). Scripture is
filled with ample examples of those who have been called by God and who
have fallen. The human frailty of priests should surprise no one: of such is
the kingdom of heaven; it is for such that Christ came. As Henri de Lubac
points out in *The Splendor of the Church*, "the Church is holy, not because
it is composed of flawless people, but because the Lord bestows holiness on
her as an entirely unmerited gift" (85). Indeed, in his weakness the priest
finds added strength in the ministry he offers God's people. What is often
seen as scandal—that is, the sinfulness of the Church and her ministers—
can be a source of comfort. "I must admit," writes Cardinal Ratzinger, "that
to me this unholy holiness of the Church has in itself something infinitely
comforting about it. Would one not be bound to despair in face of a holiness
that was spotless and could only operate on us by judging us and consuming
us by fire?" (*Introduction to Christianity*, 265).

The sacrament of confession is for the priest as well as the laity. There,
on his knees as penitent, the priest enacts his ministry and realizes it as
surely and in as sacrificial a manner as it is when he stands at the altar of
God.

—John M. Haas, "The Sacral Character of
the Priest as the Foundation for
his Moral Life and Teaching," 140–41

I reflect upon the role that the sacrament of reconciliation plays in my
spiritual life.

Priesthood, Such a Necessary Gift   September 23

> I will appoint for you shepherds after my own heart, / who will shepherd you wisely and prudently. (Jer 3:15)

In these words from the prophet Jeremiah, God promises his people that he will never leave them without shepherds to gather them together and guide them: "I will set shepherds over them [my sheep] who will care for them, and they shall fear no more, nor be dismayed (*Jer* 23:4).

The Church, the People of God, constantly experiences the reality of this prophetic message and continues joyfully to thank God for it. She knows that Jesus Christ himself is the living, supreme and definitive fulfillment of God's promise: "I am the good shepherd" (*Jn.* 10:11). He, "the great shepherd of the sheep" (*Heb.* 13:20), entrusted to the apostles and their successors the ministry of shepherding God's flock (cf. *Jn.* 21:15ff.; 1 Pt. 5:2).

Without priests the Church would not be able to live that fundamental obedience which is at the very heart of her existence and her mission in history, an obedience in response to the command of Christ: "Go therefore and make disciples of all nations" (*Mt.* 28:19) and "Do this in remembrance of me" (*Lk.* 22:19; cf. 1 *Cor.* 11:24), i.e., an obedience to the command to announce the Gospel and to renew daily the sacrifice of the giving of his body and the shedding of his blood for the life of the world.

. . . "Brother priests, we want to express our appreciation to you, who are our most important collaborators in the apostolate. Your priesthood is absolutely vital. There is no substitute for it. You carry the main burden of priestly ministry through your day-to-day service of the faithful."

—Saint John Paul II, *Pastores Dabo Vobis*, 1

Jesus, my Brother Priest, thank you for this marvelous gift that you have bestowed upon me, the gift of being called shepherd of your people. May I be ever worthy of this calling.

> "I made known to them your name and I will make it known, that the love with which you loved me may be in them and I in them." (John 17:26)

This Spirit which was "poured out" in us on the day of our ordination is now also in us in the hour of the renewal of ordination. He wants to give himself even more intimately, wants to fill all the hidden chambers of our heart and the whole extent of our life even more intimately: the Spirit of the Father and the Son; the Spirit of rebirth and the divine sonship of men; the Spirit who is Lord also of this age; the Spirit who transforms the world into a great sacrifice of praise to the Father, just as we by his power change bread and wine into the body and blood of the one victim; . . . the Spirit who alone still awakens new life out of sin and darkness . . . the Spirit of the priesthood of Jesus Christ who transforms the helpless words of our preaching into the word and act of God, who lets the forgiveness on earth become reconciliation in heaven, who turns our gestures of blessing into Christ's sacraments, who, by consecrating the quiet half hour in the morning of our days, transforms it into the reconciling act of the Lord. This Spirit was the spirit of our ordination day, this Spirit is the spirit of our renewal of ordination. If he comes down into our life, then everything we are, do and suffer can be consecrated into a priestly life. For everything was seen and loved in advance of the day we became priests; hence nothing can withstand this blessing and transforming action of God's love, if only we give it room, if only we say: do *thou* ordain us anew today.

—Karl Rahner,
"The Renewal of Priestly Ordination," 174–75

Lord Jesus, you have made me your own, and continue to strengthen me with the grace of my priestly ordination. May I daily surrender the whole of my life to your service.

Priests: Men of Personal Holiness September 25

> [B]e renewed in the spirit of your minds, and put on the new self, created in God's way in righteousness and holiness of truth. (Eph 4:23-24)

It must always be remembered that as the Council says: "Priests will acquire holiness in their own distinctive way by exercising their functions sincerely and tirelessly in the Spirit of Christ." Thus, the proclamation of the word encourages them to achieve in themselves what they teach to others. The celebration of the sacraments strengthens them in faith and in union with Christ. The whole pastoral ministry develops their charity: "While they govern and shepherd the People of God they are encouraged by the love of the Good Shepherd to give their lives for the sheep. They, too, are prepared for the supreme sacrifice." Their ideal will be to achieve unity of life in Christ, integrating prayer and ministry, contemplation and action, because they continually seek the Father's will and the gift of themselves for the flock.

Moreover, it is a source of courage and joy for the presbyter to know that his personal commitment to sanctification helps make his ministry effective. In fact, as the Council recalls: "While it is possible for God's grace to carry out the work of salvation through unworthy ministers, yet God ordinarily prefers to show his wonders through those men who are more submissive to the impulse and guidance of the Holy Spirit and who, because of their intimate union with Christ and their holiness of life, are able to say with St. Paul: 'It is no longer I who live, but Christ who lives in me.'"

—Saint John Paul II, General Audience, May 26, 1993

Lord Jesus, you have blessed me with the gift of priestly ministry. May I serve you with fidelity, and may my own commitment to holiness of life be a witness to your abiding love for those whom I serve in your name.

> The message of the cross is foolishness to those who are perishing, but to us who are being saved it is the power of God. (1 Cor 1:18)

The Church is not unaware that the choice of consecrated celibacy, since it involves a series of hard renunciations which affect the very depths of a man, presents also grave difficulties and problems to which the men of today are particularly sensitive. In fact, it might seem that celibacy conflicts with the solemn recognition of human values by the Church in the recent Council. And yet more careful consideration reveals that this sacrifice of the human love experienced by most men in family life and given up by the priest for the love of Christ, is really a singular tribute paid to that great love. For it is universally recognized that man has always offered to God that which is worthy of both the giver and the receiver.

Moreover, the Church cannot and should not fail to realize that the choice of celibacy—provided that it is made with human and Christian prudence and responsibility—is governed by grace which, far from destroying or doing violence to nature, elevates it and imparts to it supernatural powers and vigor. God, who has created and redeemed man, knows what He can ask of him and gives him everything necessary to be able to do what his Creator and Redeemer asks of him. St. Augustine, who had fully and painfully experienced in himself the nature of man, exclaimed: "Grant what You command, and command what You will."

The true, profound reason for dedicated celibacy is, as We have said, the choice of a closer and more complete relationship with the mystery of Christ and the Church for the good of all mankind: in this choice there is no doubt that those highest human values are able to find their fullest expression.

—Blessed Pope Paul VI,
Sacerdotalis Caelibatus, 50–54

What signs are there that celibacy has been a blessing in my life?

Bearing Fruit in God's Vineyard September 27

"I am the true vine, and my Father is the vine grower." (John 15:1).

Allow me to call to mind today the above words from the Gospel according to John. They are linked to the Liturgy of Holy Thursday: "Before the feast of Passover, when Jesus knew that his hour had come" (Jn. 13:1), he washed his disciples' feet, and then spoke to them intimately and with great candor, as Saint John tells us. This Farewell Discourse also contains the allegory of the vine and the branches: "I am the vine, you are the branches. He who abides in me, and I in him, he it is that bears much fruit, for apart from me you can do nothing" (Jn. 15:5). . . .

Christ is the true Vine. If the Eternal Father cultivates his vineyard in this world, he does so in the power of the Truth and Life which are in the Son. Here are found the ever-new beginning and inexhaustible source of the formation of every Christian, and especially of every priest. On Holy Thursday let us try in a particular way to grow in our awareness of this reality and in the attitude needed for us to be able to remain, in Christ, open to the breath of the Spirit of Truth, and to bear abundant fruit in God's vineyard.

Let us give thanks for the gift of the Priesthood which we share. At the same time let us pray that all those throughout the world who are offered the grace of a priestly vocation will respond to this gift, so that there will be no lack of labourers for the great harvest (cf. Mt 9:37).

—Saint John Paul II, Letter to Priests for
Holy Thursday, 1992

Lord Jesus, may I always remain convinced that without you, my priestly ministry would be fruitless. Apart from you I can do nothing.

September 28　Lord, Transubstantiate My Servitude

> For the bread of God is that which comes down from heaven and gives life to the world. (John 6:33)

O God of my vocation, I am only a poor mask, behind which You have chosen to approach others as the hidden God. Grant me the grace day by day to be ever more free from sin and self-seeking. Even then I shall remain what I can't help being, your disguise and Your unprofitable servant. But then at least I shall grow ever more like your Son, who also had to envelop the eternal light of His divinity in the form of a servant, to be found in the garb and the livery of a man.

When I bear the burden of Your calling, when Your mission weighs down heavily upon me, when Your Majesty humbles me, and my weakness is taken up into that of Your Son, then I may confidently trust that the hindrance which I have been to Your coming may still turn out to be a blessing to my brothers and sisters. Then perhaps You will transubstantiate my servitude—for only You could work such a change, unseen by me and my fellows—into a somehow sacramental form, under whose poverty You will be the bread of life for my brethren.

O God of my vocation, let my life be consumed as the Sacred Host, so that my brothers and sisters and I may live in You, and You in us, for all eternity.

—Karl Rahner, *Encounters with Silence*, 77–78

Will I make the effort this day to turn my whole life over to the transforming power of Christ, so that my life may be consumed in love?

At the Disposal of God and His Work

> Rather, he emptied himself, / taking the form of a slave, / coming in human likeness; / and found human in appearance, / he humbled himself, / becoming obedient to death, even death on a cross. (Phil 2:7-8)

Jesus was the obedient one par excellence. In the Christological hymn of the epistle to the Philippians (2:5-11), St. Paul calls out to the community: "Have the same mind in you as Christ Jesus, who . . . was obedient unto . . . the death on the cross." This obedience he understands and explains as a radical emptying of himself: Jesus keeps back nothing for himself, holds on to nothing, but humbles and surrenders himself completely. That is the fundamental shape of biblical obedience.

Obedience of this kind is essentially determined by listening. That person is obedient who does not concentrate on himself but instead is attentive to the demand of the hour, in which he discerns the will of God. He is then available and ready to do what he perceives to be God's will. Thus, an obedient person regards his whole existence as a surrender, i.e., a going out of himself when called. Another central text of the New Testament expresses the same idea in the following way: "Christ speaks at his entrance into the world: Sacrifice and oblation you did not desire, but a body you prepared for me; holocausts and sin-offerings were not pleasing to you. Then I said, Behold I have come, as it is written of me in the book, to do your will, O God" (Heb 10:5f). Thus Christ understood his whole existence (his body which is prepared for him) as something which will be given up to do the will of God. "My food is to do the will of him who sent me and to finish his work" (Jn 4:34). "My food"—what touches the innermost basis of existence, from which one lives—consists in putting myself at the disposal of God and his work.

—Gisbert Greshake, *The Meaning of Christian Priesthood*, 132–33

In what ways have I made obedience a way of life?

> [W]e always pray for you, that our God may make you worthy of his
> calling and powerfully bring to fulfillment every good purpose and
> every effort of faith, that the name of the Lord Jesus may be glorified in
> you, and you in him . . . (2 Thess 1:11-12)

We read in the Decree *Presbyterorum Ordinis*: "Hence the priesthood
of presbyters, while presupposing the sacraments of initiation, is nevertheless conferred by its own particular sacrament. Through that sacrament
presbyters, by the anointing of the Holy Spirit, are signed with a special
character and so are configured to Christ the Priest is such a way that they
are able to act in the person of Christ the Head."

This character, in those who receive it through the sacramental anointing of the Holy Spirit, is a sign of: *a special consecration*, in relationship
to Baptism and Confirmation; *a deeper configuration to Christ, the Priest*,
who makes them his active ministers in the official worship of God and in
sanctifying their brothers and sisters, the *ministerial powers* to be exercise
in the name Christ, the head and shepherd of the Church.

In the presbyter's soul the character is also a sign and vehicle of the
special graces for carrying out the ministry, graces related to the sanctifying grace that Holy Orders imparts as a sacrament both at the time it is
conferred and throughout his exercise of and growth in the ministry. It
thus surrounds and involves the presbyter in an economy of sanctification,
which the ministry itself implies both for the one who exercises it and for
those who benefit from it.

The presbyter participates ontologically in the priesthood of Christ; he
is truly consecrated, a "man of the sacred." This is the priest's truest identity.

—Saint John Paul II, General Audience,
March 31, 1993

Am I conscious of the sanctifying grace of the sacrament of holy orders in
the very exercise of my ministry?

I praise you, because I am wonderfully made; / wonderful are your works! / My very self you know. (Ps 139:14)

Thank you, O God, for the gift of the priesthood. *"Te Deum laudamus, Te Dominum confitemur . . . "* We praise you and we thank you, O God: all the earth adores you. We, your ministers, with the voices of the Prophets and the chorus of the Apostles, proclaim you as Father and Lord of life, of every form of life which comes from you alone. We recognize you, O Most Holy Trinity, as the birthplace and beginning of our vocation; You, the Father, from eternity have thought of us, wanted us and loved us; You, the Son, have chosen us and called us to share in your unique and eternal priesthood; You, the Holy Spirit, have filled us with your gifts and have consecrated us with your holy anointing.

You, the Lord of time and history, have placed us on the threshold of the Third Christian Millennium, in order to be witnesses to the salvation which you have accomplished for all humanity.

We, the Church which proclaims your glory, implore you: let there never be lacking holy priests to serve the Gospel; let there solemnly resound in every Cathedral and in every corner of the world the hymn *"Veni, Creator Spiritus."* Come, O Creator Spirit! Come to raise up new generations of young people, ready to work in the Lord's vineyard, to spread the Kingdom of God to the furthermost ends of the earth. And you, Mary, Mother of Christ, who at the foot of the Cross accepted us as beloved sons with the Apostle John, continue to watch over our vocation.

To you we entrust the years of ministry which Providence will grant us yet to live. Be near us to guide us along the paths of the world, to meet the men and women whom your Son redeemed with his blood.

Help us to fulfill completely the will of Jesus, born of you for the salvation of humanity. O Christ, you are our hope! *"In te, Domine, speravi, non confundar in aeternum."*

—Saint John Paul II, Letter to Priests for
Holy Thursday, 1996

Heavenly Father, how deeply does Saint John Paul love the priesthood of your Son Jesus Christ! Renew my own love for this precious gift.

> Rising very early before dawn, he left and went off to a deserted place, where he prayed. (Mark 1:35)

Practically every day, for the past thirty years, I have spent an hour in prayer before the Blessed Sacrament. I first heard about the idea of a daily "holy hour" when I was a seminarian. I knew that this was something for me. So, each day I rise and spend an hour before the tabernacle or at least in a quiet place if the Sacrament is not at hand.

Some priests find the prospect of an hour of prayer each day to be daunting. However, the time flies by; I start—and suddenly it is over. I typically combine quiet meditation with a slow reading of the Liturgy of the Hours. In prayer, we enter into God's timelessness.

I began this holy hour as a way to nourish my spiritual life and to be more open to the Spirit. I strongly believe that my priesthood has become more fruitful because of this "investment." I do not think I would have enough time to do all that I need to do as a priest if I did not spend this hour in prayer.

But, in the last few years, my focus has changed. I have come to treasure this time simply to be with the Lord. I feel his presence and find it brings me a deep peace and joy. I look forward to being with him.

And now, after many years, I sense that it is he who longs for these daily encounters even more than I. Just as a loving parent longs for the return of a child, so our loving God waits for us. As I step into the chapel to begin the hour, I feel a sense of relief to be back "home" and to "see" his face. But more than I, it is he who has been waiting for me.

—Stephen J. Rossetti, "God Waits for Me," 141

Lord Jesus, grace me with the courage to go daily with you into extended times of prayer and communion.

> May the Lord direct your hearts to the love of God and to the endurance of Christ. (2 Thess 3:5)

One should not be frightened by the word "contemplation" and the spiritual commitment it entails. It could be said that, independently of forms and life-styles, among which the "contemplative life" remains the most splendid jewel of Christ's Bride, the Church, the call to hear and meditate on the word of God in a contemplative spirit is valid for everyone, so that hearts and minds may be nourished on it. This helps the priest to develop a way of thinking and of looking at the world with wisdom, in the perspective of its supreme purpose: God and his plan of salvation. The synod says: "To examine the events of life in the light of the Gospel."

Herein lies supernatural wisdom, above all as a gift of the Holy Spirit, who makes it possible to exercise good judgment in the light of the "ultimate reasons," the "eternal things." Wisdom thus becomes the principal factor in identifying with Christ in thought, judgment, the evaluation of any matter however large or small, so that the priest (like every Christian only more so) reflects the light, obedience to the Father, practical zeal, rhythm of prayer and action, and one could almost say, the spiritual breath of Christ.

This goal can be reached by allowing oneself to be guided by the Holy Spirit in meditating on the Gospel, which fosters a deeper union with Christ, helps one to enter ever further into the Master's thought and strengthens the *personal* attachment to him.

—Saint John Paul II, General Audience, June 2, 1993

Lord, grant that I may be among a great number of priests who in their prayer life discover, assimilate, and taste the wisdom of God.

> Then the LORD said: "Go out and stand on the mountain before the
> LORD; the LORD will pass by." (1 Kgs 19:11)

A call is always from the Lord. He knows all the world's roads and
the needs of all engaged upon them. He continues to work redemption by
calling persons to help him in this task. That they should help, however, is
not what first becomes apparent from the call.

There are many who hear God's call over and over again without taking it seriously. They have an exact idea of what God does in order to find
workers for his vineyard. They can develop theories about the answers of
those called and they know precisely what the minimum is that a person
can offer God. They also know the maximum. But in all this they close their
hearts, as if none of it concerned them personally, as if their role were only
to be observers, or at best, witnesses. They amuse themselves speculating
who could be meant, or how this or that one ought to have answered. They
would even like to give their dear God advice as to how to make his call
even more emphatic and enticing, how to make his language more under-
standable. Only they themselves do not hear.

God calls and man has only to listen. The ear which God the Father
has given man is capable of receiving the call that goes out from God. But
it seems that it is always a long road from the ear to the will and to love.

God calls in Scripture, God calls in sermons, God also calls in every
prayer. There is no truly prayed prayer in which his call does not resound.
Whether it is the Our Father or the Hail Mary or prayer that one composes:
God's voice is always in the background.

No prayer can be uttered without man's realizing that, in it, God is
calling.

—Adrienne von Speyr, *They Followed His Call*, 13–14

Lord, may I never forget that it is your call that enlivens and sustains my
priestly ministry. Your call is ever fresh.

The Creativity of the Curé of Ars October 5

> To the weak I became weak, to win over the weak. I have become all
> things to all, to save at least some. (1 Cor 9:22)

John Mary Vianney dedicated himself essentially to teaching the faith
and to purifying consciences, and these two ministries were directed towards the Eucharist. Should we not see here, today also, the three objectives
of the priest's pastoral service?

While the purpose is undoubtedly to bring the people of God together
around the Eucharistic Mystery by means of catechesis and penance, other
apostolic approaches, varying according to circumstances, are also necessary. Sometimes it is a simple presence, over the years, with the silent
witness of faith in the midst of non-Christian surroundings; or being near
to people, to families and their concerns; there is a preliminary evangelization that seeks to awaken to the faith unbelievers and the lukewarm;
there is the witness of charity and justice shared with Christian lay people,
which makes the faith more credible and puts it into practice. These give
rise to a whole series of undertakings and apostolic works which prepare or
continue Christian formation. The Curé of Ars himself taxed his ingenuity
to devise initiatives adapted to his time and his parishioners. However, all
these priestly activities were centered on the Eucharist, catechesis and the
Sacrament of Reconciliation.

—Saint John Paul II, Letter to Priests for
Holy Thursday, 1986

How has the Holy Spirit used my creativity in addressing the many needs
of my parishioners? How has my flexibility been evident?

> Persevere in prayer, being watchful in it with thanksgiving; at the same
> time, pray for us, too . . . (Col 4:2-3)

Consecrated to the image of Christ, the priest must be a *man of prayer*
like Christ himself. This concise definition embraces the whole spiritual
life that gives the presbyter a true Christian identity, defines him as a priest
and is the motivating principle of his apostolate . . .

Those called to share Christ's mission and sacrifice find in his example
the incentive to give prayer its rightful place in their lives, as the foundation,
root and guarantee of holiness in action. Indeed, we learn from Jesus that
a fruitful exercise of the priesthood is impossible without prayer, which
protects the presbyter from the danger of neglecting the interior life for the
sake of action and from the temptation of so throwing himself into work
as to be lost in it.

After stating that "the norm of priestly life" is found in Christ's consecration, the source of his Apostles' consecration, the 1971 Synod of Bishops
also applied the norm to prayer in these words: "Following the example of
Christ who was continually in prayer, and led by the Holy Spirit in whom
we cry, 'Abba, Father,' priests should give themselves to the contemplation
of the word of God and daily take the opportunity to examine the events of
life in the light of the Gospel, so that having become faithful and attentive
hearers of the *Word* they may become true ministers of the *word*. Let them
be assiduous in personal prayer, in the Liturgy of the Hours, in frequent
reception of the sacrament of Penance and especially in devotion to the
mystery of the Eucharist."

—Saint John Paul II, General Audience, June 2, 1993

Abba, Father, pour into my heart the Spirit of your Son, Jesus, so that the
whole of my life might become a continual prayer of praise.

Mary's Presence at the Eucharistic Sacrifice

> Blessed are you who believed that what was spoken to you by the Lord would be fulfilled. (Luke 1:45)

When we celebrate the Eucharist and stand each day on Golgotha, we need to have near us the one who through heroic faith carried to its zenith her union with her Son, precisely then on Golgotha.

Has Christ not left us a special sign of this? See how during his agony on the cross he spoke the words which have for us the meaning of a testament: "When Jesus saw his mother, and the disciple whom he loved standing near, he said to his mother, 'Woman, behold, your son!' Then he said to the disciple, 'Behold, your mother!' And from that hour the disciple took her to his own home."

. . . By taking "to his own home" the Mother who stood beneath her Son's cross, he also made his own all that was within her on Golgotha: the fact that she "suffered grievously with her only begotten Son, uniting herself with a maternal heart in his sacrifice, and lovingly consenting to the immolation of this victim that she herself had brought forth." All this—the superhuman experience of the sacrifice of our redemption, inscribed in the heart of Christ the Redeemer's own Mother—was entrusted to the man who in the Upper Room received the power to make this sacrifice present through the priestly ministry of the Eucharist in the Church!

The reality of Golgotha is truly an amazing one: the reality of Christ's sacrifice for the redemption of the world! Equally amazing is the mystery of God of which we are ministers in the sacramental order. But are we not threatened by the danger of being unworthy ministers? By the danger of not presenting ourselves with sufficient fidelity at the foot of Christ's Cross as we celebrate the Eucharist?

—Saint John Paul II, Letter to Priests for
Holy Thursday, 1988

Lord God, may I strive to remain close to that Mother in whose heart is inscribed in a unique and incomparable way the mystery of the world's redemption.

October 8 Not "My" Ministry, Not "My" Priesthood

But the one who gives us security with you in Christ and who anointed us is God; he has also put his seal upon us and given the Spirit in our hearts as a first installment. (2 Cor 1:21-22)

It is in the tradition of the prophetic call that the Gospel places the priestly vocation of the Twelve Apostles by Jesus. When the priest reflects on Jeremiah's call to be prophet, he is both reassured and disturbed. "Have no fear . . . because I am with you to deliver you," says the Lord to the one whom he calls, ". . . for look, I place my words in your mouth." Who would not take heart at hearing such divine assurance? Yet when we consider why such reassurance is needed, do we not see in ourselves that same reluctance we find in Jeremiah's reply? Like him, at times, our concept of this ministry is too earth-bound; we lack confidence in him who calls us. We also become too attached to our own vision of ministry, thinking that it depends too much on our own talents and abilities, and at times forgetting that it is God who calls us, as he called Jeremiah from the womb. Nor is it our work or our ability that is primary: we are called to speak the words of God and not our own; to minister the sacraments he has given to his Church; and to call people to a love which he has first made possible.

Hence the surrender to God's call can be made with utmost confidence and without reservation. Our surrender to God's will must be total—the "yes" given once for all which has as its pattern the "yes" spoken by Jesus himself.

This call of God is grace: it is a gift, a treasure "possessed in earthen vessels to make it clear that its surpassing power comes from God and not from us" (2 Cor 4:7). But this gift is not primarily for the priest himself; it is rather a gift of God for the whole Church and for her mission to the world.

—Saint John Paul II, Homily for a Holy Mass for
the American Priests, October 4, 1979

I must always be vigilant that my priestly life is not my own, but is God's gift of love for his beloved people.

> He is able to deal patiently with the ignorant and erring, for he himself is beset by weakness and so, for this reason, must make sin offerings for himself as well as for the people. (Heb 5:2-3)

He has sent forth for the ministry of reconciliation, not Angels, but men; He has sent forth your brethren to you, not beings of some unknown nature and some strange blood, but of your own bone and your own flesh, to preach to you . . . It is your brethren whom he has appointed, and none else—sons of Adam, sons of your nature, the same by nature, differing only by grace—men, like you, exposed to temptations, to the same temptations, to the same warfare within and without; with the same three deadly enemies—the world, the flesh and the devil; with the same human, the same wayward heart: differing only as the power of God has changed and rules it. So it is; we are not Angels from heaven that speak to you, but men, whom grace, and grace alone, has made to differ from you . . .

Such are your Ministers, your Preachers, your Priests, O my brethren; not Angels, not Saints, not sinless, but those who would have lived and died in sin except for God's grace . . . Had Angels been your priests, my brethren, they could not have consoled with you, sympathized with you, have had compassion on you, felt tenderly for you, and made allowances for you, as we can; they could not have been your patterns and guides, and have led you on from your old selves into a new life, as they can who come from the midst of you.

—Blessed John Henry Newman,
Discourses Addressed to Mixed Congregations III

I take time to reflect upon the fullness of my humanity; the good and the bad, the bitter and the sweet, the crooked and the straight. This is the person whom God has called.

> Thus should one regard us: as servants of Christ and stewards of the mysteries of God. (1 Cor 4:1)

The difference between the saints and us is a difference in degree, not in kind. They possess, and we most conspicuously lack, a certain maturity and depth of soul; caused by the perfect flowering in them of self-oblivious love, joy and peace. We recognize in them a finished product, a genuine work of God. But this power and beauty of the saints is on the human side simply the result of their faithful life of prayer; and is something to which, in various degrees, every Christian worker can attain. Therefore we ought all to be a little bit like them; to have a sort of family likeness, to share the family point of view.

If we ask of the saints how they achieved spiritual effectiveness, they are only able to reply that, in so far as they did it themselves, they did it by love and prayer. A love that is very humble and homely; a prayer that is full of adoration and of confidence. Love and prayer, on their lips, are not mere nice words; they are the names of tremendous powers . . . Plainly then, it is essential to give time or to get time somehow for self-training in this love and this prayer, in order to develop those powers. It is true that in their essence they are "given," but the gift is only fully made our own by a patient and generous effort of the soul. Spiritual achievement costs much, though never as much as it is worth. It means at the very least the painful development and persevering, steady exercise of a faculty that most of us have allowed to get slack. It means an inward if not an outward asceticism: a virtual if not an actual mysticism.

—Evelyn Underhill, *Concerning the Inner Life*, 106–7

Lord Jesus, give me a depth of soul that is full of adoration and abiding trust.

A Strength of Daring Simplicity October 11

> [I]t is Christ in you, the hope for glory. It is he whom we proclaim, admonishing everyone and teaching everyone with all wisdom, that we may present everyone perfect in Christ. (Col 1:27-28)

Since the Lord chose me, unworthy as I am, for this great service, I feel I have no longer any special ties in this life, no family, no earthly country or nation, nor any particular preferences with regard to studies or projects, even good ones. Now, more than ever, I see myself only as the humble and unworthy "servant of God and servant of the servants of God." The whole world is my family. This sense of belonging to everyone must give character and vigour to my mind, my heart and my actions.

This vision, this feeling of belonging to the whole world, will give a new impulse to my constant and continual daily prayer: the Breviary, Holy Mass, the whole rosary and my faithful daily visits to Jesus in the tabernacle, all varied and ritual forms of close and trustful union with Jesus. The experience of this first year gives me light and strength in my efforts to straighten, to reform, and tactfully and patiently to make improvements in everything.

Above all, I am grateful to the Lord for the temperament he has given me, which preserves me from anxieties and tiresome perplexities. I feel I am under obedience in all things and I have noticed that this disposition, in great things and in small, gives me, unworthy as I am, a strength of daring simplicity, so wholly evangelical in its nature that it demands and obtains universal respect and edifies many. Lord, I am not worthy. O Lord, be always my strength and the joy of my heart. My God, my mercy.

—Saint John XXIII, *Journal of a Soul*, 349

In my priestly ministry, have I truly come to see the whole world as my family? How can my disposition become more revealing of gospel simplicity?

The Amen, the faithful and true witness, the source of God's creation, says this: " . . . I wish you were either cold or hot. So, because you are lukewarm, neither hot nor cold, I will spit you out of my mouth." (Rev 3:14-16)

To those who . . . came to [St. John Vianney] already desirous of and suited to a deeper spiritual life, he flung open the abyss of God's love, explaining the untold beauty of living in union with Him and dwelling in His presence: "Everything in God's sight, everything with God, everything to please God. . . . How beautiful it is!" And he taught them to pray: "My God, grant me the grace to love You as much as I possibly can."

In his time the Curé of Ars was able to transform the hearts and the lives of so many people because he enabled them to experience the Lord's merciful love. Our own time urgently needs a similar proclamation and witness to the truth of Love. Thanks to the Word and the Sacraments of Jesus, John Mary Vianney built up his flock, although he often trembled from a conviction of his personal inadequacy, and desired more than once to withdraw from the responsibilities of the parish ministry out of a sense of his unworthiness. . . .

He sought to remain completely faithful to his own vocation and mission through the practice of an austere asceticism: "The great misfortune for us parish priests—he lamented—is that our souls grow tepid"; meaning by this that a pastor can grow dangerously inured to the state of sin or of indifference in which so many of his flock are living. He himself kept a tight rein on his body, with vigils and fasts, lest it rebel against his priestly soul. Nor did he avoid self-mortification for the good of the souls in his care and as a help to expiating the many sins he heard in confession. To a priestly confrere he explained: "I will tell you my recipe: I give sinners a small penance and the rest I do in their place."

—Pope Benedict XVI, Letter Proclaiming
a Year for Priests, June 16, 2009

Lord Jesus, deliver me from halfhearted and tepid ministry!

O Great Sacrament of Faith October 13

[T]herefore, he had to become like this brothers in every way, that he might be a merciful and faithful high priest before God to expiate the sins of the people. (Heb 2:17)

On this day every year we renew the promises we made in connection with the Sacrament of the Priesthood. These promises have great implications. What is at stake is the word we have given to Christ himself. Fidelity to our vocation builds up the Church, and every act of infidelity is a painful wound to the Mystical Body of Christ. And so, as we gather together and contemplate the mystery of the institution of the Eucharist and the Priesthood, let us implore our High Priest who, as Sacred Scripture says, showed himself to be faithful (cf. Heb 2:17), that we too may remain faithful. In the spirit of this "sacramental brotherhood" let us pray for one another—priests for priests! May Holy Thursday become for us a renewed call to cooperate with the grace of the Sacrament of the Priesthood! Let us pray for our spiritual families, for those entrusted to our ministry. Let us pray particularly for those who in a special way expect our prayers and are in need of them. May our fidelity to prayer ensure that Christ will become ever more the life of our souls.

O great Sacrament of Faith, O holy Priesthood of the Redeemer of the world! Lord Jesus Christ, how grateful we are to you for having brought us into communion with you, for having made us one community around you, for allowing us to celebrate your unbloody sacrifice and to be ministers of the sacred mysteries in every place: at the altar, in the confessional, the pulpit, the sickroom, prisons, the classroom, the lecture hall, the offices where we work. All praise to the Most Holy Eucharist! I greet you, the Church of God, his priestly people (cf. 1 Pet 2:9), redeemed by his Precious Blood!

—Saint John Paul II, Letter to Priests for
Holy Thursday, 1994

I pray again, with great devotion: "O great Sacrament of Faith . . ."

As the deer longs for streams of water, / so my soul longs for you, O God. / My soul thirsts for God, the living God. (Ps 42:2-3)

There is something in the depths of our being that hungers for wholeness and finality. Because we are made for eternal life, we are made for an act that gathers up all the powers and capacities of our being and offers them simultaneously and forever to God. The blind spiritual instinct that tells us obscurely that our own lives have a particular importance and purpose, and which urges us to find out our vocation, seeks in so doing to bring us to a decision that will dedicate our lives irrevocably to their true purpose. The man who loses this sense of his own personal destiny, and who renounces all hope of having any kind of vocation in life, has either lost all hope of happiness or else has entered upon some mysterious vocation that God alone can understand.

Most human vocations tend to define their purpose not only by placing the one called in a definite relation to God, but also by giving him a set place among his fellow men. The vocation of each one of us is fixed just as much by the need others have for us as by our own need for other men and for God. Yet when I speak here of a need, I do not mean to exclude the untrammeled exercise of spiritual freedom. If I am called to the priesthood, it may be because the Church has need of priests and, therefore, that she had need of me. And it may also happen that my own peace and spiritual balance and the happiness of my whole life may ultimately depend on my becoming a priest. But the Church is not determined to accept me as a priest simply because she needs priests, nor am I forced to become a priest by the pressure of my own spiritual condition.

—Thomas Merton, *No Man Is an Island*, 113

Can my daily celebration of the Eucharist "gather up all the powers of my being and offer them forever to God"?

Making the Best of What Time Remains   October 15

[B]ut when you grow old, you will stretch out your hands, and someone else will dress you and lead you where you do not want to go. (John 21:18)

I shall often return to these considerations, trying to foster in myself a desire and holy longing to suffer with Jesus who suffers, lovingly to accept my present inactivity without being impatient to do more, and to love this semi-obscurity in which the Lord keeps me, preventing me from doing anything else, though this would be my inclination and desire. . . .

I am in the fiftieth year of my life: therefore a mature man on the road to old age: perhaps death is near. I have achieved very little in half a century of life and of following a priestly vocation. I feel humble and ashamed before the Lord, and ask his pardon "for my countless sins," but I look to the future with imperturbable and confident serenity, "Heart of Jesus in which the Father is well pleased." This invocation has made a great impression on me during this retreat. When the Father's voice was heard expressing his pleasure, Jesus had as yet done nothing in his life except live in obscurity, in silence and humble prayer, doing the humblest work. Oh what great comfort there is in this teaching!

I go on my way once more, ever more determined to make the most of the time that yet remains. I must persevere, driving my body and soul without mercy. I will, I must be of more use, even in my present ministry. Therefore a more conscientious use of my time: everything to be done at once, speedily and well; no waiting about, no putting lesser things before the more important; always alert, busy and serene.

But above all and in all things I must endeavor to express in my inner life and outward behavior the Image of Jesus, "gentle and lowly of heart." May God help me.

—Saint John XXIII, *Journal of a Soul*, 278

Jesus, my brother, deliver me from any desire to have places of honor in my ministry. Give me your gentle and humble heart.

[I wish] to know [Christ] and the power of his resurrection and [the] sharing of his sufferings by being conformed to his death, if somehow I may attain the resurrection from the dead. (Phil 3:10-11)

Saint John Mary Vianney did not content himself with the ritual carrying out of the activities of his ministry. It was his heart and his life which he sought to conform to Christ.

Prayer was the soul of his life: silent and contemplative prayer, generally in his church at the foot of the tabernacle. Through Christ, his soul opened to the three divine Persons, to whom he would entrust "his poor soul" in his last will and testament. "He kept a constant union with God in the middle of an extremely busy life." And he did not neglect the office or the rosary. He turned spontaneously to the Virgin.

His poverty was extraordinary. He literally stripped himself of everything for the poor. And he shunned honours. Chastity shone in his face. He knew the value of purity in order "to rediscover the source of love which is God." Obedience to Christ consisted, for John Mary Vianney, in obedience to the Church and especially to the bishop. This obedience took the form of accepting the heavy charge of being a parish priest, which often frightened him.

But the Gospel insists especially on renouncing self, on accepting the cross. Many were the crosses which presented themselves to the Curé of Ars in the course of his ministry: calumny on the part of the people, being misunderstood by an assistant priest or other confreres, contradictions, and also a mysterious struggle against the powers of hell, and sometimes even the temptation to despair in the midst of spiritual darkness . . .

—Saint John Paul II, Letter to Priests for
Holy Thursday, 1986

Lord Jesus, in my darkest hours of ministry, may I have the grace to turn trustingly to you, conforming my life to your own.

> But I say to you, love your enemies, and pray for those who persecute you . . . (Matt 5:44)

Like the stones of a temple, cut for a building for God the Father, you have been lifted up to the top by the crane of Jesus Christ, which is the Cross, and the rope of the Holy Spirit. For your faith has drawn you up and charity has been the road leading to God. You are all fellow pilgrims, carrying with you God and His temple; you are the bearers of Christ and of holy offerings, decked out in the commandments of Jesus Christ. And with this letter I am able to take part in your festivity, to be of your company, to share in the joy that comes from setting your heart not on what is merely human life, but on God.

And so do not cease to pray for all persons, for there is hope for their conversion and of their finding God. Give them the chance to be instructed, at least by the way you behave. When they are angry with you, be meek; answer their words of pride by your humility, their blasphemies by your prayers, their error by your steadfastness in faith, their bullying by your gentleness. Let us not be in a hurry to give them tit for tat, but, by our sweet reasonableness, show that we are their brothers. Let us rather be eager to imitate the Lord, striving to be the first in bearing wrongs, in suffering loss, in being despised, so that no weed of the evil one may be found among you; but abide in Jesus Christ in perfect purity and temperance of body and soul.

—Saint Ignatius of Antioch, *Letter to the Ephesians*

How well do I love the difficult people in my life?

October 18   Open Your Hearts to the Spirit of Christ

> He stood up to read and was handed a scroll of the prophet Isaiah. He unrolled the scroll and found the passage where it was written: / "The Spirit of the Lord is upon me, / because he has anointed me / to bring glad tidings to the poor." (Luke 4:16-18)

Let us open our hearts, these hearts which he has created anew by his divine power. He has created them anew with the grace of the priestly vocation, and within them he is continually at work. Every day he creates: he creates in us, ever anew, that reality which constitutes the essence of our Priesthood—which confers upon each of us full identity and authenticity in priestly service—which enables us to "go and bear fruit" and which ensures that this fruit "abides."

It is he, the Spirit of the Father and the Son, who enables us to rediscover ever more deeply the mystery of that friendship to which Christ the Lord called us in the Upper Room: "No longer do I call you servants . . . , but I have called you friends." For while the servant does not know what his master is doing, the friend is familiar with the secrets of his Lord. The servant can only be obliged to work. The friend rejoices that he has been chosen by the one who has entrusted himself to him and to whom he too entrusts himself, entrusts himself totally.

So today let us pray to the Holy Spirit and ask him always to visit our thoughts and our hearts. His visit is the prerequisite for remaining in Christ's friendship. It also guarantees for us an ever deeper, ever more stirring knowledge of the mystery of our Master and Lord. We share in the mystery in a singular way: we are its heralds, and, above all, its stewards. This mystery fills us and, through us, like the vine, brings to birth the branches of divine life. How desirable therefore is the time of the coming of this Spirit who "gives life"!

—Saint John Paul II, Letter to Priests for
Holy Thursday, 1990

Come, Holy Spirit, renew this priestly heart with the fire of your love.

> Now I rejoice in my sufferings for your sake, and in my flesh I am filling up what is lacking in the afflictions of Christ on behalf of his body, which is the church . . . (Col 1:24)

My life as a priest, or rather—as I am called to my honor and shame—as Prince of the whole priesthood of Christ, in his name and by his power, unfolds before the eyes of my divine Master, the great Lawgiver. He looks down on me as he hangs on the Cross, his body torn and stained with blood. His side is wounded, his hands and feet are pierced. He looks at me and invites me to gaze on him. Justice led him straight to love, and love immolated him. This must be my lot: "The disciple is not above his master."

O Jesus, here I am before you. You are suffering and dying for me, old as I am now and drawing near the end of my service and my life. Hold me closely, and near to your heart, letting mine beat with yours. I love to feel myself bound for ever to you with a gold chain, woven of lovely, delicate links.

The first link: the justice which obliges me to find my God wherever I turn.
The second link: the providence and goodness which will guide my feet.
The third link: love for my neighbour, unwearying and most patient.
The fourth link: the sacrifice that must always be my lot,
    and that I will and must welcome at all times.
The fifth link: the glory that Jesus promises me in this life and in eternity.

O crucified Jesus, "my love and my mercy now and for ever." "Father, if thou art willing, remove this cup from me; nevertheless not my will, but thine be done" (Luke 22:42).

—Saint John XXIII, *Journal of a Soul*, 362

Jesus, my brother, give me the grace and honesty to allow the whole of my priestly life to open to your loving and healing gaze, especially my painful secrets and memories.

> Do not lord it over those assigned to you, but be examples to the flock. And when the chief Shepherd is revealed, you will receive the unfading crown of glory. (1 Pet 5:3-4)

Let us now take a closer look at the three fundamental affirmations of Jesus on the good shepherd. The first one, which very forcefully pervades the whole discourse on shepherds, says: the shepherd lays down his life for the sheep. The mystery of the Cross is at the centre of Jesus' service as a shepherd: it is the great service that he renders to all of us.

He gives himself and not only in a distant past. In the Holy Eucharist he does so every day, he gives himself through our hands, he gives himself to us. For this good reason the Holy Eucharist, in which the sacrifice of Jesus on the Cross remains continually present, truly present among us, is rightly at the centre of priestly life.

And with this as our starting point, we also learn what celebrating the Eucharist properly means: it is an encounter with the Lord, who strips himself of his divine glory for our sake, allows himself be humiliated to the point of death on the Cross and thus gives himself to each one of us.

The daily Eucharist is very important for the priest. In it he exposes himself ever anew to this mystery; ever anew he puts himself in God's hands, experiencing at the same time the joy of knowing that He is present, receives me, ever anew raises and supports me, gives me his hand, himself. The Eucharist must become for us a school of life in which we learn to give our lives.

> —Pope Benedict XVI, Homily for the Ordination to
> the Priesthood, May 7, 2006

How do I experience daily Eucharist and daily ministry as a sustaining experience of Christ Jesus?

> Everything that the Father has is mine; for this reason I told you that he [the Paraclete] will take from what is mine and declare it to you. (John 16:15)

On this Holy Thursday, as we go back to the origin of the Priesthood of the new and everlasting Covenant, each one of us recalls, at the same time, that day which is inscribed in the history of our personal lives as the beginning of our sacramental Priesthood, which is service in Christ's Church. The voice of the Church, which invokes the Holy Spirit on that day so decisive for each of us, alludes to Christ's promise in the Upper Room: "I will pray the Father, and he will give you another Counselor, to be with you for ever, even the Spirit of Truth." The Counselor, the Paraclete! The Church is certain of his saving and sanctifying presence. It is he "who gives life." "The Spirit of Truth, who proceeds from the Father . . . whom I shall send to you from the Father," is he who has generated in us that new life which is called and which really is the ministerial Priesthood of Christ. He says: "He will take what is mine and declare it to you." It happened exactly like this.

The Spirit of Truth, the Paraclete, "has taken" from that one Priesthood which is in Christ and has revealed it to us as the path of our vocation and our life. It was on that day that each of us saw himself, in the Priesthood of Christ in the Upper Room, as a minister of the Eucharist and, seeing ourselves in this way, we began to walk along this path. It was on this day that each of us, by virtue of the sacrament, saw this Priesthood as accomplished in himself, as imprinted on his soul in the form of an indelible seal: "You are a priest forever, after the order of Melchizedek."

—Saint John Paul II, Letter to Priests for
Holy Thursday, 1990

Lord Jesus, give me the grace to recognize that the Spirit of God, poured out upon me at ordination, can be renewed whenever I cry out, "Come, Holy Spirit, renew my heart."

> Thus should one regard us: as servants of Christ and stewards of the
> mysteries of God. Now it is of course required of stewards that they be
> found trustworthy. (1 Cor 4:1-2)

In this personal testimony, I also feel the need to go beyond the mere
recollection of events and individuals in order to take a deeper look and to
search out, as it were, the mystery which for fifty years has accompanied
and enfolded me.

What does it mean to be a priest? According to Saint Paul, it means
above all to be a steward of the mysteries of God: "This is how one should
regard us, as servants of Christ and stewards of the mysteries of God. Now
it is required of stewards that they be found trustworthy" (1 Cor 4:1-2).
The word "steward" cannot be replaced by any other. It is deeply rooted
in the Gospel: it brings to mind the parable of the faithful steward and the
unfaithful one (cf. Lk 12:41-48). The steward is not the owner, but the one
to whom the owner entrusts his goods so that he will manage them justly
and responsibly. In exactly the same way the priest receives from Christ the
treasures of salvation, in order duly to distribute them among the people
to whom he is sent. These treasures are those of faith. The priest is thus
a man of the word of God, a man of sacrament, a man of the "mystery of
faith." Through faith he draws near to the invisible treasures which constitute the inheritance of the world's Redemption by the Son of God. No
one may consider himself the "owner" of these treasures; they are meant
for us all. But, by reason of what Christ laid down, the priest has the task
of administering them. The priestly vocation is a mystery. . . . A man
offers his humanity to Christ, so that Christ may use him as an instrument
of salvation, making him as it were into another Christ.

—Saint John Paul II, *Gift and Mystery*, 71–72

Each day that I celebrate the Eucharist, do I consciously offer the whole
of my humanity to the service of Christ and his people?

> Take as your norm the sound words that you heard from me, in the faith and love that are in Christ Jesus. Guard this rich trust with the help of the holy Spirit that dwells within us. (2 Tim 1:13-14)

You went away by means of the cross, becoming "obedient unto death," and "emptying Yourself" through the love with which You loved us to the end; and so, after Your resurrection, the Holy Spirit was given to the Church, the Holy Spirit who came to dwell in her "forever."

It is the Spirit who "by the power of the Gospel preserves the Church's youth, continually renews her and leads her to perfect union with You."

Each one of us is aware that through the Holy Spirit, working through the power of Your cross and resurrection, we have received the ministerial Priesthood in order to serve the cause of man's salvation in Your Church; and

—we ask today, on this day which is so holy for us, that Your Priesthood may be continually renewed in the Church, through Your Spirit who in every epoch of history must "preserve the youth" of this beloved Bride of yours;

—we ask that each one of us will find again in his heart, and will unceasingly confirm through his life, the genuine meaning that his personal priestly vocation has both for himself and for all people,

—so that in an ever more mature way we may see with the eyes of faith the true dimension and beauty of the Priesthood,

—so that we may persevere in giving thanks for the gift of his vocation, as for an undeserved grace,

—so that, giving thanks unceasingly, we may be strengthened in fidelity to this holy gift, which, precisely because it is completely gratuitous, imposes a proportionately greater obligation.

> —Saint John Paul II, Letter to Priests for
> Holy Thursday, 1982

Lord Jesus, give me the grace daily to recognize the sacredness of the gift of priesthood that has been given to me for the service of your Body, the church.

> Every high priest is taken from among men and made their representa-
> tive before God, to offer gifts and sacrifices for sins. (Heb 5:1)

As the people redeemed in Jesus Christ, we offer the sacrifice of the
new covenant on the altars of our Church. More than this we cannot do,
even on the most special occasions. For there is no greater deed than this
and there is no way in which its value can really be increased: the Lord of
ages becomes present in our midst—He who is the heart of the world, and
whose act of love moves the stars and takes up everything with Him into
the glory of God.

And yet on the day of a priest's first Mass we do offer the everlasting
thanksgiving prayer in a special way. For we celebrate the hour when a
man, consecrated to be a priest of Jesus Christ, performs for the first time
that act which in a noble God-like monotony he is to perform every day
for the rest of his life, until his life is finally consumed in that sacrifice that
he daily celebrates and in whose acceptance alone all earthly reality sees
itself accepted before the infinite majesty of God.

Why do we celebrate such a day? Does the Church invite Her faithful to
make a kind of first installment of the laurels to a young man who has not
yet done anything else but offer God his heart and his life, when actually it
is only the completed sacrifice that ought to be celebrated? No, we are not
honoring any man. We are honoring only the priesthood of Jesus Christ.
We are honoring the Church, the entire Church of all those redeemed, made
holy, and called to eternal life. We are honoring Her to whom we all belong,
whether we are priests or "merely" believers and sanctified. For we are all
knit so closely into one body that the grace, dignity, or power that comes
to one man graces and lifts all the others, and in one man's being called to
service we glimpse the holy dignity of all.

—Karl Rahner, *Meditations on the Sacraments*, 60

I remember my own first Mass, and ask that God renew within me the grace-
filled zeal and overwhelming joy with which I began my priestly ministry.

I have already said that you are in our hearts, that we may die together and live together. I have great confidence in you, I have great pride in you; I am filled with encouragement, I am overflowing with joy all the more because of all our affliction. (2 Cor 7:3-4)

. . . I doubt that I will be able to convey to you my love for the priesthood and for each one of you priests of God . . . It is important for us the laity to communicate to you, dear Fathers, both our feelings and our needs . . . I wish convey to you the need we laity have of being guided by our shepherds. We long to hear your voices echoing the call of the one shepherd you represent so tangibly for us . . . If we do not hear his voice through you, how shall we hear it? Lately, your reassuring voices have either been muted or simply drowned out by the din of a noisy and confused world. We need to hear your voices clearly and we need to hear them now. Our pastures once so green and nourishing for us are being scorched by the searing heat of materialism, selfishness, and doubt. Only your voices united with the voice of the Good Shepherd can lead us to verdant fields once again. The Prince of Darkness is clouding minds, frightening the flock, forcing us to huddle together, uncertain of the direction we must travel in. But in the present twilight, we the laity are confident that in the face of danger, dear Fathers, you will stand by us and lead us.

. . . We call you "Father" because you begot us in the mystery of a tremendous love affair between you and God. Because you participate in the one priesthood of Christ, you are wedded to the Church, his bride. . . . We call you "Father" and we are your "family."

—Catherine de Hueck Doherty, *Dear Father*, 12

Lord Jesus, help me appreciate the love which the laity has for priests, and to faithfully endure the indifference that I at times experience from them.

October 26   Calling the Young to Full Personhood

> He replied and said to him, "Teacher, all of these I have observed from my youth." Jesus, looking at him, loved him and said to him, "You are lacking in one thing. Go, sell what you have, and give to [the] poor and you will have treasure in heaven; then come, follow me." (Mark 10:20-21)

Love enables us to propose what is good. Jesus "looked" at his young questioner in the Gospel "with love" and said to him: "Follow me." This good that we can propose to young people is always expressed in this exhortation: Follow Christ! We have no other good to propose; no one has a better good to propose. To say "Follow Christ!" means, above all, try to find yourself as a person. For—as the Council teaches—it is precisely Christ who "fully reveals man to himself and brings to light his highest calling."

And so: Follow Christ! Which means try to discover the calling that Christ makes known to man: that calling which is the realization of man and of his unique dignity. Only in the light of Christ and of his Gospel can we fully understand what it means that man has been created in the image and likeness of God himself. Only by following him can we fill this eternal image with a content of actual life. This content is very diversified: many are the vocations and duties of life before which young people must decide their own path. But on each of these paths it is a question of following a fundamental vocation: to be a person! To be so in a Christian way! To be a person "in the measure of the gift of Christ."

If there is love of young people in our priestly hearts, we shall know how to help them to find the answer to what constitutes the life vocation of each one. We will know how to help them while leaving them fully free to seek and choose . . .

—Saint John Paul II, Letter to Priests for
Holy Thursday, 1985

Lord Jesus, I beg you to fill my heart with love for each young person I meet, so that I may readily invite them by my word and my life to follow you unreservedly.

The Village of Ars and a Saintly Priest   October 27

Amen, amen, I say to you, unless a grain of wheat falls to the ground
and dies, it remains just a grain of wheat; but if it dies, it produces much
fruit. (John 12:24)

Through John Mary Vianney, who consecrates his whole strength and
his whole heart to him, Jesus saves souls. The Saviour entrusts them to
him, in abundance.

First his parish—which numbered only 230 people when he arrived—
which will be profoundly changed. One recalls that in that village there
was a great deal of indifference and very little religious practice among the
men. The bishop had warned John Mary Vianney: "There is not much love
of God in that parish, you will put some there." But quite soon, far beyond
his own village, the Curé becomes the pastor of a multitude coming from
the entire region, from different parts of France and from other countries.
It is said that 80,000 came in the year 1858! People sometimes waited for
days to see him, to go to confession to him. What attracted them to him
was not merely curiosity nor even a reputation justified by miracles and
extraordinary cures, which the saint would wish to hide. It was much more
the realization of meeting a saint, amazing for his penance, so close to God
in prayer, remarkable for his peace and humility in the midst of popular
acclaim, and above all so intuitive in responding to the inner disposition of
souls and in freeing them from their burdens, especially in the confessional.
Yes, God chose as a model for pastors one who could have appeared poor,
weak, defenseless and contemptible in the eyes of men. He graced him
with his best gifts as a guide and healer of souls. While recognizing the
special nature of the grace given to the Curé of Ars, is there not here a sign
of hope for pastors today who are suffering from a kind of spiritual desert?

—Saint John Paul II, Letter to Priests
for Holy Thursday, 1986

"While recognizing the special nature of the grace given to the Curé of Ars,
is there not here a sign of hope for pastors today who are suffering from a
kind of spiritual desert?"

We are afflicted in every way, but not constrained; perplexed, but not driven to despair; persecuted, but not abandoned; struck down, but not destroyed . . . (2 Cor 4:8-9)

Do we experience a loneliness which can make our eagerness for earthly fulfillment so very hard and unbearable? In our "yes," this emptiness of our heart becomes the wide vacuum filled by God's love. Our sins? In our concrete "yes," which allows God to be greater than our sins, we learn the greatness of our office of reconciliation and compassion with sinners. Our lack of courage? Our "yes" turns it into a weakness which is simply the hiddenness of the sole victory of God. The inescapable darkness of the future? Our "yes" turns its burden into a proof of faith, for faith is truest when we believe in the love of the Father even in correction (cf. Heb 12:7-13). The particular duty within the sacerdotal sphere which is not "in our line"? Our "yes" to this duty bursts wide open that "diabolical circle" . . . in which we keep circling around ourselves in a self-seeking way, and renders us truly free for the first time.

. . . Our ordination to the priesthood has established one final fact in our life. Whatever we do, we never escape this law of our life. Everything we do is unavoidably and inexorably either a "yes" or a "no" to this action of God in our life. Today, let us with all the power of the heart at our disposal give a pure, believing, loving, unconditional "yes" to this priesthood, a "yes" to everything it entails and imposes on us. This "yes"—even one already caused by God—is the condition and sign that God accomplishes his work in us, that he makes us anew today what we already are: priests of God.

—Karl Rahner,
"The Renewal of Priestly Ordination," 175–76

Lord Jesus, bless me with a sensitivity to the many resistances that I bring to ministry, and free me for a complete commitment to your service.

"Whoever loves me will keep my word, and my Father will love him, and we will come to him and make our dwelling with him." (John 14:23)

The priest's fundamental relationship is to Jesus Christ, head and shepherd. Indeed, the priest participates in a specific and authoritative way in the "consecration/anointing" and in the "mission" of Christ (cf. Lk. 4:18-19). But intimately linked to this relationship is the priest's relationship with the Church. It is not a question of "relations" which are merely juxtaposed, but rather of ones which are interiorly united in a kind of mutual immanence. The priest's relation to the Church is inscribed in the very relation which the priest has to Christ, such that the "sacramental representation" to Christ serves as the basis and inspiration for the relation of the priest to the Church.

In this sense the synod fathers wrote: "Inasmuch as he represents Christ the head, shepherd and spouse of the Church, the priest is placed not only in the Church but also in the forefront of the Church. The priesthood, along with the word of God and the sacramental signs which it serves, belongs to the constitutive elements of the Church. The ministry of the priest is entirely on behalf of the Church; it aims at promoting the exercise of the common priesthood of the entire People of God; it is ordered not only to the particular Church but also to the universal Church (*Presbyterorum Ordinis*, 10), in communion with the bishop, with Peter and under Peter. Through the priesthood of the bishop, the priesthood of the second order is incorporated in the apostolic structure of the Church. In this way priests, like the apostles, act as ambassadors of Christ (cf. 2 Cor. 5:20). This is the basis of the missionary character of every priest."

—Saint John Paul II, *Pastores Dabo Vobis*, 16

Heavenly Father, may my love for Christ and for the universal church nurture a missionary spirit within me.

> So, as you received Christ Jesus the Lord, walk in him, rooted in him and built upon him and established in the faith as you were taught, abounding in thanksgiving. See to it that no one captivate you with an empty, seductive philosophy . . . (Col 2:6-8)

The priest should apply himself above all else to developing, with all the love grace inspires in him, his close relationship with Christ, and exploring this inexhaustible and enriching mystery; he should also acquire an ever deeper sense of the mystery of the Church. There would be the risk of his state of life seeming unreasonable and unfounded if it is viewed apart from this mystery.

Priestly piety, nourished at the table of God's word and the Holy Eucharist, lived within the cycle of the liturgical year, inspired by a warm and enlightened devotion to the Virgin Mother of the supreme and eternal High Priest and Queen of the Apostles, will bring him to the source of a true spiritual life which alone provides a solid foundation for the observance of celibacy.

In this way the priest, with grace and peace in his heart, will face with generosity the manifold tasks of his life and ministry. If he performs these with faith and zeal he will find in them new occasions to show that he belongs entirely to Christ and His Mystical Body, for his own sanctification and the sanctification of others. The charity of Christ which urges him on, will help him not to renounce his higher feelings but to elevate and deepen them in a spirit of consecration in imitation of Christ the High Priest, who shared intimately in the life of men, loved and suffered for them, and of Paul the Apostle who shared in the cares of all in order to bring the light and power of the Gospel of God's grace to shine in the world.

—Blessed Pope Paul VI,
Sacerdotalis Caelibatus, 75–77

Do I walk with Christ? Am I rooted in Christ? Is my priestly life built upon Christ?

The Man with the Pierced Heart October 31

> [O]ne soldier thrust his lance into his side, and immediately blood and water flowed out. (John 19:34)

Tomorrow's priest will be the man with the pierced heart, from which alone he draws strength for his mission. With the pierced heart: pierced through by the godlessness of life, pierced through by the folly of love, pierced through by the lack of success, pierced through by the experience of his own wretchedness and profound unreliability, believing that only such a heart communicates the strength for his mission, that all the authority of office, all the objective validity of the word, all the efficacy of the sacraments, are only turned into the event of salvation by the grace of God if they come to man through the ineffable channel of the pierced heart.

I say he is the man with the pierced heart because he is to lead others to the very core of their existence, to their inmost heart, because he can only do so if he has found his own heart, because he and others can only find this center of existence, the heart, if they accept its being pierced, pierced by the incomprehensibility of love that is pleased to conquer only in death.

When the priest of tomorrow anxiously asks himself where he can always contemplate in its archetypal simplicity what he himself should be, then there is only one thing for him to do: turn to the Lord whom he serves, look on him whom they pierced, and venerate the pierced heart of Jesus Christ.

—Karl Rahner, *Servants of the Lord*, 113–15

In what ways have the piercings of my heart nurtured Christ-like compassion for others?

November 1 Strive to Be "Artists" of Pastoral Work

[The Lord has poured Wisdom] forth upon all his works, / upon every living thing according to his bounty, / lavished her upon those who love him. (Sir 1:9-10)

The special care for the salvation of others, for truth, for the love and holiness of the whole People of God, for the spiritual unity of the Church—this care that has been entrusted to us by Christ, together with the priestly power, is exercised in various ways. Of course there is a difference in the ways in which you, dear brothers, fulfill your priestly vocation. Some in the ordinary pastoral work of parishes; others in mission lands; still others in the field of activities connected with the teaching, training and education of youth, or working in the various spheres and organizations whereby you assist in the development of social and cultural life; yet others near the suffering, the sick, the neglected, and sometimes, you yourselves bedridden and in pain. These ways differ from one another, and it is just impossible to name them all one by one. They are necessarily numerous and different, because of the variety in the structure of human life, in social processes, and in the heritage and historical traditions of the various cultures and civilizations. Nevertheless, within all these differences, *you are always and everywhere the bearers of your particular vocation:* you are bearers of the grace of Christ, the eternal Priest, and bearers of the charism of the Good Shepherd. And this you can never forget; this you can never renounce; this you must put into practice at every moment, in every place and in every way. In this consists that "supreme art" to which Jesus Christ has called you. "The Supreme art is the direction of souls," wrote St. Gregory the Great. I say to you therefore, quoting these words of his: Strive to be "artists" of pastoral work.

—Saint John Paul II, Letter to Priests for
Holy Thursday, 1979

Lord, give me daily consciousness of my ministry as a bearer of the wisdom and grace of Christ.

The Shepherd-Lamb

> I myself will pasture my sheep; I myself will give them rest—oracle of the Lord GOD. The lost I will search out, the strays I will bring back, the injured I will bind up, and the sick I will heal . . . (Ezek 34:15-16)

We priests are not only shepherds, but also lambs. Was not Our Lord Himself both the "Good Shepherd" and the "Lamb of God" (Jn 1:29)? As the Offerer, He is the Shepherd. As the Offered, He is the Lamb. It is this dual role of Christ that explains why He spoke at certain times during His trial and at other times was silent. He spoke as the Shepherd; He was silent as the Lamb.

The priest too is not only the shepherd who cares for his sheep; he is also the lamb who is offered in caring for them. This caring is what distinguishes him from the hireling. One who cares for another assumes the weight of the other's condition on his own heart and bears it in love. The parishioners are not disturbers; they are our heart, our body, our blood.

The priest playing the role of a shepherd often goes to his death as a lamb. The shepherd who would give more abundant life to the lost sheep is bound to have wolves howling about him and thus be led ultimately to his death. It was only the sight of the Shepherd crucified that made the sheep realize how much the Shepherd cared. It is interesting that Saint Peter described Our Lord as "your Shepherd, who keeps watch over your souls" (1 Pet 2:25).

The shepherd's primary duty is to search out the lost sheep and stay with it once found. . . . So with the priest. Contact with people for Christ's sake is the victimhood that makes the priesthood. Only by also being a lamb offered through forgetfulness of worldly superiority does the priest become the shepherd of souls.

—Fulton J. Sheen, *The Priest Is Not His Own*, 29–30

Lord Jesus, may I be forever conscious that it is the sacrificial nature of my life that most identifies me with Christ the Good Shepherd.

> Now to him who is able to accomplish far more than all we ask or imagine, by the power at work within us, to him be glory in the church and in Christ Jesus to all generations, forever and ever. Amen. (Eph 3:20-21)

Unless we grasp the mystery of this "exchange," the *wondrous exchange between God and man*, we will not understand how it can be that a young man, hearing the words "Follow me!" can give up everything for Christ, in the certainty that if he follows this path he will find complete personal fulfillment.

In our world, is there any greater fulfillment of our humanity than to be able to re-present every day *in persona Christi* the redemptive sacrifice, the same sacrifice which Christ offered on the Cross? In this sacrifice, on the one hand, the very mystery of the Trinity is present in the most profound way, and, on the other hand, the entire created universe is "united" (cf. Eph 1:10). The Eucharist is also celebrated in order to offer "on the altar of the whole earth the world's work and suffering," in the beautiful expression of Teilhard de Chardin. This is why in the thanksgiving after Holy Mass the Old Testament canticle of the three young men is recited: *Benedicite omnia opera Domini Domino*. For in the Eucharist all creatures seen and unseen, and man in particular, bless God as Creator and Father; they bless him with the words and the action of Christ, the Son of God.

"I thank you, Father, Lord of heaven and earth, that you have hidden these things from the wise and understanding and revealed them to babes. . . . No one knows who the Son is except the Father, or who the Father is except the Son and anyone to whom the Son chooses to reveal him" (Lk 10:21-22). These words of Saint Luke's Gospel lead us to the heart of the mystery of Christ and enable us to draw near to the mystery of the Eucharist.

—Saint John Paul II, *Gift and Mystery*, 73–74

In what ways do I sense the unity of all creation in the celebration of the Eucharist?

"He Has Placed Heaven in My Hand" November 4

> Jesus answered and said to him, "Whoever loves me will keep my word, and my Father will love him, and we will come to him and make our dwelling with him. (John 14:23)

It is particularly as the ministers of Jesus Christ in the great sacrifice which is constantly renewed with abiding power for the salvation of the world, that we have the duty of conforming our minds to that spirit in which he offered himself as an unspotted victim to God on the altar of the Cross. . . . "More resplendent than the sun must be the hand that divides this Flesh, the mouth that is filled with spiritual fire, the tongue that is reddened by this Blood!" (John Chrysostom).

Saint Charles Borromeo gave apt expression to this thought when, in his discourses to the clergy, he declared: "If we would only bear in mind, dearly beloved brethren, the exalted character of the things that the Lord God has placed in our hands, what unbounded influence would not this have in impelling us to lead lives worthy of ecclesiastics! Has not the Lord placed everything in my hand, when he put there his only-begotten Son, coeternal and coequal with himself? In my hand he has placed all his treasures, his sacraments, his graces; he has placed there souls, than whom nothing can be dearer to him; in his love he has preferred them to himself, and redeemed them by his Blood; he has placed heaven in my hand, and it is in my power to open and close it to others . . . How, then, can I be so ungrateful for such condescension and love as to sin against him, to offend his honor, to pollute this body which is his? How can I come to defile this high dignity, this life consecrated to his service?"

—Saint Pius X, *Haerent Animo*

I must never take lightly my responsibility to mirror the loving heart of Christ.

> So when he had washed their feet [and] put his garments back on and
> reclined at table again, he said to them, "Do you realize what I have
> done for you?" (John 13:12)

Mysterium fidei! This is what the celebrant proclaims after saying the
words of the consecration. And the liturgical assembly responds, joyfully
expressing its faith and adherence filled with hope. The Eucharist is a truly
great mystery! A mystery "incomprehensible" to the human mind, but so
full of light to the eyes of faith! The Table of the Lord in the simplicity of
the Eucharistic symbols—the shared bread and wine—are also revealed
as the table of concrete brotherhood. The message that radiates from them
is too clear to be missed: those who take part in the Eucharistic Celebration cannot remain impervious to the expectations of the poor and needy.

It is precisely in this prospective that I would like the collection taken
during this Celebration to go to alleviate the urgent needs of all those in
Iraq who are suffering the consequences of the war. A heart that has known
the love of the Lord opens spontaneously to charity for his brethren.

"*O sacrum convivium, in quo Christus sumitur.*" We are all invited this
evening, until well on into the night, to celebrate and adore the Lord who
made himself food for us pilgrims in time, offering to us his flesh and his
blood. . . .

Adoro te devote, latens Deitas! We adore you, O wonderful Sacrament
of the presence of the One who loved his own "to the end." We thank you,
O Lord, who edifies, gathers together and gives life to the Church.

O divine Eucharist, flame of Christ's love that burns on the altar of the
world, make the Church, comforted by you, ever more caring in wiping
away the tears of the suffering and in sustaining the efforts of all who yearn
for justice and peace.

—Saint John Paul II, Homily for the Mass of
the Lord's Supper, April 17, 2003

Am I consciously living a eucharistic life, so that my daily priestly duties
flow from and to the altar of Christ's sacrificial love?

[The Lord said to Moses,] Now go, I will assist you in speaking and teach you what you are to say. (Exod 4:12)

Would that all pastors of souls would exert as much effort as the Curé of Ars did to overcome difficulties and obstacles in learning, to strengthen memory through practice, and especially to draw knowledge from the Cross of Our Lord, which is the greatest of all books. This is why his Bishop made this reply to some of his critics: "I do not know whether he is learned; but a heavenly light shines in him."

This is why Our predecessor of happy memory, Pius XII, was perfectly right in not hesitating to offer this country Curé as a model for the preachers of the Holy City: " . . . the clear, lofty, living thoughts of his mind were reflected in the sound of his voice and shone forth from his glance, and they came out in the form of ideas and images that were so apt and so well fitted to the thoughts and feelings of his listeners and so full of wit and charm that even St. Francis de Sales would have been struck with admiration. This is the kind of speaker who wins the souls of the faithful. A man who is filled with Christ will not find it hard to discover ways and means of bringing others to Christ."

These words give a wonderful picture of the Curé of Ars as a catechism teacher and as a preacher. And when, towards the end of his life on earth, his voice was too weak to carry to his listeners, the sparkle and gleam of his eyes, his tears, his sighs of divine love, the bitter sorrow he evidenced when the mere concept of sin came to his mind, were enough to convert to a better way of life the faithful who surrounded his pulpit. How could anyone help being moved deeply with a life so completely dedicated to Christ shining so clearly there before him?

—Saint John XXIII,
Sacerdotii Nostri Primordia, 79–80

In what measure are those whom I serve able to see the love of Christ shining through my priestly life?

November 7 To Be with Jesus, in All Circumstances

He called a child over, placed it in their midst, and said, "Amen, I say to you, unless you turn and become like children, you will not enter the kingdom of heaven. Whoever humbles himself like this child is the greatest in the kingdom of heaven." (Matt 18:2-4)

We pass the passion to reach childhood. I regard the priesthood as a life of joy, and as I reflect on my experience through the years I often think of the joy our vocation has brought me. I remember the challenging times, too, and though they were certainly no fun I can see God's hand at work. He nudged me, challenged me, stretched me, awakened me—and invited me to understand better how as a priest I would always be linked to the cross of Christ. Suffering has the potential to make us bitter, cynical, and hopeless, and one might at first think that only those with adult sensibilities can navigate through it successfully. We certainly don't have to like it, much less seek it out. But when suffering enters our lives in its various forms, so do the many aspects of the passion of Jesus: trust, fidelity, perseverance, and most especially love. It was love above all that took Jesus in his passion, as a child trustingly dependent on his Father, through death to resurrection.

It is no easier for us priests than for anyone else to childlike; perhaps in some ways it is more difficult. Still, as those joined to Jesus at the deepest level of our being, as sons of the Father and brothers to one another, our vocation calls us unremittingly in that direction: to be, with Jesus, one with the Father. To be, in Jesus, one with each other. To love, with the love of Jesus, the people we serve. To trust, with Jesus, that the Father's will is being done even if we don't understand how. To see our suffering, our passion, as joined to that of Jesus, and to know that the Father will help us through it—for our sake and for the sake of those to whom he sends us.

—Archbishop J. Peter Sartain,
Strengthen Your Brothers, 42

Lord Jesus, renew within me a spirit of childlike trust!

Our Mothers and the Priesthood November 8

And Mary kept all these things, reflecting on them in her heart.
(Luke 2:19)

The first and most basic relationship which any human being establishes with a woman is precisely the relationship of the child to its mother. Each of us can express his love for his earthly mother just as the Son of God did and still does for his. Our mother is the woman to whom we owe our life. She conceived us in her womb and brought us into the world amid the pains which are part of the experience of every woman who gives birth. Through childbirth a special and almost sacred bond is established between a human being and his mother.

Having brought us into the world, our parents then enabled us to become in Christ, through the Sacrament of Baptism, adopted children of God. All this further deepened the bond between us and our parents, and in particular between us and our mothers. The prototype here is Christ himself, Christ the Priest, who addresses his Eternal Father in these words: "Sacrifices and offerings you have not desired, but a body you have prepared for me. In burnt offerings and sin offerings you have taken no pleasure. Then I said, 'Lo, I have come to do your will, O God'" (Heb 10:5-7). These words in some way also involve his Mother, since the Eternal Father formed Christ's body by the power of the Holy Spirit in the womb of the Virgin Mary, thanks also to her consent: "Let it be to me according to your word" (Lk 1:38).

How many of us also owe to our mothers our very vocation to the priesthood! Experience shows that very often it is the mother who for years nurtures in her own heart a desire for a priestly vocation for her son, and obtains it by praying with persevering trust and deep humility.

—Saint John Paul II, Letter to Priests for
Holy Thursday, 1995

Mary, Mother of Priests, renew within me the grace of ordination, the grace of wholehearted service to your Son Jesus Christ.

> Do not conform yourselves to this age but be transformed by the re-
> newal of your mind, that you may discern what is the will of God, what
> is good and pleasing and perfect. (Rom 12:2)

There are some who think, and even declare openly, that the true measure of the merits of a priest is his dedication to the service of others;
consequently, with an almost complete disregard for the cultivation of the
virtues which lead to the personal sanctification of the priest (these they
describe as passive virtues), they assert that all his energies and fervor
should be directed to the development and practice of what they call the
active virtues. One can only be astonished by this gravely erroneous and
pernicious teaching.

Our predecessor of happy memory [Leo XIII] in his wisdom spoke as
follows of this teaching: "To maintain that some Christian virtues are more
suited to one period than to another is to forget the words of the Apostle:
Those whom he foreknew he also predestined to be conformed to the image
of his Son" (Rom. 8:29). Christ is the teacher and the model of all sanctity;
all who desire to take their place in the abode of the blessed must adapt
their conduct to the standard which he has laid down. Now Christ does not
change with the passing of the centuries: He is the same yesterday and today
and forever (Heb 13,8). The words: Learn of me because I am meek and
humble of heart (Mt 11,29) apply to men of every age; at all times Christ
reveals himself obedient unto death (Phil 2,8), true for every age are the
words of the Apostle: "They that are Christ's have crucified the flesh, with
the vices and concupiscences" (Gal 5,24).

—Saint Pius X, *Haerent Animo*

I too often fall into the "heresy of hyperactivity," considering my busyness
as an esteemed virtue rather than what it truly is, a distraction from the
work of personal transformation.

The Preacher's Imagination

> Look at the birds in the sky; they do not sow or reap, they gather nothing into barns, yet your heavenly Father feeds them. (Matt 6:26)

Imagination helps me begin the task [of preparing to preach]. Imagination can consider the strangeness of the texts, the otherness and surprise of the lives of the people who will assemble, the manifold variety of both the wretchedness and the blessedness of the world, and the resonances of meaning that will occur as Word and Sacrament are set side by side in this present world. Indeed, I need imagination and attention to reflect on how, by the power of the Spirit, the cross and the resurrection of Jesus Christ gather all these things into the mercy of God, proposing justice and love.

Because I am a preacher of the church, continual practice in attention and imagination must be a part of my daily round. I read novels and go to a few films, chosen with critical discretion, so that I might image the situation of other people and pay attention to the ways fine artists envision the world. I read a little history and some ethnography, and I try to listen carefully to the personal stories that are told me, not immediately imposing my meaning on them. . . . I watch the trees and birds outside my window. I walk on the streets of my city, watching faces, and I walk in the nearby woods, attending to the actual place on the earth where I live. In both places—streets and woods—I try to see what is happening. I pursue interests in other cultures than here, other places away from here. I go to museums and to art shows. . . . I do not watch much television, my feeling that there is usually very little there that will surprise me. I read the Scripture alone, seeking to hold myself before Christ in the text, continually surprised by Christ in the text, eating and drinking the body and blood of Christ in the text. . . . It is attention and imagination I must bring to the preparation for preaching.

—Gordon W. Lathrop, *The Pastor: A Spirituality*, 56

When the whole of my preaching comes from books, and I forget about my people, their world and their needs, I realize that I am not preaching as Jesus did, nor will I embody his sensitivity and compassion.

> To me, the very least of all the holy ones, this grace was given, to preach
> to the Gentiles the inscrutable riches of Christ, and to bring to light [for
> all] what is the plan of the mystery hidden from ages past in God who
> created all things . . . (Eph 3:8-9)

The church is Catholic. For the first time in its long history, the universality of the Catholic Church has become a tangible reality, with local churches burgeoning on every continent. The visible appearance of the church's catholicity occurs at a time when nation-states appear ever weaker and when, in Samuel Huntington's phase, a clash of cultures grows ever more evident. The Catholic Church is one of the major transnational, transcultural actors on the world stage.

As the church in the United States becomes more American, the role of the priest as symbol and agent of Catholicity looms as especially important. While valuing the local church, he needs to remind Catholics that the church is wider than the parish, the diocese, and the United States; further, that the local church bears a measure of responsibility for churches elsewhere, especially those that are just beginning or are poor. Such stewardship is made concrete, for example, in the twinning of parishes with those in poor countries.

As the church becomes truly universal, there is a danger that a world church could become little more than a loose federation of national churches, a kind of British commonwealth of nations in which the fellowship of the Holy Spirit is reduced to a set of bureaucratic ties. The unity of the church must become a concern of all its catholic parts. It is a paramount duty of priests to remind themselves and their people that this wider church is always intimately present to every local church.

A universal point of view also makes it easier to identify the strengths and the weaknesses of American culture, especially those that may run counter to the Gospel like materialism, individualism, and neglect of the family.

—Howard P. Bleichner, *View from the Altar*, 160–61

When I move beyond the possessive—"my" parish, "my" diocese, "my" ministry—and embrace a global vision, I am enriched and strengthened with the perspective of Christ himself.

Accessibility to Youth

> As [Jesus] was setting out on a journey, a man ran up, knelt down before
> him, and asked him, "Good teacher, what must I do to inherit eternal
> life?" (Mark 10:17)

In the field of *pastoral work with youth*, Jesus Christ is the most perfect
model. His conversation with the young man, which we find in the text of
all three Synoptic Gospels constitutes an inexhaustible source of reflection
on this theme. . . . In this concern Jesus Christ must remain for us the first
and fundamental source of inspiration.

The Gospel text indicates that the young man had easy access to Jesus.
For him, the Teacher from Nazareth was someone to whom he could turn
with confidence: someone to whom he could entrust his essential questions; someone from whom he could expect a true response. All this is for
us, too, an indication of fundamental importance. Each one of US must
be distinguished by an accessibility similar to that of Christ. Young people
should find no difficulty in approaching the Priest, and should discover
in him the same openness, benevolence and amiability with regard to the
problems troubling them. Even when by temperament they are a little shy or
reserved, the priest's attitude should help them to overcome the resistances
which derive from that.

Moreover, there are various ways of beginning and forming the contact
which can be summed up as "the dialogue of salvation." . . . The Priest's
accessibility to young people means not only ease of contact with them,
both inside and outside church, wherever young people feel drawn in harmony with the healthy characteristics of their age . . . The accessibility of
which Christ gives us an example consists in something more. The Priest
ought to evoke trust in young people as the confidant of their problems of
a fundamental nature, questions regarding their spiritual life and questions
of conscience.

—Saint John Paul II, Letter to Priests for
Holy Thursday, 1985

In what ways is ministry to young people an essential part of my life as a
priest, as it was a part of the life of Christ himself?

November 13   Our "Five Loaves and Two Fishes"

"There is a boy here who has five barley loaves and two fish; but what good are these for so many?" (John 6:9)

The People which has been entrusted to us to be educated, sanctified and governed are not a reality that distracts us from "our life" but the Face of Christ that we contemplate daily, as the face of his beloved for the bridegroom and the Church his Bride for Christ. The People entrusted to us are the indispensable path for our holiness, in other words the path on which Christ manifests through us the Glory of the Father.

"Whoever causes one of these little ones who believe in me to sin, it would be better for him to have a great millstone fastened round his neck and to be drowned in the depth of the sea . . . those on the other hand who send to perdition an entire people . . . what should they suffer and what punishment should they receive?" (St John Chrysostom, *De Sacerdotio VI*, 1,498). In the face of the awareness of such a serious task and such a great responsibility for our life and our salvation, in which faithfulness to Christ coincides with "obedience" to the needs dictated by the redemption of those souls, there is not even room to doubt the grace received. We can only ask to surrender as much as possible to his Love so that he will act through us, for either we let Christ save the world, acting in us, or we risk betraying the very nature of our vocation. The measure of dedication, dear confreres, is totality, again and anew. Yes, "five loaves and two fishes" are not many but they are all! God's Grace makes of all our littleness the Communion that satisfies the People. Elderly and sick priests who exercise the divine ministry daily, uniting themselves with Christ's Passion and offering their own priestly existence for the true good of the Church and the salvation of souls, share especially in this "total dedication."

—Pope Benedict XVI, Letter on the Occasion of the
World Day of Prayer for the Sanctification of Priests

For my ministry to be fruitful, I must continually remind myself that it is Christ who is acting in and through me. Apart from him I can do nothing.

> "For who is greater: the one seated at table or the one who serves? Is it not the one seated at table? I am among you as the one who serves." (Luke 22:27)

The state of life of the Christian priest, because it participates in the eternal priesthood of Christ and its continuation in the Church for the sake of all, is shaped within the obediential love, the poverty of kenosis and the chaste fruitfulness of the Son. These are transposed in modes of ministerial presence and pastoral love. They are what constitute the transforming ministry of the Christian priest, and before a priest becomes part of the outreach of that transforming love, he must first allow himself to be drawn into its depth. Interiority and mission are intrinsically woven together in Christ.

The spirit of the Counsels guarantees the radical reversal of authority and power that Jesus specifically refers to as the pattern of those who are called to leadership in the community. It is a pattern that completely undermines relationships of domination and control which have characterized every human society. The paradox of the institution and of the office of priesthood is precisely that it is to exemplify only the pattern of Christ who was sent as a servant.

As men constrained by their Lord to a pattern of humility and service, those called to ministerial priesthood find the source of this self-renunciation in the living out of the Counsels. Balthasar speaks of this as the humble obedience of the man who holds office becoming completely transparent to Christ only by completely losing himself and submitting his entire existence to the demands that this office brings.

—Dermot Power, *A Spiritual Theology of the Priesthood*, 98–99

Am I conscious throughout the day that I am called to serve, and not to be served?

I remind you to stir into flame the gift of God that you have through the imposition of my hands. (2 Tim 1:6)

Being converted means "to pray continually and never lose heart." *In a certain way prayer is the first and last condition for conversion*, spiritual progress and holiness. Perhaps in these recent years at least in certain quarters—there has been too much discussion about the Priesthood, the priest's "identity," the value of his presence in the modern world, etc., and on the other hand there has been too little praying. There has not been enough enthusiasm for actuating the Priesthood itself through prayer, in order to make its authentic evangelical dynamism effective, in order to confirm the priestly identity. It is prayer that shows the essential style of the priest; without prayer this style becomes deformed. Prayer helps us always to find the light that has led us since the beginning of our priestly vocation, and which never ceases to lead us, even though it seems at times to disappear in the darkness. Prayer enables us to be converted continually, to remain in a state of continuous reaching out to God, which is essential if we wish to lead others to Him. Prayer helps us to believe, to hope and to love, even when our human weakness hinders us.

Prayer likewise enables us continually to rediscover the dimensions of that kingdom for whose coming we pray every day, when we repeat the words that Christ taught us. Then we realize what *our place is in the realization of the petition*: "Thy kingdom come," and we see how necessary we are in its realization. And perhaps, when we pray, we shall see more easily those "fields . . . already white for harvest" and we shall understand the meaning of Christ's words as He looked at them: "So ask the Lord of the harvest to send laborers to his harvest."

—Saint John Paul II, Letter to Priests for
Holy Thursday, 1979

In what way is my daily life of prayer a source of the daily conversion to Christ?

The Flood of Divine Mercy

Have mercy on me, God, in accord with your merciful love; / in your abundant compassion blot out my transgressions. (Ps 51:3)

The Curé of Ars dealt with different penitents in different ways. Those who came to his confessional drawn by a deep and humble longing for God's forgiveness found in him the encouragement to plunge into the "flood of divine mercy" which sweeps everything away by its vehemence. If someone was troubled by the thought of his own frailty and inconstancy, and fearful of sinning again, the Curé would unveil the mystery of God's love in these beautiful and touching words: "The good Lord knows everything. Even before you confess, He already knows that you will sin again, yet He still forgives you. How great is the love of our God: He even forces Himself to forget the future, so that He can grant us His forgiveness!"

But to those who made a lukewarm and rather indifferent confession of sin, he clearly demonstrated by his own tears of pain how "abominable" this attitude was: "I weep because you don't weep," he would say. "If only the Lord were not so good! But He is so good! One would have to be a brute to treat so good a Father this way!" He awakened repentance in the hearts of the lukewarm by forcing them to see God's own pain at their sins reflected in the face of the priest who was their confessor. To those who, on the other hand, came to him already desirous of and suited to a deeper spiritual life, he flung open the abyss of God's love, explaining the untold beauty of living in union with Him and dwelling in His presence: "Everything in God's sight, everything with God, everything to please God. . . . How beautiful it is!" And he taught them to pray: "My God, grant me the grace to love You as much as I possibly can."

—Pope Benedict XVI, Letter Proclaiming
a Year for Priests, June 16, 2009

Lord Jesus, renew within me a deepening love for the sacrament of penance—in my personal life and in my ministry to your people.

> Then he took the bread, said the blessing, broke it, and gave it to them, saying, "This is my body, which will be given for you; do this in memory of me." And likewise the cup after they had eaten, saying, "This cup is the new covenant in my blood, which will be shed for you." (Luke 22:19-20)

We turn to You, O Christ of the Upper Room and of Calvary, on this day which is the feast of our Priesthood. To You we turn, all of us, bishops and priests, gathered together in the priestly assemblies of our churches, and at the same time joined together in the universal unity of the holy and apostolic Church.

Holy Thursday is the birthday of our Priesthood. It is on this day that we were all born. As a child is born from its mother's womb thus were we born, O Christ, from Your one and eternal Priesthood. We were born in the grace and strength of the new and eternal Covenant from the Body and Blood of Your redeeming sacrifice: from the Body that was given for us, and from the Blood that was poured out for us all.

We were born at the Last Supper, and at the same time at the foot of the cross on Calvary: the place which is the source of new life and of all the sacraments of the Church is also the place where our Priesthood begins.

We were also born together with the whole People of God of the new Covenant, whom You, the beloved of the Father, made "a kingdom, priests to your God and Father."

We have been called to be servants of this people, which brings to the eternal tabernacles of the thrice holy God its "spiritual sacrifices." The Eucharistic Sacrifice is the "source and summit of all Christian life." It is a single sacrifice that embraces everything. It is the greatest treasure of the Church. It is her life.

—Saint John Paul II, Letter to Priests for
Holy Thursday, 1982

Eucharistic Lord, may I always approach your table with reverence and recollection, joyfully placing in the cup the sacrifices of my priestly life.

Embracing the Spirit of the Cross

> My eager expectation and hope is that I shall not be put to shame in any way, but that with all boldness, now as always, Christ will be magnified in my body, whether by life or by death. (Phil 1:20)

I understand very well the reluctance of my nature, but I rely on the grace of God which, on this foundation of perfect humility, was able to work the sanctification of so many other souls who were to become instruments of his glory and illustrious apostles for the cause of Holy Church.

I feel ever more strongly a love for my Lord's Cross, especially in these days. O blessed Jesus, do not let this be a spurt of flame to flicker out in the first shower of rain, but a burning, inextinguishable fire.

During this retreat I have come across another beautiful prayer which corresponds very well to the state of my spiritual life. It is by a recently canonized saint, St. John Eudes. I humbly make it my own, and hope this is not too presumptuous on my part. In its context it is called: *"A profession of love for the Cross."*

"O Jesus, my crucified love, I worship you in all your sufferings. I ask your pardon for all the times I have failed you in the afflictions you have been pleased to send me till now. I embrace the spirit of your Cross, and in this spirit, as in all love of heaven or earth, I welcome with all my heart, for love of you, all the afflictions of body and soul which you may send me. And I promise to find all my glory, my treasure and my joy in your Cross, that is in humiliations, privations and sufferings, saying with St. Paul: 'Far be it from me to glory except in the Cross of our Lord Jesus Christ' (Gal 6:14). As for me, I want no other paradise in this world than the Cross of my Lord Jesus Christ."

—Saint John XXIII, *Journal of a Soul*, 274

In what ways is my priestly ministry a profession of love for the cross?

> Yet just as from the heavens / the rain and snow come down / And do not return there / till they have watered the earth, . . . So shall my word be / that goes forth from my mouth; / It shall not return to me empty, / but shall do what pleases me, / achieving the end for which I sent it. (Isa 55:10-11)

The word of God has carried me. The Bible has influenced me since childhood and still affects me, and is decisive for my priesthood. I would not want to let a single day pass without spending some time quietly with the Bible. During Mass the reader proclaims at the end of the lesson: "This is the word of God." It has become a catchword for me. The Bible, as I hold it today, is the word of the living God—Word, not words which have been written by Paul or whomsoever. The word in the sense of message as a whole comes from the living God who is still speaking to me today. Looking at the Bible in this way has given me new perspectives regarding exegesis. When one accepts the Bible as the word of God one can, with unshakable confidence, discuss questions relating to historicity, form-critic and investigation of source without it putting one's faith in jeopardy.

I will give an example: in our youth group we read the high priestly prayer of Christ (Jn 17:1 ff.). As usual after the reading I asked the question: "What has affected you particularly?" One boy answered: "The full stop in the first verse. It says there: 'This Jesus said. And he raised his eyes to heaven and spoke.' Then follows the long prayer. It has occurred to me that all the talk about God must at some time come to a full stop and must change into speech with God."

—Gertrude Resseguier, *The First Love*, 16–17

What has been my relationship with Sacred Scripture? In what ways has it been my daily bread?

We Invite to the Priesthood by Our Lives
November 20

> At the sight of the crowds, his heart was moved with pity for them because they were troubled and abandoned, like sheep without a shepherd. (Matt 9:36)

Young people must be helped . . . to discover their own vocation. They must also be supported and strengthened in their desire to transform the world, to make it more human and more fraternal. And these are not just words; it is a question of the whole reality of the "path" that Christ points out for a world made in just this way.

. . . When Christ says to the young man: "Follow me," in that concrete Gospel circumstance it is a call to "leave everything" and to follow the path taken by Christ's Apostles. Christ's conversation with the young man is the prototype of countless other conversations in which the prospect of a vocation to the Priesthood or religious life opens up before a young soul. Dear brother Priests and Pastors, we must know how to recognize these vocations. Truly, "the harvest is plentiful but the labourers are few!" Here and there they are extremely few! Let us ask "the Lord of the harvest to send out labourers into his harvest." Let us pray ourselves, and let us ask others to pray for this. And above all, let us endeavor to make our very lives a concrete point of reference for priestly and religious vocations: a concrete model. Young people have an extreme need of such a concrete model in order to discover in themselves the possibility of following a similar path. In this area our Priesthood can bear fruit in an extraordinary way. Work for this, and pray that the Gift which you have received may become the source of a similar gift to others: precisely to the young!

> —Saint John Paul II, Letter to Priests for
> Holy Thursday, 1985

I reflect upon the way in which my priestly life has been a personal invitation to the young to consider a vocation to the priesthood, to the following of Christ.

"[W]hoever wishes to be great among you shall be your servant; whoever wishes to be first among you shall be your slave. Just so, the Son of Man did not come to be served but to serve and to give his life as a ransom for many." (Matt 20:26-28; cf. Mark 10:43-45)

Another characteristic [of Holy Orders] which derives from this sacramental union with Christ is a *passionate love for the Church*. Let us think of that passage from the Letter to the Ephesians in which St. Paul states that Christ "loved the Church and gave himself up for her, that he might sanctify her, having cleansed her by the washing of water with the word, that he might present the Church to himself in splendour, without spot or wrinkle or any such thing" (5:25-27). Through Holy Orders the minister dedicates himself entirely to his community and loves it with all his heart: it is his family. The bishop and the priest love the Church in their own community, they love it greatly. How? As Christ loves the Church. . . .

Finally, the Apostle Paul recommends to the disciple Timothy that he not neglect, indeed, that *he always rekindle the gift that is within him*. The gift that he has been given through the laying on of hands (cf. 1 Tim 4:14; 2 Tim 1:6). When the ministry is not fostered—the ministry of the bishop, the ministry of the priest—through prayer, through listening to the Word of God, through the daily celebration of the Eucharist and also through regularly going to the Sacrament of Penance, he inevitably ends up losing sight of the authentic meaning of his own service and the joy which comes from a profound communion with Jesus.

The bishop who does not pray, the bishop who does not listen to the Word of God, who does not celebrate every day, who does not regularly confess—and the same is true for the priest who does not do these things—in the long run lose their union with Jesus and become so mediocre that they do not benefit the Church. That is why we must help bishops and priests to pray, to listen to the Word of God which is one's daily nourishment, to celebrate the Eucharist each day and to confess regularly. This is so important precisely because it concerns the sanctification of bishops and priests.

—Pope Francis, General Audience, March 26, 2014

Lord Jesus, give me greater attentiveness to all that can lead me into deeper friendship with you and to a more passionate love for your people.

> Jesus said to them, "My food is to do the will of the one who sent me and to finish his work." (John 4:34)

[The Vatican Council] talks about the difficult problem of how the priest, torn between the plethora of his often quite varied tasks, may be able to preserve the unity of his life—a problem that is threatening, with an increasing shortage of priests, to become the real crisis in the daily lives of priests. A parish priest who may today be in charge of three or four parishes is forever traveling from one place to another; this situation, well known to missionaries, is becoming more and more the rule in the heartlands of Christianity. The priest has to try to guarantee the availability of the sacraments to the communities; he is oppressed by administrative work; problems of all kinds make their demands on him in addition to the personal troubles of so many people, for whom he can often—because of all the rest—hardly find any time. Torn to and fro between such activities, he feels empty, and it becomes more and more difficult for him to find time for recollection, from which he can draw new strength and inspiration. Outwardly torn apart and inwardly emptied, he loses all joy in his calling, which ends by seeming nothing but a burden and scarcely bearable any longer. Escape increasingly seems the obvious course.

The Council offered three initiatives toward controlling this situation. The basic theme is inner fellowship with Christ, whose food was to do the will of the Father (Jn 4:34). It is important for the priest's ontological unity with Christ to be alive in his consciousness and, thus, in his actions: Everything I do, I do in fellowship with him. In the very act of doing it, I am with him. The great variety of my activities, and what are outwardly even contradictions in them, nonetheless amount to a calling: all of it is being together with Christ . . .

—Pope Benedict XVI,
Pilgrim Fellowship of Faith, 169

Are all my actions done in fellowship with Christ? How does this give unity to my life?

This is how all will know that you are my disciples, if you have love for one another. (John 13:35)

Who can explain the bond of the charity of God? Who can express the splendor of its beauty? The height to which charity lifts us is inexpressible. Charity unites us to God, "Charity covers a multitude of sins"; charity bears all things, is long-suffering in all things. There is nothing mean in charity, nothing arrogant. Charity knows no schism, does not rebel, does all things in concord. In charity all the elect of God have been made perfect. Without charity nothing is pleasing to God. In charity the Lord received us: out of charity which he has for us, Jesus Christ our Lord gave his blood for us by the will of God, and His flesh for our flesh, and His life for our lives.

You see, dearly beloved, how great and wonderful is charity, and that its perfection is beyond expression. Who is good enough to be found in it except those whom God makes worthy? Let us pray, therefore, and beg of his mercy that we may be found in charity, without human partisanship, free from blame. All the generations from Adam to this day have passed away; but those who were made perfect in charity by the grace of God live among the saints; and they shall be made manifest at the judgment of the Kingdom of Christ. . . . Blessed are we, dearly beloved, if we fulfilled the commandments of God in the harmony of charity, that our sins were forgiven through charity. . . . This benediction came to those who are chosen by God through Jesus Christ our Lord, to whom be glory forever and ever. Amen.

—Saint Clement of Rome,
Letter to the Corinthians 49.1–50.3, 5, 7

In what ways have I made charity the hallmark of my priestly life?

But the tax collector stood off at a distance and would not even raise his eyes to heaven but beat his breast and prayed, "O God, be merciful to me a sinner." (Luke 18:13)

When the Epistle to the Hebrews speaks of the priest, the first thing it says is that he is taken from among men. So much so that even the eternal high priest Jesus Christ wanted to be born of a woman, subject to the Law, a pilgrim through the valley of this transitory world, the Son of Man, a man, making himself like us in everything. The priest is a man. He is not made from another kind of clay than the rest of us. He is your brother. He continues to share the lot of man after the hand of God has rested on him in the form of the bishop's hand. The lot of the weak and the weary, the lot of the discouraged, the unsuccessful, and the sinner.

But men are offended when someone appears to do God's business and still is only a man. They want messengers who speak more brilliantly, heralds who preach more persuasively, hearts that burn with a hotter flame. They would gladly receive God's representative, provided he always had the upper hand, had an answer for everything, could handle every problem. But what is the terrible and happy truth? Those who come are weak men, who live in fear and trembling, men who themselves must pray over and over, "Lord, I believe, help my unbelief!" men who themselves must keep beating their breast, "Lord, be merciful to me, a sinner!" And still they preach the faith that conquers the world and bring the grace that makes redeemed saints out of lost sinners. God sends men.

—Karl Rahner, *Meditations on the Sacraments*, 61

Are there times when I think that because I am a priest, I am a bit more worthy or deserving than another? May I never forget my frail and fallible humanity.

> And when I saw [the vision of the likeness of the glory of the Lord],
> I fell on my face and heard a voice speak. The voice said to me: Son
> of man, stand up! I wish to speak to you. As he spoke to me, the spirit
> entered into me and set me on my feet, and I heard the one who was
> speaking say to me: Son of man, I am sending you to the Israelites, a
> nation of rebels who have rebelled against me . . . (Ezek 1:28–2:3)

Prophecy is the rarest voice. The Old Testament reminds us that there are schools only for false prophets, not true ones. The true prophetic call descends on the individual vertically and inexplicably. No instruction manual accompanies it. Priests in our tradition are institutional figures who belong to a worldwide order of priests. They are not the usual recipients of such a call. Experience also teaches that claimants to extraordinary gifts deserve close scrutiny. A noted biblical scholar once wryly observed that in all Israel only a handful of prophets appeared, a fact that gave him pause in the late 1960s when divinity schools seemed regularly to graduate twenty to thirty prophets a year. Yet if the prophetic charism is rare, it is also an enduring form of the Word, which appears when and where it chooses.

In recent years, some Catholic priests and bishops have been impelled to act in a prophetic way to be faithful to their duties as shepherds. Bishop Robert Bello in East Timor and Archbishop Oscar Romero in El Salvador are but two of those who, in the name of human rights, have felt compelled to raise a prophetic voice. A witness to their authenticity is that they did not choose to become prophets. Rather, the role was thrust on them. It is not surprising that large institutions are seldom entirely comfortable with a prophet in their midst. Who is?

The more common translation of the prophetic challenge for priests is that they be persons of character who act with integrity. From time to time, they may find it necessary to speak out publicly on injustice in society and wrong policies in government. Such preaching is effective only if one's personal life is marked by integrity.

—Howard P. Bleichner, *View from the Altar*, 172–73

Rather than embracing the role of the prophet in speaking out against injustice, do I sometimes suffer from terminal caution, fearing the slightest negative response?

Put on then, as God's chosen ones, holy and beloved, heartfelt compassion, kindness, humility, gentleness, and patience, bearing with one another, and forgiving one another . . . And over all these put on love, that is, the bond of perfection. (Col 3:12-14)

Moreover, priestly chastity is increased, guarded and defended by a way of life, surroundings and activity suited to a minister of God. For this reason the "close sacramental brotherhood" which all priests enjoy in virtue of their ordination must be fostered to the utmost. Our Lord Jesus Christ has taught the urgency of the new commandment of charity. He gave a wonderful example of it when He instituted the sacrament of the Eucharist and the Catholic priesthood, and prayed to His Heavenly Father that the love the Father bore for Him from all eternity should be in His ministers and that He too should be in them.

So the unity of spirit among priests should be active in their prayers, friendship and help of all kinds for one another. One cannot sufficiently recommend to priests a life lived in common and directed entirely toward their sacred ministry; the practice of having frequent meetings with a fraternal exchange of ideas, counsel and experience with their brother priests; the movement to form associations which encourage priestly holiness.

Priests should reflect on the advice of the Council, which reminds them of their common sharing in the priesthood so that they may feel a lively responsibility for fellow priests troubled by difficulties which gravely endanger the divine gift they have. They should have a burning charity for those who have greater need of love, understanding and prayer, who have need of prudent but effective help, and who have a claim on their unbounded charity as those who are, and should be, their truest friends.

—Blessed Pope Paul VI,
Sacerdotalis Caelibatus, 78–81

There are few things more toxic in the priesthood than gossip about brother priests. Lord Jesus, bless me with the grace always to live in charity with my brothers.

> Then the angel showed me the river of life-giving water, sparkling like crystal, flowing from the throne of God and of the Lamb down the middle of its street. (Rev 22:1-2)

Priests are conformed to the sublime image of Christ, the eternal Priest and most pure Victim of the salvific sacrifice. . . . It is necessary for the clergy to be faithful to that image, which mirrors the living truth of Christ the Priest and Victim.

The reproduction of that image in priests is attained primarily through their life-giving participation in the Eucharistic mystery, to which the Christian priesthood is essentially ordered and linked. The Council of Trent emphasized that the bond between the priesthood and sacrifice comes from the will of Christ, who conferred upon his ministers "the power to consecrate, to offer and to distribute his Body and his Blood." In this there is a mystery of communion with Christ in *being* and *doing*, which must be translated into a spiritual life imbued with faith in and love for the Eucharist.

The priest is quite aware that he cannot count on his own efforts to achieve the purposes of his ministry, but rather that he is called to serve as an instrument of the victorious action of Christ whose sacrifice, made present on the altars, obtains for humanity an abundance of divine gifts. However, he also knows that in order to worthily pronounce the words of consecration in the name of Christ—"This is my Body," "This is the cup of my Blood"—he must be profoundly united to Christ and seek to reproduce Christ's countenance in himself. The more intensely he lives in Christ, the more authentically he can celebrate the Eucharist.

—Saint John Paul II, General Audience, June 9, 1993

Lord Jesus, deepen my love for the eucharistic sacrifice of the Mass, and grace me with the generosity to place the whole of my life upon the altar.

Courageous Fidelity

> Here is my servant whom I uphold, / my chosen one with whom I am pleased. / Upon him I have put my spirit . . . (Isa 42:1)

The harshness of life—and its grandeur—will not let us dabble, committing ourselves only "until further notice." Every choice is a decision about a misty, unpredictable future—getting married, embarking on a profession, any other important choice in a person's life. Why should it be otherwise in the case of the priest? Why should a man of 28 or 35—supposing that is to be the age of ordination—not be able to say to himself: Relying on the Gospel, I am irrevocably choosing a form of life; I do not know what abysses, crises, defeats, despairs, desolations may lie ahead; for all I know—perhaps when I have barely taken my decision, perhaps when I am 40 or 50 or 60—I may suddenly meet the woman who seems to be the only happiness there is in this world.

But I have made my choice; I will pass by, I will stick to my vocation and the work I have to do because I am a believer, because I want to be faithful, because I want the tremendous gift of eternal life and God's love, want to confess the cross of Christ, to be realized in me in *this* way. Even lapses in our faithfulness confirm the virtue of faithfulness. It is fitting and necessary in this life that we make decisions which carry us into an unpredictable future. It cannot be done, of course, without faith, without accepting the incomprehensible folly of the cross, without hoping against hope, without the blind obedience of Abraham, without prayer.

—Karl Rahner, *Servants of the Lord*, 159

Is the bedrock of my priestly vocation, always and in all ways, prayer?

"This is my commandment: love one another as I love you. No one has greater love than this, to lay down one's life for one's friends." (John 15:12-13)

By virtue of their consecration, priests are configured to Jesus the good shepherd and are called to imitate and to live out his own pastoral charity. The internal principle, the force which animates and guides the spiritual life of the priest inasmuch as he is configured to Christ the head and shepherd, is pastoral charity, as a participation in Jesus Christ's own pastoral charity, a gift freely bestowed by the Holy Spirit and likewise a task and a call which demand a free and committed response on the part of the priest.

The essential content of this pastoral charity is the gift of self, the total gift of self to the Church, following the example of Christ. "Pastoral charity is the virtue by which we imitate Christ in his self-giving and service. It is not just what we do, but our gift of self, which manifests Christ's love for his flock. Pastoral charity determines our way of thinking and acting, our way of relating to people."

With pastoral charity, the priest, who welcomes the call to ministry, is in a position to make this loving choice, as a result of which the Church and souls become his first interest, and with this concrete spirituality he becomes capable of loving the universal Church and that part of it entrusted to him with the deep love of a husband for his wife.

—Saint John Paul II, *Pastores Dabo Vobis*, 22–23

In what ways is "pastoral charity" the loving choice that I make daily in the service of God's people?

Faithfully Preaching the Gospel

> I charge you in the presence of God and of Christ Jesus . . . : proclaim the word; be persistent whether it is convenient or inconvenient; convince, reprimand, encourage through all patience and teaching. (2 Tim 4:1-2)

For presbyters, it can be said that *proclaiming the word of God is the first task to be carried out*, because the basis of personal and communal Christian life is faith, which results from the word of God and is nourished on this word.

The preaching of presbyters is not a mere exercise of the word that answers a personal need to express oneself and to communicate one's own thought, nor can it consist solely in sharing one's personal experience. This psychological element, which can have a didactic-pastoral role, is neither the reason for nor the principle element in preaching. "The experience of life, whether of men in general or of priests, which must be kept in mind and always interpreted in the light of the Gospel, cannot be either the sole or the principal norm of preaching."

The mission of preaching is entrusted by the Church to presbyters as a sharing in Christ's mediation, to be exercised by virtue of and according to the demands of his mandate: priests, "in the degree of their ministry, share in the office of the one Mediator, Christ, and proclaim to all the divine word." This expression cannot fail to make us reflect: it is a "divine word," which therefore is not "ours" and cannot be manipulated, changed or adapted at will, but must be proclaimed in its entirety.

—Saint John Paul II, General Audience, April 21, 1993

What are the indications in my ministry that I consider preaching the word of God to be of supreme importance?

"This is why the Father loves me, because I lay down my life in order to take it up again." (John 10:17)

The Priesthood calls for a particular integrity of life and service, and precisely such integrity is supremely fitting for our priestly identity. In that identity there are expressed, at the same time, the greatness of our dignity and the "availability" proportionate to it: it is a question of the humble readiness to accept the gifts of the Holy Spirit and to transmit to others the fruits of love and peace, to give them that certainty of faith from which derive the profound understanding of the meaning of human existence and the capacity to introduce the moral order into the life of individual and of the human setting.

Since the Priesthood is given to us so that we can unceasingly serve others, after the example of Christ the Lord, the Priesthood cannot be renounced because of the difficulties that we meet and the sacrifices asked of us. Like the apostles, "we have left everything to follow Christ." Therefore we must persevere beside Him also through the Cross . . .

As I write, there pass before the eyes of my soul the vast and varied areas of human life, areas into which you are sent, dear brothers, like laborers into the Lord's vineyard. But for you there holds also the parable of the flock, for, thanks to the priestly character, you share in the *pastoral charism*, which is a sign of a special relationship of *likeness to Christ, the Good Shepherd*. You are precisely marked with this quality in a very special way.

—Saint John Paul II, Letter to Priests for
Holy Thursday, 1979

I contemplate the ways in which my priestly life is seen and respected as one of personal integrity and generous service.

Embracing an Apostolic Faith December 2

> They devoted themselves to the teaching of the apostles and to the communal life, to the breaking of the bread and to the prayers. (Acts 2:42)

The church is rooted in the faith of the apostles. Apostolic faith is a living tradition that each generation seeks to pass down intact to those who follow. In a world that changes ever more swiftly, an old tradition is a repository of stabilizing wisdom. Apostolic faith gives both perspective and the wisdom of age, bringing a discerning eye to modern dilemmas. It helps to distinguish new human problems from perennial ones, to which faith gives the same reliable answer, phrased slightly differently in every generation.

Inevitably, the modern world has a tendency to view the wisdom of an old tradition as antiquated. The Catholic Church has learned to bear such reactions with patient equanimity, teaching the same truths with consistency and perseverance. Short-term skepticism often gives way to persistent effort. In this regard, the way the church has dealt with questions about the sanctity of life is exemplary. Slowly, the position of the church has come to look more persuasive and convincing.

The passing down of the tradition is never an impersonal affair, a matter of books and regulations. Teaching must come alive, for only a living tradition can be handed on. Priests have always played an active role in this transmission. But to play such a role effectively, priests themselves must be steeped in the apostolic faith, and that is no simple task. Rather, it is the fruit of a long education that has been internalized. But every preacher must eventually answer the question that St. Paul rightly poses to him: whose wisdom do you teach, that of the world or of Christ crucified? Only the latter gives life.

—Howard P. Bleichner, *View from the Altar*, 161–62

Lord Jesus, give me the wisdom and initiative to embrace a life of study and reflection, realizing that I am forever a student of the Sacred Scriptures and the rich tradition of the church.

December 3   The Daily Newness of the Eucharist

It is good to give thanks to the LORD, / to sing praise to your name, Most High, / To proclaim your love at daybreak, / your faithfulness in the night . . . (Ps 92:2-3)

Some of my brothers have the habit of keeping an account of the Masses that they have celebrated, beginning with their ordination. . . . I never felt this need because it has always seemed to me that in one Mass there would be all Masses and what counted was not the number but one's interior devotion. Thank God, having completed fifty-six years of priesthood, there has been granted to me the gift of celebrating the Eucharist almost every day and, often, many times a day—without ever taking these rituals for granted, but experiencing a new appreciation each time.

Naturally, I ought to speak about what the Eucharistic presence in the tabernacle means to me. I discovered it in all its power when I was about eleven years old, praying in a church in the mountains before a tabernacle where there was a lit candle. The thought that there was a living presence within that tabernacle made a great impression on me, and I spent a long time in prayer. From that time, in order to find my bearings in a given location, I keep in mind the places where the Most Blessed Sacrament is kept. On some trips abroad, I recall the pain I experienced while thinking that within the range of a few kilometers, even in a large city, the presence of Jesus in the Eucharist did not exist.

But above all, I am thankful for the great gift which has been given me of not ever taking the Mass for granted, but finding again and again the newness of its mystery. The Vatican II reforms have been easy for me to accept because they corresponded with my experience. I truly hope that there will not be any turning back from that maturity in understanding the Eucharist reached in the Church, especially in *Sacrosanctum Concilium.*

—Carlo Maria Cardinal Martini,
"A Few Thoughts on the Eucharist," 81–82

Lord Jesus, grant me the grace to give my fullest attention to the mystery of the daily Eucharist.

Eucharist as Act and Gift December 4

He loved his own in the world and he loved them to the end. (John 13:1)

Let us also enter the "large upper room furnished and ready" (Mk 14:15), and dispose ourselves to listen to the most intimate thoughts that he wants to confide to us; in particular, let us be ready to receive the act and the gift that he has prepared in view of this final meeting.

So, while they are eating, Jesus rises from the table and begins to wash the disciples' feet. At first Peter resists, then he understands and accepts. We too are asked to understand: the first thing the disciple must do is to prepare himself to listen to the Lord, opening his heart to accept the initiative of his love. Only then will he be invited, in turn, to do what the Teacher did. He too must be committed to "washing the feet" of his brothers and sisters, expressing in gestures of mutual service that love which is the synthesis of the whole Gospel (cf. Jn 13:1-20).

Also during the Supper, knowing that his "hour" had now come, Jesus blesses and breaks the bread, then gives it to the Apostles saying: "This is my body"; he does the same with the cup: "This is my blood." And he commands them: "Do this in remembrance of me" (1 Cor 11:24-25). Truly this is the witness of love taken "to the end" (Jn 13:1). Jesus gives himself as food to his disciples to become one with them. Once again the "lesson" emerges that we must learn: the first thing to do is to open our hearts to welcoming the love of Christ. It is his initiative: it is his love that enables us, in turn, to love our brethren.

—Saint John Paul II, Homily for the Mass of
the Lord's Supper, April 17, 2003

In what ways do I see my daily pastoral ministry as eucharistic? Or have I limited Eucharist to the altar?

It was not you who chose me, but I who chose you and appointed you to go and bear fruit that will remain . . . (John 15:16)

We are taught total dedication by the One who loved us first. "I was ready to be found by those who did not seek me. I said, 'Here am I, here am I' to a nation that did not call on my name" (Is. 65, 1). The place of totality par excellence is the Eucharist since, "in the Eucharist Jesus does not give us a 'thing' but himself; he offers his own body and pours out his own blood" (*Sacramentum Caritatis*, n. 7).

Let us be faithful, dear brothers, to the daily Celebration of the Most Holy Eucharist, not solely in order to fulfill a pastoral commitment or a requirement of the community entrusted to us but because of the absolute personal need we have of it, as of breathing, as of light for our life, as the one satisfactory reason for a complete priestly existence.

. . . Since the missionary spirit is intrinsic in the very nature of the Church, our mission is likewise innate in the priestly identity, which is why missionary urgency is a matter of self-awareness. Our priestly identity is edified and renewed day after day in "conversation" with Our Lord. An immediate consequence of our relationship with him, continuously nourished in constant prayer, is the need to make all those around us share in it. The holiness we ask for daily, in fact, cannot be conceived according to a sterile and abstract individual acceptance but is necessarily Christ's holiness, which is contagious for everyone: "Being in communion with Jesus Christ draws us into his 'being for all'; it makes it our own way of being" (Benedict XVI, *Spe Salvi*, n. 28).

> —Pope Benedict XVI, Letter on the Occasion of the
> World Day of Prayer for the Sanctification of Priests

How can I make certain that my celebration of the Eucharist does not become routine, but remains the fresh and living water of grace for my priestly life?

The Unchanging Heart of Christ December 6

[O]ne soldier thrust his lance into his side, and immediately blood and water flowed out. (John 19:34)

Changed in the depths of his being so that he acts and speaks in the person of Christ, the priest shares in a particularly intimate relationship with Christ and through Christ with the beloved Father, in the power of the Holy Spirit, who is the gift of divine love in person. These are personal relationships that, far from being abstract, are more real than any relationship with another human person. Yet, like all relationships, the relationship between Christ and the priest must be developed and nourished through priestly ministry and life—a life lived in total self-giving, together with the self-gift of Christ, renewed constantly through the Eucharist and deepened in a loving communion of prayer. As the priest is a man of communion, that communion must first and foremost be grounded in the source of all communion, in our one God, who is a communion of three Persons. It is impossible to build community in the Church or anywhere else if one does not partake of the profound reality of that communion in God. The priest must be a man of prayer; only in prayerful communion with the Trinity will anything else about his priesthood make sense, either on a supernatural or natural level. Only then can we rightly understand what is changing in the priesthood by gazing into its unchanging heart—the unchanging heart of the person of Christ, in whom the priest now lives and acts from the depth of his being.

. . . There is no room for vainglory in priestly consecration. To be set apart in this way is to serve all the rest rather than to be served by them. The mystery of this vocation lays a tremendous responsibility upon the priest. Set apart as he is, his life will never again be his own as it had seemed to be before.

—Thomas Acklin,
The Unchanging Heart of the Priesthood, 22

As a man of communion, what concrete steps might I take to strengthen my relationship with Christ?

December 7   **Precious Vessels, Not Made of Gold**

"For where your treasure is, there also will your heart be." (Matt 6:21)

For He who sent the apostles without gold also brought together churches without gold. The Church has gold, not to store up, but to lay out, to spend on those in need. What necessity is there to guard what is of no good? Do we not know how much gold and silver the Assyrians took out of the temple of the Lord? Is it not much better that the priests should melt it down for the sustenance of the poor, if other supplies fail, than that a sacrilegious enemy should carry it off and defile it? Would not the Lord himself say: why did you suffer so many needy to die of hunger? Surely you had gold? You should have given them sustenance . . . It had been better to preserve living vessels than gold ones.

For what would you say: I feared that the temple of God would need its ornaments? He would answer: The sacraments need not gold, nor are they proper to gold only—for they are not bought with gold. The glory of the sacraments is the redemption of captives. Truly they are precious vessels, for they redeem men from death. That, indeed, is the true treasure of the Lord which effects what His blood effected . . . How beautifully it is said when long lines of captives are redeemed by the Church: These Christ has redeemed. Behold the gold that can be tried, behold the useful gold of Christ which frees from death, behold the gold whereby modesty is redeemed and chastity is preserved.

—Saint Ambrose, *Duties of the Clergy* II

Have I kept the proper perspective regarding the resources of the church and their use for pastoral ministry? Do I regard my ministry as my greatest treasure?

Our Souls Proclaim God's Greatness December 8

The Mighty One has done great things for me, / and holy is his name. (Luke 1:49)

As we celebrate the Eucharist at so many altars throughout the world, let us give thanks to the Eternal Priest for the gift which he has bestowed on us in the sacrament of the Priesthood. And in this thanksgiving may there be heard the words which the Evangelist puts on Mary's lips on the occasion of her visit to her cousin Elizabeth: "The Almighty has done great things for me, and holy is his name." Let us also give thanks to Mary for the indescribable gift of the Priesthood, whereby we are able to serve in the Church every human being. May gratitude also reawaken our zeal! Is it not through our priestly ministry that there is accomplished what the next verses of Mary's Magnificat speak of? Behold, the Redeemer, the God of the Cross and of the Eucharist, indeed "lifts up the lowly" and "fills the hungry with good things." He who was rich, yet for our sake became poor, so that by his poverty we might become rich, has entrusted to the humble Virgin of Nazareth the admirable mystery of his poverty which makes us rich. And he entrusts the same mystery to us too through the sacrament of the Priesthood.

Let us unceasingly give thanks for this. Let us give thanks with the whole of our lives. Let us give thanks with all our strength. Let us give thanks together with Mary, the Mother of priests. "How can I repay the Lord for his goodness to me? The cup of salvation I will raise; I will call on the Lord's name."

—Saint John Paul II, Letter to Priests for
Holy Thursday, 1988

I spend some moments in silent reflection on the many personal blessings that God has given me throughout my priestly ministry. May Mary's Magnificat be my own.

Then he summoned his twelve disciples and gave them authority over unclean spirits to drive them out and to cure every disease and every illness. (Matt 10:1)

Priestly office is a *spiritual* ministry which cannot be fulfilled except by a *spiritual* man. "Such a man does not regard what is visible, manageable, calculable as the sole reality. He makes room for the free, un-covenanted action of the Spirit of God, and lives from the freedom of that Spirit" (W. Kaspar). Yet inasmuch as the kingdom of God and the activity of the Spirit go beyond the dimensions of the immediate situation, spiritual ministry is not purely spiritual: it is concerned with setting up in this world, here and now, visible signs of the kingdom, signs by which the coming sovereignty of God is sketched out in anticipatory outline. Such signs are to some extent concrete, visible, "corporal."

At particular times and in particular situations these signs may certainly take the form of youth work and social work and work to relieve human needs and cares. Jesus also healed the sick, fed the hungry, consoled the lonely, called men together out of their isolation into a community. But this he did not do in order to make the world better "in itself" and thus endorse it "in itself": through healing, helping and consoling he has established signs of hope which make credible the announcement of the kingdom of God, which breaks through the limits of the world. In the same way the spiritual ministry, as part of the community and forming with the community "God's model society" (N. Lohfink), is called upon to set up for the world the signs of the kingdom which can bring about mutual reconciliation among men, enabling them to live in mutual love, brotherly peace and shared joy, in the expectation of ultimate happiness.

—Gisbert Greshake, *The Meaning of Christian Priesthood*, 107–8

In what ways am I conscious that *all* my activities can be signs of the coming of the kingdom of God?

A person should examine himself, and so eat the bread and drink the cup. For anyone who eats and drinks without discerning the body, eats and drinks judgment on himself. (1 Cor 11:28-29)

The Curé of Ars was convinced that the fervour of a priest's life depended entirely upon the Mass: "The reason why a priest is lax is that he does not pay attention to the Mass! My God, how we ought to pity a priest who celebrates as if he were engaged in something routine!" He was accustomed, when celebrating, also to offer his own life in sacrifice: "What a good thing it is for a priest each morning to offer himself to God in sacrifice!"

This deep personal identification with the Sacrifice of the Cross led him—by a sole inward movement—from the altar to the confessional. Priests ought never to be resigned to empty confessionals or the apparent indifference of the faithful to this Sacrament. In France, at the time of the Curé of Ars, confession was no more easy or frequent than in our own day, since the upheaval caused by the revolution had long inhibited the practice of religion. Yet he sought in every way, by his preaching and his powers of persuasion, to help his parishioners to rediscover the meaning and beauty of the Sacrament of Penance, presenting it as an inherent demand of the Eucharistic presence. He thus created a "virtuous" circle. By spending long hours in church before the tabernacle, he inspired the faithful to imitate him by coming to visit Jesus with the knowledge that their parish priest would be there, ready to listen and offer forgiveness.

Later, the growing numbers of penitents from all over France would keep him in the confessional for up to sixteen hours a day. It was said that Ars had become "a great hospital of souls."

—Pope Benedict XVI, Letter Proclaiming
a Year for Priests, June 16, 2009

I consider how I might more effectively preach the relationship between the Eucharist and the sacrament of penance.

> [H]earing of your faith in the Lord Jesus and of your love for all the holy ones, do not cease giving thanks for you, remembering you in my prayers . . . (Eph 1:15-16)

A priest's sense of ministry needs nourishment and we ought never grow apart or aloof from the people we serve. Even the continual respect people show a priest renews his awareness of the "treasure we hold in common clay pots," for they salute the office as much as the man.

The trusting way in which people ask for our intercessory prayer, as well as invigorating our own weakness, reminds us of that commitment made at ordination to "maintain and deepen a spirit of prayer appropriate to our way of life, and in keeping with what is required of us, to celebrate faithfully the liturgy of the hours *for the Church and for the world.*"

People keep reminding us that we are appointed priests on their behalf and that we have the responsibility of bringing their needs with us to prayer. When we pray the Prayer of the Church for the world, we are exercising the mediatorship of the priesthood. The high priest Aaron, in case he might forget his continued duty to pray on behalf of his people, always brought the sign of the people on his breast when he went into the Holy of Holies to pray. A priest's breviary, just like his celebration of the liturgy, contributes to his own holiness when it is not divorced from his daily activities but in fact expresses what he tries to live day by day. He intercedes for the people but he also shows genuine care and compassion for their needs. He celebrates the sacred mysteries but tries in his life to epitomize the word he preaches and the sacrifice he makes present. Otherwise his celebration is mere ritual and has only shallow significance. He develops spiritually "through his liturgical ministry only if he stands judged in his own life by the word he proclaims to others and challenged to the same conversion, faith and love that he preaches to his people."

—Gerard McGinnity, *Christmen: Experience*
of Priesthood Today, 56–57

Lord Jesus, help me to more deeply realize that my prayer for your people is of infinite worth, and is in faithful imitation of your own prayer in the Upper Room.

A Committed Friendship with Christ   December 12

[L]et us rid ourselves of every burden and sin that clings to us and persevere in running the race that lies before us while keeping our eyes fixed on Jesus, the leader and perfecter of faith. (Heb 12:1-2)

Speaking from the Cross on Golgotha, Christ said to the disciple: "Behold your mother." And the disciple "took her to his own home" as Mother. Let us also take Mary as Mother into the interior "home" of our Priesthood. For we belong to the "faithful in whose rebirth and development" the Mother of God "cooperates with a maternal love." Yes, we have, in a certain sense, a special "right" to this love in consideration of the mystery of the Upper Room. Christ said: "No longer do I call you servants . . . , but I have called you friends." Without this "friendship" it would be difficult to think that, after the apostles, he would entrust to us the sacrament of his Body and Blood, the sacrament of his redeeming death and resurrection, in order that we might celebrate this ineffable sacrament in his name, indeed, *in persona Christi*. Without this special "friendship" it would also be difficult to think about Easter evening, when the Risen Lord appeared in the midst of the apostles, saying to them: "Receive the Holy Spirit. Whose sins you forgive are forgiven them, and whose sins you retain are retained."

Such a friendship involves a commitment. Such a friendship should instill a holy fear, a much greater sense of responsibility, a much greater readiness to give of oneself all that one can, with the help of God. In the Upper Room such a friendship has been profoundly sealed with the promise of the Paraclete: "He will teach you all things, and bring to your remembrance all that I have said to you. . . . He will bear witness to me, and you also are witnesses."

—Saint John Paul II, Letter to Priests for
Holy Thursday, 1988

Christ Jesus, I am with you in the Upper Room, receiving your Spirit and renewing my desire to give myself completely to your service.

So do not be ashamed of your testimony to our Lord, nor of me, a prisoner for his sake; but bear your share of hardship for the gospel with the strength that comes from God. (2 Tim 1:8)

By reason of his celibacy the priest is a man alone: that is true, but his solitude is not meaningless emptiness because it is filled with God and the brimming riches of His kingdom. Moreover, he has prepared himself for this solitude—which should be an internal and external plenitude of charity—if he has chosen it with full understanding, and not through any proud desire to be different from the rest of men, or to withdraw himself from common responsibilities, or to alienate himself from his brothers, or to show contempt for the world. Though set apart from the world, the priest is not separated from the People of God, because he has been "appointed to act on behalf of men," since he is "consecrated" completely to charity and to the work for which the Lord has chosen him.

At times loneliness will weigh heavily on the priest, but he will not for that reason regret having generously chosen it. Christ, too, in the most tragic hours of His life was alone—abandoned by the very ones whom He had chosen as witnesses to, and companions of, His life, and whom He had loved "to the end"—but He stated, "I am not alone, for the Father is with me." He who has chosen to belong completely to Christ will find, above all, in intimacy with Him and in His grace, the power of spirit necessary to banish sadness and regret and to triumph over discouragement. He will not be lacking the protection of the Virgin Mother of Jesus nor the motherly solicitude of the Church, to whom he has given himself in service. He will not be without the kindly care of his father in Christ, his bishop; nor will the fraternal companionship of his fellow priests and the love of the entire People of God, most fruitful of consolations, be lacking to him.

—Blessed Pope Paul VI,
Sacerdotalis Caelibatus, 58–59

How do I live my solitude? With the constant distraction of entertainment, or with a nurturing sense of peace as a "friend of God"?

Cherish the Gift of Priesthood

So you, my child, be strong in the grace that is in Christ Jesus. (2 Tim 2:1)

Dear brothers: you who have borne "the burden of the day and the heat": who have put your hand to the plough and do not turn back, and perhaps even more those of you who are doubtful of the meaning of your vocation or of the value of your service: think of the places where people anxiously await a priest, and where for many years, feeling the lack of such a priest, they do not cease to hope for his presence. And sometimes it happens that they meet in an abandoned shrine, and place on the altar a stole which they still keep, and recite all the prayers of the Eucharistic Liturgy; and then, at the moment that corresponds to the transubstantiation a deep silence comes down upon them, a silence sometimes broken by a sob . . . so ardently do they desire to hear the words that only the lips of a priest can efficaciously utter. So much do they desire Eucharistic Communion, in which they can share only through the ministry of a priest, just as they also so eagerly wait to hear the divine words of pardon: *Ego te absolvo a peccatis tuis!* So deeply do they feel the absence of a priest among them! . . . Such places are not lacking in the world. So if one of you doubts the meaning of his Priesthood, if he thinks it is "socially" fruitless or useless, reflect on this!

We must be converted every day, we must rediscover every day the gift obtained from Christ Himself in the sacrament of Orders, by penetrating the importance of the salvific mission of the Church and by reflecting on the great meaning of our vocation in the light of that mission.

—Saint John Paul II, Letter to Priests for
Holy Thursday, 1979

May I never forget the share that I have been given in the redemptive work of Christ, who continues his healing ministry in my priestly life.

For God did not give us a spirit of cowardice but rather of power and love and self-control. (2 Tim 1:7)

If, the priest is a "man of God" and if personal following of Christ and being possessed by the kingdom of God belong to his office, then there is inherent in him an impulse towards radicalism which persists in all the concrete details of his life.

Wherever this radicalism is moderated and adulterated for any worldly reason, the priest's office will be less effective and less credible. It is no coincidence that in St. John's Gospel, in which the handing over of the pastoral office to Peter stands as a model for all transmission of office, the love of God is named as the one condition: "Do you love me more than these?" (Jn 21:15). Significantly, no question is asked about readiness for self-sacrifice for the sake of mankind, but only for Christ: since it is only from this that that self-sacrifice can arise whereby Christ the Shepherd gave himself up for the flock and which he expects from the disciples he has commissioned.

In these ways Holy Scripture gives many indications that only a union of vocation and lifestyle, a mutual interpenetration of the objective sacramental holiness of the office and personal holiness, can meet the requirements of priestly ministry. When Francis de Sales says that "the difference between the written word of the Gospels and the life of the Saints is the same as the difference between a musical score and its performance," this means that the priest should not merely pass on the score but must also take part in the performance, and in fact must be himself a "hymn."

—Gisbert Greshake, *The Meaning of
Christian Priesthood*, 115–16

May the whole of my priestly life, O God, become a hymn of lasting, joyous praise!

> For you know the gracious act of our Lord Jesus Christ, that for your sake he became poor although he was rich, so that by his poverty you might become rich. (2 Cor 8:9)

As leader of the community the priest is, above all, to be honest and responsible in his administration of the goods of the community, committed to equitable distribution of goods among the presbyterate itself and a facilitator of a preferential option for the poor among the community and society at large. Here the Holy Father underlines the prophetic role of the priest in his proclamation of the Gospel to and presence among those on the margins of society. This is an urgent task for the ministerial priesthood in the light of the tyranny of consumerist values in contemporary society. If the Christian priest as prophet is to witness to a new pattern of liberated life in Christ which refuses to become a slave to worldly things in its freedom for the values of the Kingdom, then he must first embrace these values in a life that strives toward the freedom of the Gospel. This prophetic role leads to a closer configuration with Christ who brings "his pastoral charity to perfection on the Cross with a complete exterior and interior emptying of self."

The spirit of poverty drives the priest towards the total and absolute claims of the Gospel as the criterion of both his personal and professional existence and involves him in a process of self-emptying that is always "for others."

—Dermot Power, *A Spiritual Theology of the Priesthood*, 104–5

Does my way of life indicate that I have chosen to imitate Christ in his poverty?

> Oh, the depths of the riches and wisdom and knowledge of God! (Rom 11:33)

Mystagogy seeks to enable a genuine and deep conversion to Jesus in holiness of life. It aims to move Christians from the *notional* to the *real*, to use the expression of Cardinal Newman. Christian faith is not about "ideas one has thought," but about "a divine relationship fully lived." We need to lead our people to understand the holy signs that we celebrate. It is our job to allow the rites to speak as fully as they can through the quality of our performance of the liturgy. As bearers of the mystery, our ritual leadership will invest the sacraments with dignity and integrity. This helps the faithful see how the rites express God's presence, God's claim upon them, and their vocation to be living witnesses to the Church as a sign and sacrament of salvation.

The missionary ecclesiology of a priestly people can only emerge from lay faithful who are living a transforming faith. The pressure of numbers and the limited cadre of priests often make us settle for sacramental celebrations that are religious but not really faith experiences. They are religious because they address the craving of those who come for spiritual comfort and some level of religious nurture. But they are not faith experiences in the full sense because the people do not understand the fundamental realities that the liturgy celebrates; that the sacraments are the common work of a priestly people, and what we offer to God is the sacrifice of the whole Christ—the Head and members together, and that the "Church gathered" has been called together to be sent out on mission to proclaim the kingdom of God.

In terms of priestly spirituality, being a bearer of the mystery demands an appreciation of ritual, a symbolic literacy, and a passion to share the meaning of the liturgy. The mystagogue can never be satisfied to allow the holy signs that the Church celebrates to become merely a means of satisfying human curiosity or a craving for religious experience. Rather he will work unceasingly to explain the unspeakable mercy of adoption, whereby God adds men and women to the body of Christ through the sacraments and the gifts of the Holy Spirit.

—Paul J. Philibert, *Stewards of God's Mysteries*, 35–36

I will only be a "bearer of mystery" if my own life is immersed in the paschal mystery of Christ.

Never Cease Praying for Vocations December 18

> The harvest is abundant but the laborers are few; so ask the master of the harvest to send out laborers for his harvest. (Luke 10:2)

The Eucharist is first and foremost a gift made to the Church. An inexpressible gift. The Priesthood too is a gift to the Church, for the sake of the Eucharist. Today, when it is said that the community has a right to the Eucharist, it must be remembered in particular that You urged Your disciples to "pray . . . the Lord of the harvest to send out laborers into his harvest."

If people do not "pray" with fervor, if they do not strive with all their strength to ensure that the Lord sends to communities good ministers of the Eucharist, can they say with inner conviction that "the community has a right . . . "? If it has a right, then it has a right to the gift! And a gift cannot be treated as if it were not a gift. Unceasing prayers must be offered to obtain that gift. We must ask for it on our knees.

And so, since the Eucharist is the Lord's greatest gift to the Church, we must ask for priests, because the Priesthood too is a gift to the Church. We beg You, Lord, to grant that we may always be intensely aware of the greatness of the gift which is the Sacrament of Your Body and Blood.

Grant that, in inner accord with the economy of grace and the law that governs gifts, we may continually "pray the Lord of the harvest," and that our cry may come from a pure heart, a heart that has the simplicity and sincerity of true disciples. Then, Lord, You will not reject our plea.

—Saint John Paul II, Letter to Priests for
Holy Thursday, 1982

Lord, I received your call to the priesthood through the prayer, encouragement, and example of other priests. May I be such a light for the young men of today.

December 19   Ministers of the Future of the World

> The one who gives this testimony says, "Yes, I am coming soon." Amen!
> Come, Lord Jesus! (Rev 22:20)

We ourselves must have a renewed certainty: he [Jesus Christ] is the Truth; only by walking in his footsteps do we go in the right direction, and it is in this direction that we must walk and lead others.

. . . In all this suffering, not only should we keep our certainty that Christ really is the Face of God, but we should also deepen this certainty and the joy of knowing it and thus truly be ministers of the future of the world, of the future of every person. We should deepen this certainty in a personal relationship with the Lord because certainty can also grow with rational considerations. A sincere reflection that is also rationally convincing but becomes personal, strong and demanding by virtue of a friendship lived personally, every day, with Christ, truly seems to me to be very important . . .

And it is therefore important to live in the reality of the presbyterate, of the community of priests who help one another, who are journeying on together with solidarity in their common faith. This also seems to me to be important, for if young people see priests who are very lonely, sad and tired, they will think: "If this is my future, then it is not for me." A real communion of life that shows young people: "Yes, this can be a future for me too, it is possible to live like this," must be created.

—Pope Benedict XVI, Address to a Meeting with
Diocesan Clergy of Aosta, July 25, 2005

In what ways is my ministry enlivened by Christian hope, and reflective of the joyful Christ?

> Do you not know that your body is a temple of the holy Spirit within you, whom you have from God, and that you are not your own? (1 Cor 6:19)

With the one definitive sacrifice of the cross, Jesus communicated to all his disciples the dignity and mission of priests of the new and eternal covenant. And thus the promise which God had made to Israel was fulfilled: "You shall be to me a kingdom of priests and a holy nation" (Ex. 19:6). According to St. Peter, the whole people of the new covenant is established as "a spiritual house, a holy priesthood, to offer spiritual sacrifices acceptable to God through Jesus Christ" (1 Pt. 2:5). The baptized are "living stones" who build the spiritual edifice by keeping close to Christ, "that living stone . . . in God's sight chosen and precious" (1 Pt. 2:4). The new priestly people which is the Church not only has its authentic image in Christ, but also receives from him a real ontological share in his one eternal priesthood, to which she must conform every aspect of her life.

For the sake of this universal priesthood of the new covenant Jesus gathered disciples during his earthly mission (cf. Lk. 10:1-12) . . . Already during his public ministry (cf. Mt. 16:18), and then most fully after his death and resurrection (cf. Mt. 28; Jn. 20; 21), Jesus had conferred on Peter and the Twelve entirely special powers with regard to the future community and the evangelization of all peoples. After having called them to follow him, he kept them at his side and lived with them, imparting his teaching of salvation to them through word and example, and finally he sent them out to all mankind.

—Saint John Paul II, *Pastores Dabo Vobis*, 13–14

Lord Jesus, you have given me a special ministry so that I might call all believers to their dignity as members of a royal priesthood and a holy nation. May I do so with all humility and gratitude!

> For the Father himself loves you, because you have loved me and have come to believe that I came from God. (John 16:27)

Christ loves his priests. It is incomprehensible to us how much he loves his priests. He loves them like brothers. But what is more, he loves them as himself. Because, you see, a priest is Christ, and the Father loves them because he loves the Son, and the Icon of the Son is in the heart of every priest. And so the Father bends over each heart with a love that surpasses all understanding, and the Holy Spirit sends his fire and flame constantly upon you. You have a Pentecost every day.

It is hard for you to realize this because you usually look upon yourself only as a man. If only you could see yourself as the Father sees you, as the Son sees you, as the Holy Spirit sees you. Yes, loneliness is yours, but don't you understand, dearly beloved Father, that your loneliness is shared with Jesus Christ—with the Trinity. The Apostles were asleep in Gethsemane. But Christ never sleeps. He is always at your side and he shares your loneliness.

Does it ever occur to you, dearly beloved Father, that he also shares with you his joy, providing you look for it? . . . Loneliness shared with Christ, with a deep understanding as to why you are sharing it, turns to joy. But this is a kind of joy that stays deep within the priestly heart. It remains there. It is like a little brook watering the deserts that are so often in men's hearts, especially priestly hearts.

—Catherine de Hueck Doherty, *Dear Father*, 25

I consider the times I have felt loneliness in my ministry, and now share those times with Christ. He wishes nothing more than to be at my side.

> This is how all will know that you are my disciples, if you have love for
> one another. (John 13:35)

If it is true that the priest genuinely possesses and fulfills his priestly
nature only when he personally believes, hopes, loves, and is justified and
holy, then his relationship to the other person must as such be sustained
by that infused, divine virtue of supernatural love in the Holy Spirit which
justifies man and places him in an intimate relationship to God himself and
his neighbor. This neighbor is really and truly loved in and with God, for
God's sake and in the light of God, and can be loved deeply and intimately
only through the supernatural deifying power of the Holy Spirit whom
God has given to us in the supernatural life of grace . . . Nothing can be
greater or more important than this grace . . . It follows that, whenever the
priest fails to realize in his priestly calling this most radical relationship to
his fellow man which exists in God himself and in his divine life, he will
also fail to come up to the requirements of his work as a priest. It follows
likewise that all inner vitality, closeness, and personal esteem for the other
person must be included in the "heart to heart" of Christian love of neighbor.
   . . . The priest has to deal with human beings and when he really loves
these human beings in a priestly spirit, in labor and sacrifice, he has really
fulfilled his Christianity and his own proper destiny. For it is true that the
law is summed up in the one commandment of love of neighbor (Mt. 22:39)
and the person who selflessly finds his neighbor has also found God.

—Karl Rahner,
Meditations on Priestly Life, 138–39, 146

Jesus, my Brother, grace me with a genuine priestly heart that is animated
daily by your selfless love for all.

May the peoples praise you, God; / may all the peoples praise you!
(Ps 67:4)

God's glory is written in the order of creation and in the order of redemption; the priest is called to live this mystery in its fullness in order to
participate in the great *officium laudis* which is unceasingly taking place
in the universe. Only by living in depth the truth of the redemption of the
world and of humanity can he come close to the sufferings and problems
of individuals and families, and fearlessly face as well the reality of evil
and sin, with the spiritual strength necessary to overcome them.

. . . In every situation, the priest's task is to show God to man as the
final end of his personal existence. The priest becomes the one to whom
people confide the things most dear to them and their secrets, which are
sometimes very painful. He becomes the one whom the sick, the elderly
and the dying wait for, aware as they are that only he, a sharer in the priesthood of Christ, can help them in the final journey which is to lead them to
God. As a witness to Christ, the priest is the messenger of man's supreme
vocation to eternal life in God. And while he accompanies his brothers
and sisters, he prepares himself: the exercise of the ministry enables him
to deepen his own vocation to give glory to God in order to have a share
in eternal life. He thus moves forward towards the day when Christ will
say to him: "Well done, good and faithful servant, . . . enter into the joy
of your master" (Mt 25:21).

—Saint John Paul II, Letter to Priests for
Holy Thursday, 1996

Lord Jesus, the whole of my life I dedicate to your glory and to the dignity
of every person to whom I am sent.

Suffering and Consolation in Ministry   December 24

> For as Christ's sufferings overflow to us, so through Christ does our encouragement also overflow. (2 Cor 1:5)

The trials of the ministry are various: physical and nervous exhaustion, bad moods, the daily grind, states of repugnance, negative states in which we feel like rejecting people and situations. These states affect us physically and psychologically and yet we can withhold ourselves from them. We do not look them in the face, we deny them, we put them aside, perhaps because we are afraid that we cannot face them openly. In some way or other we consider them as side effects of our lives, that should not occur, and which are better re-assimilated unconsciously. We inject a sort of psychological anesthetic into these trials.

I think we often deprive ourselves of the strength we could gain from entering into Christ's sufferings, because when we face them we hold our breath, close our eyes, go on just the same. We do not confront them in prayer or in conversation with Christ. We do not take them into ourselves and so our trials remain like foreign bodies, they are not integrated into our experience and therefore they cannot be transformed into comfort.

It is very significant that Saint Paul speaks of Christ's sufferings in us, because it is not a question of my weaknesses, my failures, my personal defeats. It is a question of Christ's sufferings in me and this makes things different. I understand that suffering is a way in which Christ works in me, and that it is he himself who suffers from my weakness in the difficulties of the ministry.

—Carlo Maria Cardinal Martini,
In the Thick of His Ministry, 22–23

How can I more readily accept my sufferings as a share in the sufferings of Christ?

And the Word became flesh / and made his dwelling among us, / and
we saw his glory, / the glory as of the Father's only Son, / full of grace
and truth. (John 1:14)

"Godhead here in hiding, whom I do adore." On this Night, the opening words of this celebrated Eucharistic hymn echo in my heart. These
words accompany me daily in this year dedicated to the Eucharist. In the
Son of the Virgin, "wrapped in swaddling clothes and lying in a manger"
(Lk 2:12), we acknowledge and adore "the Bread which came down from
heaven" (Jn 6:41, 51), the Redeemer who came among us in order to bring
life to the world.

Bethlehem! The city where Jesus was born in fulfillment of the Scriptures, in Hebrew means "house of bread." It was there that the Messiah was
to be born, the One who would say of himself: "I am the bread of life" (Jn
6:35, 48). In Bethlehem was born the One who, under the sign of broken
bread, would leave us the memorial of his Pasch. On this Holy Night,
adoration of the Child Jesus becomes Eucharistic adoration.

We adore you, Lord, truly present in the Sacrament of the Altar, the
living Bread which gives life to humanity. We acknowledge you as our one
God, a little Child lying helpless in the manger! "In the fullness of time,
you became a man among men, to unite the end to the beginning, that is,
man to God" (cf. Saint Irenaeus, *Adversus Haereses*, IV, 20, 4).

You are born on this Night, our divine Redeemer, and, in our journey
along the paths of time, you become for us the food of eternal life. Look
upon us, eternal Son of God, who took flesh in the womb of the Virgin
Mary! All humanity, with its burden of trials and troubles, stands in need
of you. Stay with us, living Bread which came down from heaven for our
salvation! Stay with us forever! Amen!

—Saint John Paul II, Homily for Midnight Mass,
December 24, 2004

As I read this last Christmas homily of Pope John Paul II, I pray that I might
have as deep a love for the Eucharist as did he!

> My son, do not forget my teaching, / take to heart my commands; / For many days, and years of life, / and peace, will they bring you. (Prov 3:1-2)

John M. Vianney was an outstanding model of voluntary mortification of the body as well as of detachment from external things. "There is only one way"—he used to say—"for anyone to devote himself to God as he should through self-denial and the practice of penance: that is by devoting himself to it completely." Throughout his whole life, the holy Curé of Ars carried this principle into practice energetically in the matter of chastity . . .

The ascetic way of life, by which priestly chastity is preserved, does not enclose the priest's soul within the sterile confines of his own interests, but rather it makes him more eager and ready to relieve the needs of his brethren. St. John Mary Vianney has this pertinent comment to make in this regard: "A soul adorned with the virtue of chastity cannot help loving others; for it has discovered the source and font of love—God."

What great benefits are conferred on human society by men like this who are free of the cares of the world and totally dedicated to the divine ministry so that they can employ their lives, thoughts, powers in the interest of their brethren! How valuable to the Church are priests who are anxious to preserve perfect chastity! For We agree with Our predecessor of happy memory, Pius XI, in regarding this as the outstanding adornment of the Catholic priesthood and as something "that seems to Us to correspond better to the counsels and wishes of the Most Sacred Heart of Jesus, so far as the souls of priests are concerned." Was not the mind of John Mary Vianney soaring to reach the counsels of this same divine charity when he wrote this lofty sentence: "Is not the priesthood love of the Most Sacred Heart of Jesus?"

—Saint John XXIII, *Sacerdotii Nostri Primordia*

Lord Jesus, help me to appreciate my promise of chaste celibacy, not as a limitation, but as a sacred freedom to love as you have loved.

Oh, the depth of the riches and wisdom and knowledge of God! How inscrutable are his judgments and how unsearchable his ways! (Rom 11:33)

The Catechism is entrusted above all to us, the Pastors of God's People, in order to strengthen our deep bonds of communion in the same apostolic faith. *As a compendium of the one perennial Catholic faith*, it constitutes a trustworthy and authoritative means for bearing witness to and ensuring that unity in faith for which Christ himself prayed fervently to the Father as his "hour" drew near (cf. Jn 17:21-23).

The Catechism sets forth once more the fundamental and essential contents of Catholic faith and morality as they are believed, celebrated, lived and prayed by the Church today. It is thus *a special means* for deepening knowledge of the inexhaustible Christian mystery, for encouraging fresh enthusiasm for prayer intimately united with the prayer of Christ and for strengthening the commitment of a consistent witness of life.

At the same time, this Catechism is given to us as *a sure point of reference* for fulfilling the mission, entrusted to us in the Sacrament of Orders, of proclaiming the "Good News" to all people *in the name of Christ and of the Church.* Thanks to it, we can put into practice in a constantly renewed way Christ's perennial command: "Go therefore and make disciples of all nations . . . teaching them to observe all that I have commanded you" (Mt 28:19-20).

Indeed, in this summary of the deposit of faith, we can find *an authentic and sure norm* for teaching Catholic doctrine, for catechetical activity among the Christian people, for that "new evangelization" of which today's world has such immense need.

—Saint John Paul II, Letter to Priests for
Holy Thursday, 1993

Lord Jesus, grant me the discipline to make full use of the Catholic Catechism in my life of personal prayer and reflection.

A Priest's Life of Virtue December 28

Blessed is the man who does not walk / in the counsel of the wicked, / Nor stand in the way of sinners, / nor sit in company with scoffers. / Rather, the law of the LORD is his joy; / and on his law he meditates day and night. (Ps 1:1-2)

Just as the failings of a priest can weaken the entire Body of Christ, so too can his virtue strengthen it. But it is important to understand how the grace of God works so that no priest is ever lulled into a false sense of security by thinking that the sacrament of orders confers in some magical way a greater ability to lead the moral life. The only way in which one can become moral is by doing the good that one ought to do and by avoiding moral evil. Nothing else works. One may consume all the communions one can. One may celebrate Mass every day of his priestly life. But unless the priest chooses and does that which is moral, he will not become virtuous. . . . With the sacrament of orders God will also provide the graces necessary for the priest to live in conformity with his nature. But the priest must cooperate with the graces given. The only way he can become moral is by acting morally . . .

The natural moral virtues must be built up in the priest by the performance, with God's help, of virtuous acts. The priest [must] heed the exhortation of Saint Paul: "Finally, brothers, whatever is true, whatever is honorable, whatever is just, whatever is pure, whatever is lovely, whatever is gracious, if there is any excellence and if there is anything worthy of praise, think about these things. Keep on doing what you have learned and received and heard and seen in me" (Ph 4:8).

—John M. Haas, "The Sacral Character of the Priest as
the Foundation for his Moral Life and Teaching," 139

Just as I become weak if I do not exercise the body, so my moral strength is diminished if I do not actively practice virtue.

December 29   The Eucharist and Daily Self-Surrender

> For the sake of the joy that lay before him he endured the cross, despising its shame, and has taken his seat at the right of the throne of God. (Heb 12:2)

The cross of Golgotha always overshadows and hovers over our life. We are always living within sight of this tree of life. God always looks out on us in his merciful love from the cross. We are always sustained by this event. This sacrifice of the Mass is not what brings us first of all into contact with the sacrifice of the cross; but that which always holds for us and for our life becomes visible in a substantial way, although only sacramentally, in the sacrifice of the Mass. Our life is sustained by this act of obedience and love on the part of the Son of God, so that this sacramental anamnesis of the cross of Christ occurs as sacrifice in the Mass; but this does not mean that we enter into a relationship with the cross of Christ only at these moments of time in our life. Everywhere the cross sustains us; whenever man in belief, hope and love, reaches out for God, he realizes also this existential of his life, the cross of Christ.

But this very personal entry into the sacrifice of Christ on the Cross has its peak in our actual wretched life and rarely indeed at the point where we put on our priestly vestments and celebrated the Holy Eucharist. It is in our ordinary dress, at our death-bed, in humiliation, in the steady fulfillment of our duty that this self-surrender occurs concretely and radically; there too the sacrifice takes place which we celebrate in fact with good will, but first of all liturgically, sacramentally in the Mass. Hence our whole life is ultimately part of this Eucharist as worship of God.

—Karl Rahner, *Meditations on Priestly Life*, 208, 211

Loving Father, help me to appreciate that the daily routine of my priestly life is truly a share in the eucharistic sacrifice of your Son. May my whole life be an act of worship.

> He saved us and called us to a holy life, not according to our works but according to his own design and the grace bestowed on us in Christ Jesus before time began . . . (2 Tim 1:9)

A division between evangelization and the celebration of the sacraments "would divide the heart of the Church to the point of imperiling the faith." One can never doubt that for presbyters teaching and preaching, even at the highest academic and scholarly level, must always retain their purpose of serving the ministry of sanctification through the sacraments.

In the present economy of salvation, however, Christ makes use of the presbyters' ministry to sanctify believers. Acting in the name of Christ, the priest achieves effective sacramental action through the Holy Spirit, the Spirit of Christ, the principle and source of the holiness of the "new life."

The new life that the priest imparts, nurtures, restores and increases through the sacraments is a life of faith, hope and love. Faith is the basic divine gift: "This makes clear the great importance of preparation and of a disposition of faith on the part of the person who receives the sacraments; it also makes clear *the necessity for a witness of faith on the part of the minister in his entire life and especially in the way he values and celebrates the sacraments themselves.*"

The faith communicated by Christ through the sacraments is unfailingly accompanied by a "living hope," which instills in the hearts of the faithful a powerful dynamism of spiritual life, and impulse towards "what is above." On the other hand, faith "works through love," the love of charity, which springs from the Savior's heart and flows through the sacraments to spread throughout Christian life.

—Saint John Paul II, General Audience, May 5, 1993

Do I celebrate the sacraments with devotion, inspiring God's people to charity?

> Rather, he emptied himself, / taking the form of a slave, / coming in human likeness; / and found human in appearance, / he humbled himself, / becoming obedient to death, / even death on a cross. (Phil 2:7-8)

The obedience asked of a priest becomes the foundation of his own authentic ministry of preaching and teaching: "Only the person who knows how to obey in Christ is really able to require obedience from others in accordance with the Gospel." This aspect of the priest's obedience demands a marked spirit of asceticism in the letting go of personal preferences and points of view and in the collaboration with others that is a mark of the unity of the presbyterate . . . The radical availability for mission in which the priest is to find his true freedom is therefore an obediential state of life that transcends the juridical structure and finds its origins in Christ's own obediential stance before His Father which constitutes the very heart of His own Priesthood.

"The more unostentatiously the priest dedicates himself to his ministry in order to live only for it, the better he fulfills it. In such self-surrender, the priest 'loses his soul'—his subjectivity—in the act of obedience that is an essential part of every special election and mission. The authority represented and exercised by the ecclesial minister is that of Christ, the Redeemer, who was obedient unto death. It not only demands obedience; obedience is its very nature . . . It is not only authority *as* service; it is also, and explicitly, authority *for* service, for participation in the responsibility of the divine Shepherd who gives his life for his sheep (Jn 10:15)."

—Dermot Power, *A Spiritual Theology of
the Priesthood*, 102–3

Do I have an inner disposition of obedience? Can I make it the hallmark of the coming year?

References

Acklin, Thomas. *The Unchanging Heart of the Priesthood: A Faith Perspective on the Mystery and the Reality of Priesthood in the Church.* Steubenville, OH: Emmaus Road, 2005.

Ambrose, Saint. *Duties of the Clergy.* In *Ambrose: Select Works and Letters.* 61–65. Nicene and Post-Nicene Fathers 10. Translated by H. de Romestin. Peabody, MA: Hendrickson, 1994.

Arrupe, Pedro. *The Spiritual Legacy of Pedro Arrupe, S.J.* (Rome: Jesuit Curia, 1985).

Benedict XVI, Pope. Letter Proclaiming a Year for Priests. June 16, 2009.

———. Address to the Members of the Congregation for the Clergy. March 16, 2009.

———. Homily for the Chrism Mass. Saint Peter's Basilica, March 20, 2008.

———. Address to the Lenten Meeting of the Clergy of Rome. February 22, 2007.

———. Homily for the Ordination to the Priesthood. May 7, 2006.

———. *Pilgrim Fellowship of Faith: The Church as Communion.* San Francisco: Ignatius, 2005.

———. Letter on the Occasion of the World Day of Prayer for the Sanctification of Priests. May 8, 2008.

Bernardin, Joseph. *Homilies and Teaching Documents.* Vol. 1 of *Selected Works of Joseph Cardinal Bernardin.* Edited by Alphonse P. Spilly. Collegeville, MN: Liturgical Press, 2000.

Bleichner, Howard P. *View from the Altar: Reflections on the Rapidly Changing Catholic Priesthood.* New York: Crossroad, 2004.

Chrysostom, Saint John. *Six Books on the Priesthood*. Translated by Graham Neville. Crestwood, NJ: St. Vladimir's Seminary Press, 1996.

Clement of Rome, Saint. Letter to the Corinthians. In *The Apostolic Fathers*, 9–60. The Fathers of the Church 1. Translated by Francis X. Glimm. Washington, DC: Catholic University of America Press, 1947.

Doherty, Catherine de Hueck. *Dear Father: A Message of Love to Priests*. 1st ed. New York: Alba House, 1979.

Francis, Pope. *Evangelii Gaudium*. November 24, 2013.

———. Homily for the Chrism Mass. Saint Peter's Basilica, March 28, 2013.

———. Homily at Mass with Bishops, Priests, Religious and Seminarians. Cathedral of San Sebastian, Rio de Janeiro, July 27, 2013.

George, Francis. "Universal Communion." In *Born of the Eucharist: A Spirituality for Priests*, edited by Stephen J. Rossetti, 45–46. Notre Dame, IN: Ave Maria, 2009.

Greshake, Gisbert. *The Meaning of Christian Priesthood*. Dublin: Four Courts, 1988.

Haas, John M. "The Sacral Character of the Priest as the Foundation for his Moral Life and Teaching." In *The Catholic Priest as Moral Teacher and Guide: Proceedings of a Symposium Held at St. Charles Borromeo Seminary, Overbrook, Pennsylvania, January 17-20, 1990*, 123–47. San Francisco: Ignatius, 1990.

Hume, Basil. *Light in the Lord: Reflections on Priesthood*. Collegeville, MN: Liturgical Press, 1993.

Ignatius, Saint. Letter to the Ephesians. In *The Apostolic Fathers*, 38–50. The Fathers of the Church 1. Translated by Francis X. Glimm. Washington, DC: Catholic University of America Press, 1947.

John XXIII, Saint. *Sacerdotii Nostri Primordia*. August 1, 1959.

———. *Journal of a Soul: The Autobiography of Pope John XXIII*. New York: McGraw-Hill, 1965.

John Paul I, Pope. Address to a Meeting of Roman Clergy. September 7, 1978.

John Paul II, Saint. Letter to Priests for Holy Thursday. Various years posted at http://www.vatican.va.

———. Message to the Participants in the Fourth International Meeting of Priests. June 19, 1999.

———. *Pastores Dabo Vobis*. March 25, 1992.

———. General Audiences. http://www.vatican.va.

———. *Letters to My Brother Priests: Complete Collection of Holy Thursday Letters (1979–2005)*. 5th ed. Edited by James Socias. Woodridge, IL: Midwest Theological Forum, 2006.

———. Homily at the Liturgy of Vespers. Chapel of Saint Joseph's Seminary, Yonkers, NY, October 6, 1995.

———. *Gift and Mystery: On the Fiftieth Anniversary of My Priestly Ordination*. New York: Doubleday, 1996.

———. Homily for the Chrism Mass. Saint Peter's Basilica, April 17, 2003.

———. Homily for Priests at the Jubilee of Redemption, April 24, 1984.

———. Homily for a Holy Mass for the American Priests. Philadelphia, October 4, 1979.

Lathrop, Gordon W. *The Pastor: A Spirituality*. Minneapolis: Fortress, 2006.

Leen, Edward. *In the Likeness of Christ*. New York: Sheed & Ward, 1936.

Marmion, Columba. *Christ: The Ideal of the Priest*. St. Louis: Herder, 1952.

Martini, Carlo-Maria. *In the Thick of His Ministry*. Collegeville, MN: Liturgical Press, 1991.

———. "A Few Thoughts on the Eucharist." In *Born of the Eucharist: A Spirituality for Priests,* edited by Stephen J. Rossetti, 81–82. Notre Dame, IN: Ave Maria, 2009.

McCormack, John B. "The Eucharist Strengthens Us in Difficult Times." In *Born of the Eucharist: A Spirituality for Priests,* edited by Stephen J. Rossetti, 63–64. Notre Dame, IN: Ave Maria, 2009.

McGinnity, Gerard. *Christmen: Experience of Priesthood Today*. Dublin: Four Courts, 1985.

Merton, Thomas. *No Man Is an Island*. New York: Harcourt, Brace, 1955.

Newman, John Henry. *Meditations and Devotions*. Edited by Ian Ker. Mahwah, NJ: Paulist Press, 2010.

———. Parochial and Plain Sermons. 8 volumes. London: Longman, Green, 1891.

O'Donnell, Gabriel B. "The Eucharist—Heart of the Priest's Life." In *Born of the Eucharist: A Spirituality for Priests,* edited by Stephen J. Rossetti, 127–40. Notre Dame, IN: Ave Maria, 2009.

Oelrich, Anthony. "Communion in a Fractured World." In *Born of the Eucharist: A Spirituality for Priests,* edited by Stephen J. Rossetti, 65–66. Notre Dame, IN: Ave Maria, 2009.

Olier, Jean Jacques. "Introduction to the Christian Life and Virtues." In *Berulle and the French School*, 244–47. Translated by Lowell M.

Glendon. Edited by William Thompson. Classics of Western Spirituality. Mahwah, NJ: Paulist, 1989.

Paul VI, Blessed Pope. *Sacerdotalis Caelibatus.* June 24, 1967.

———. Homily in the Manila Metropolitan Cathedral-Basilica. November 27, 1970.

———. Address to the Newly Ordained Priests of the Pontifical College of Propagande Fide and the Pontifical Beda College. March 20, 1972.

Philibert, Paul J. *Stewards of God's Mysteries: Priestly Spirituality in a Changing Church.* Collegeville, MN: Liturgical Press, 2004.

Pius X, Saint. *Haerent Animo.* August 4, 1908.

Pius XI, Pope. *Ad Catholici Sacerdotii.* December 20, 1935.

Polycarp of Smyrna, Saint. The Letter to the Philippians. In *The Apostolic Fathers*, 135–43. The Fathers of the Church 1. Translated by Francis X. Glimm. Washington, DC: Catholic University of America Press, 1947.

Power, Dermot. *A Spiritual Theology of the Priesthood: The Mystery of Christ and the Mission of the Priest.* Edinburgh: T & T Clark, 1998.

Radcliffe, Timothy. *Sing a New Song: The Christian Vocation.* Springfield, IL: Templegate, 1999.

Rahner, Karl. *Meditations on the Sacraments.* New York: Seabury, 1977.

———. "The Renewal of Priestly Ordination." *Theological Investigations.* Translated by Karl-H. and Boniface Kruger. Baltimore, MD: Helicon, 1967. 3:171–76.

———. *Servants of the Lord.* New York: Herder & Herder, 1968.

———. *Encounters with Silence.* Westminster, MD: Newman, 1960.

———. *Prayers for a Lifetime.* Edited by Albert Raffelt. New York: Crossroad, 1984.

———. *Meditations on Priestly Life.* Translated by Edward Quinn. London: Sheed & Ward, 1970.

———. *Watch and Pray with Me.* Translated by William V. Dych. London: Burns & Oates, 1968.

Resseguier, Gertrude. *The First Love: About Joy in the Priesthood.* Petersham, MA: Saint Bede's, 1998.

Rossetti, Stephen J. "God Waits for Me." In *Born of the Eucharist: A Spirituality for Priests,* edited by Stephen J. Rossetti, 141–42. Notre Dame, IN: Ave Maria, 2009.

Sartain, J. Peter. *Strengthen Your Brothers: Letters of Encouragement from an Archbishop to His Priests.* Collegeville, MN: Liturgical Press, 2012.

Sheen, Fulton J. *The Priest Is Not His Own.* San Francisco, Ignatius, 2004.

Speyr, Adrienne von. *They Followed His Call: Vocation and Asceticism.* New York: Alba House, 1979.

Suhard, Emmanuel-Célestin. *The Church Today: The Collected Writings of Emmanuel Cardinal Suhard.* Chicago: Fides, 1953.

Teilhard de Chardin, Pierre. *Writings in Time of War.* Translated by René Hague. New York: Harper & Row, 1968.

———. "The Mass on the World." *Hymn of the Universe*, 9–32. Translated by Gerald Vann. New York: Harper & Row, 1961.

Underhill, Evelyn. *Concerning the Inner Life with the House of the Soul.* New York: E. P. Dutton, 1926.

Permissions